The Congress of Prague

The Congress of Prague

Revitalizing the Atlantic Alliance

Gerald Frost and William E. Odom,
editors

The AEI Press

Publisher for the American Enterprise Institute
WASHINGTON, D.C.
1997

Available in the United States from the AEI Press, c/o Publisher Resources Inc., 1224 Heil Quaker Blvd., P.O. Box 7001, La Vergne, TN 37086-7001. Distributed outside the United States by arrangement with Eurospan, 3 Henrietta Street, London WC2E 8LU England.

Library of Congress Cataloging-in-Publication Data

The Congress of Prague: revitalizing the Atlantic Alliance / Gerald Frost and William E. Odom, editors.
    p. cm.
    Includes index.
    ISBN 0-8447-4020-9. — ISBN 0-8447-4021-7 (pbk.)
    1. North Atlantic Treaty Organization—Congresses. 2. World politics — 1989- —Congresses. 3. Europe—Defenses—Congresses. I. Frost, Gerald. II Odom, William E.
    D860.C665   1997
    909.82—dc2   97-10771
                                                                              CIP

1 3 5 7 9 10 8 6 4 2

THE AEI PRESS
Publisher for the American Enterprise Institute
1150 17th Street, N.W., Washington, D.C. 20036

Printed in the United States of America

Contents

1

Introduction

Gerald Frost

On May 10–12, 1996, more than 300 leaders of intellectual and political opinion met in the glittering chambers of the Cernin Palace in the Czech capital to convene the Congress of Prague. Welcomed by Václav Havel, the Czech president, their purpose was to celebrate the achievements of Western civilization and to affirm the values on which that civilization is based. This event, held under the auspices of the New Atlantic Initiative, concluded with a declaration of common principles: an eloquent and unapologetic statement of belief in individual liberty, the market economy, and democratic pluralism, which those present were invited to sign. The chapters in this volume derive from the addresses and policy discussions at the congress, the first stage of the initiative that has the practical aim of bringing about a renewal of the Western Alliance and a reshaping of its institutions to meet new conditions.

Perhaps in the hope that the West would help prolong its rapidly waning life, the former Soviet apparatchik Georgi Arbatov once said that the West needed Soviet communism in much the same way as Roman Catholicism required the Devil. In his speech to the Congress of Prague Václav Klaus, the Czech prime minister, expressed a diametrically opposite view when he spoke of "ideas, not enemies": that now, as in the past, the West owes its identity and its strength to common values, not to a common foe. The implication of the Czech prime minister's assertion is clear: that following the collapse of the Soviet Empire, there is nothing to prevent the redrawing of political and economic boundaries so that these correspond more closely to

1

those of the civilization on whose behalf the cold war was waged. This sentiment, combined with a warning of the dangers arising from continued Western introspection, was a common theme of contributions to the Congress of Prague, one from which there was virtually no dissent.

The congress received worldwide media coverage; this edited volume is being published because it provides a more detailed and comprehensive guide to the complex issues involved in rethinking the purpose and means of Western cooperation than could be achieved in press reports.

In assessing the significance of the congress, readers may benefit from a brief explanation of the origins of the New Atlantic Initiative. The initiative was conceived entirely by those outside of government: an ad hoc group of scholars, journalists, and former public servants reflecting a range of political allegiances and beliefs that expanded as plans developed. It came into existence through a shared anxiety about the influence of a pervasive but in our view mistaken belief that the Atlantic relationship was now an expendable legacy of history. It seemed to us that this mood was not so much the consequence of rigorous appraisals of national interests but of introspection, drift, and the thoughtless subordination of fundamental and long-term interests to parochial and short-term ones. The consequence was that an important opportunity to seize the moment in the interests of liberal democracy was being neglected. What was needed, we concluded, was a considered reappraisal of the role and rationale of Atlantic institutions, combined with an imaginative response to the deeply felt desire of the Central and Eastern European states to be accommodated within them. The purpose of the initiative is to start that process and to encourage others to participate in it, an ambition already partly realized.

In preparation for a major international congress at which our concerns might be aired, four policy committees—on political cooperation, security, trade and economics, and culture and art—were created. The committees met on November 24–26, 1995, subsequently producing reports for presentation to the Congress of Prague. These were intended purely to stimulate discussion, an aim that was amply realized and should not be taken as expressing the views or carrying the approval of those present at Prague; these appear as chapters 3, 4, 5, and 6 in this volume. Those with a taste for historical irony may be interested that the venue for the committees' deliberation on ways of enlarging Western forms of political cooperation was the Grand Hotel Pupp in the Czech spa town of Karlovy Vary, where more than a quarter of a century earlier the Soviet Politburo promulgated the Brezhnev doctrine, specifically and absolutely dismissing the possibility of any such development.

As our plans progressed, it became clear that the ability of Europe and the United States to redefine and rebuild the forms of Western cooperation would be influenced significantly by the ability of Western states to overcome a range of domestic economic and social problems of a possibly systemic kind. The program of the Congress of Prague was therefore expanded to provide the opportunity to analyze these and to discuss alternative approaches to their solution.

Of necessity, this volume cannot convey the full range of discussion and debate that those who attended the conference experienced firsthand. Nevertheless, I believe that it provides a unique guide to the issues that will determine the profiles and fault lines of a fluid and uncertain international order. No less important, it provides a description of the means available to persons in and outside government who are prepared to act on the conviction of those who organized the Congress of Prague: that the best hope of enhancing international stability, of raising standards of prosperity, and of expanding the area of individual liberty depends crucially on the rejuvenation of the Atlantic partnership.

2

Declaration of Atlantic Principles

We the undersigned have convened in Prague, a city that has borne witness to both the glories and the cruelties of Europe's modern history. It is where Charles IV built the first university in Central Europe, and Mozart conducted the premiere of *Don Giovanni*. It is also the city that suffered the betrayal of Munich, the defenestration of democracy in 1948, and the brutal Soviet invasion twenty years later—until at last it overcame the iron fist of tyranny with its velvet revolution.

We have convened here, first, to celebrate the high achievements of European civilization. From the glory of Greece and Rome, to the Renaissance and Enlightenment, it is in the countries of Europe that our modern concepts of freedom evolved and flowered—spiritual freedom, intellectual freedom, economic freedom, and political freedom. Today's universal principles of liberty under the law, constitutional democracy, pluralism, and human rights were nurtured here. It is the continent of Magna Carta and the Rights of Man, of Blackstone and Beethoven, Copernicus and Kossuth, Montesquieu and Masaryk.

We have convened, second, to celebrate the gratitude which the free peoples of Europe owe to the United States, that other Europe across the Atlantic where liberty grew tall under spacious skies. Twice in this century, America came to Europe's rescue. Ever generous with its abundance, ever willing to share its strength, the United States remains a natural and valued leader of the democratic world. Its continued leadership is indispensable.

We have convened, third, to celebrate the Atlantic community,

the worthy heir of these traditions, whose staunch partnership preserved European civilization in this century's great struggle against
the totalitarians. The link between America and Europe—political,
economic, and moral—cannot be broken except at grave peril to both.
Making common cause, Europe and America can help build a new
global community based on the principles of liberty that they have
conceived and championed.

We have convened, finally, to celebrate Central Europe's place
in this family. The peoples of this region were an integral part of
Europe's free civilization and the Atlantic world until artificially and
cruelly separated from them by the totalitarians. From 1939 to 1989,
Central Europe was the main arena of this century's epic battle of
freedom against tyranny. The revolution that liberated Central Europe was the beacon of the West´s victory in the cold war.

Our mission at this Congress of Prague, therefore, is to reunite
the family of Western civilization, and so to ensure its future. There
is grave danger that the links among us might be broken again, or
gradually erode, owing to shortsightedness and the failure of states-
manship on all sides. We must not allow that. In politics, economics,
and culture we are one civilization. We share common security interests. We seek a world of greater opportunities for all our people. These
common purposes and aspirations must be reflected in our institutions and practices. Just as the Atlantic community preserved the
freedom of Western Europe and America in the past fifty years, so it
must now entrench that freedom, build upon it, and reaffirm common purposes for a new era:

• In our cultural life, the democratic world has gained a new
and needed infusion of spirit from those who know and love liberty
well because they were so long deprived of it. Those in the West who
took their freedom for granted can only be inspired by the glowing
courage of those who kept faith with that ideal where it was forbid-
den. We must help ensure that freedom of expression and access to
the media are entrenched and developed throughout the Atlantic
world.

• In economic life, our common civilization will be more du-
rable if it rests on common foundations. A Transatlantic Free Trade
Area, obeying the rules of international trade but solidifying the partnership of Europe and America, must become an urgent objective of
Atlantic politics. Across the Atlantic, NAFTA is already growing into

a Western Hemispheric Free Trade Area. It must become Europe's partner or it will become Europe's rival. In parallel, incorporating the Central European democracies into the European Union is a moral and strategic imperative as well as an economic one. The inclusion of Central Europe in an Atlantic economic space is essential not only to spread prosperity, but also to reinforce its place in the Atlantic world and to strengthen stability.

• In political life, all good things rest ultimately on our willingness to defend them. Our cultural and economic community will be secure only if it is allied to a diplomatic partnership and common security. The NATO alliance is today the expression of Atlantic partnership and the guarantor of our common security. Central Europe's admission to it is another imperative.

Ours is not an exclusionary vision. No new final line is being drawn between nations and associations within the Atlantic Community and those beyond. But to refrain from offering close cooperation to neighbors who have achieved full democracy and liberty against great odds would be to cling to the absurd and obsolete scission of the Europe of 1945.

Relations with Russia, moreover, should be friendly, constructive, and open to increasing cooperation. No offensive threat or provocation is part of this enterprise. Mutual reassurance is readily attainable. There is no objective reason for great power conflict in Europe—provided that the outcome of 1989 is accepted as irreversible: namely, that the new democracies are sovereign, independent, and free to exercise their choice of association.

The long-term relationship of Russia with Europe and America will ultimately be shaped by Russia's political, economic, and cultural evolution. It will always find us willing partners and hopeful friends.

Therefore, we, assembled in solemn Congress in Prague on May 12, 1996, pledge ourselves to work toward the goals of a New Atlantic Cooperation, to translate our common heritage into new realities of political and economic association among free peoples, while ensuring that we together maintain our strength and the will to defend ourselves against those who might seek to diminish our liberty, the source of our strength and purposes.

PART ONE
Policy Papers

3

Political Cooperation

The Nature of Atlanticism

There are rare moments when history is open and its course may be altered. The end of the cold war provided just such an occasion. But five years have now passed since the Soviet collapse and very little has been done either to consolidate the gains achieved or to question whether Western institutions need to be adapted in response to new conditions. Current problems are proving difficult to deal with partly because they *are* new—and therefore not necessarily susceptible to traditional policy approaches—and partly because they are more complex than the ones encountered in the relatively stable cold war world of clear-cut distinctions and divisions.

Some have suggested that Western states cannot remain in a cohesive alignment in the absence of a common enemy and that it therefore makes no sense to talk in terms of a common response to new and emerging dangers (this view was anticipated by a Soviet apparatchik who remarked that the West needed communism in much the same way as the Roman Catholic church needed the Devil). If membership of the West did indeed depend purely on the existence of a common foe there might be little point in seeking common responses to the problems thrown up in the wake of Soviet collapse. But membership of the transatlantic community—the West, to use the more familiar term—has always depended on common characteristics derived from shared values and historical experience.

The most important of these are the rule of law, individual liberty, democratic institutions, the existence of civil society, and the development of scientific and technological innovation. The principles of limited government and public accountability are also defining characteristics of the Western democratic tradition whose origins are to be found in the Enlightenment, in the attempt to distill our Judaeo-Christian inheritance in the form of a secular political philosophy.

The Atlantic community is not a fixed geographical entity. It grew during the world war years to include all of the free countries of Europe; it also includes former colonies such as Australia and New Zealand. There are presently powerful reasons for welcoming its further expansion.

Atlantic-*ism* remains an innovative and flexible approach, enabling us to build a future that preserves and extends what is most of value in our inheritance. We believe that in present conditions it ought to imply the adaptation of Western institutions to anchor more securely to the West those Central and East European states which display underlying Western characteristics. Although some valuable opportunities have been missed, that possibility remains open; it is most unlikely to remain open indefinitely.

The Need for Widening the Atlantic Circle

Most Central and East European states are now beyond the painful, critical early stages of reform; nearly all have achieved substantial progress in liberalizing their economies and introducing democratic political structures, even if ex-Communists and ex-nationalists continue to command a disturbing degree of support. Most of their economies are growing at impressive rates—at present averaging around 5 percent per annum—and their conversion to free market disciplines is judged by the World Bank to have passed the point of no return.

The desire to participate fully in the economic and political life of the West was a natural extension of the desire for political freedom and national sovereignty. A refusal to recognize those ambitions when entry requirements are being met—except on grudging or partial terms—is likely to weaken the champions of political pluralism. Equally, it is likely to strengthen those whose commitment to democratic values is limited or suspect. In the long run a negative response from the West could be damaging to its own security and economic interests.

In some respects, however, the West's welcome has grown cooler as the Central Europeans have moved steadily closer to achieving the goals set for them. The recent talk of "partial membership" of the EU which would give the new entrants a measure of influence over some aspects of EU policy, but deny them the solid benefits of belonging to a single market, is merely one instance. In the immediate aftermath of Soviet collapse such measures might have had some merit as transitional steps toward a fuller accommodation. In present circumstances limited association with the EU is bound to be regarded as inadequate. Moreover, when the obstacles to the enlargement of the Atlantic community are seen to flow from the parochial short-term political interests of the more prosperous existing members, the consequence is likely to be cynicism among the applicants. That could make it harder for Central and East Europeans to nurture those notions of civic courage and obligation upon which civil society depends, while encouraging their governments to adopt narrow, short-term interpretations of their own interests.

The inclusion of the Central and East states in the broad Atlantic community would provide its members, old and new, with a common unifying purpose. Not to embrace the challenge of expanding the Western circle would, in a sense, diminish the West's achievement in opposing totalitarianism. While its victory over Soviet communism has led to the emergence of new threats and problems we should not compound these by denying the emerging democracies the chance to participate fully in the economic and political life of the West.

In our view Western governments are mistaken if they believe that they will be better placed to solve their own problems arising from rapid economic and technological change by postponing discussion of these crucial political issues. Indeed, cooperation on economic and trade matters may well become more difficult to solve unless our political elites are able to raise their sights from purely domestic considerations to the broader strategic implications of a Europe that remains divided.

We acknowledge the strength of the domestic political pressures which push the European Union toward insularity and protectionism—and therefore away from enlargement—but we believe that the long-term interests of EU members will best be served if, in resisting those pressures, it does enlarge to the east, while becoming more outward-looking to the United States. Unless discouraged, such forces

11

could encourage similar pressures in the United States which are both considerable and growing— to the detriment of both parties.[1]

Most disturbingly, there is the very real danger that, in the absence of a clear and persuasive rationale for its continuing commitment to Europe, the United States will turn its back on Europe in favor of a strong involvement with a dynamic Asia. Recognizing such dangers, Newt Gingrich, Speaker of the U.S. House of Representatives, said recently that new transatlantic initiatives which have recently appeared on the international agenda should make Europeans and Americans excited at being on the same team, adding, "Because if we are not actively on the same team in a practical way, we will inevitably, in the long run, not be on the same team." For the time being, however, concerns about Russian attitudes are inhibiting serious discussion of NATO expansionism among Allies while the EU appears to take the position that all talk of a Trans Atlantic Free Trade Area (TAFTA) is premature until discussion about the EU's own future is settled at the forthcoming Inter-Governmental Conference. These passive stances risk a serious souring of relations with the Central and East European states and a consequent damage to Western cohesion.

Western leaders should acknowledge this reality, and seek public support for progress toward NATO enlargement and freer trade. There are a number of reasons for supposing that the prospects for achieving these goals are better than in the recent past.

First, gradual economic recovery in most Western countries should make it somewhat easier for governments to look beyond their immediate domestic agendas and to prepare the path toward realistic trade liberalization.

Second, the progress of Central and East Europeans in introducing democratic systems and market economies and in seeking to restore civil society undeniably strengthens their claims to membership that simply cannot be refused for narrow domestic reasons.

Third, enhanced fears of a resurgent and politically unstable Russia, which have grown markedly since the December 1995 elections to the Duma, reinforce the case for a sustaining and continuing U.S. presence in Europe based on the strengthening of economic and strategic commitments to embrace the broadest possible community of democratic nations in the West.

Fourth, there is a widespread perception that events in ex-Yugoslavia have further demonstrated the indispensability of U.S. military power and diplomatic muscle as a necessary condition of

European security in the most salutary possible way. Europe presently lacks the political cohesion and confidence to deal with such problems, even when military strength is probably sufficient to achieve the desired outcome, and in our view this is likely to remain true for the foreseeable future.

Forms and Institutions

The profound changes which have occurred in the international order during the last five years make it necessary to examine whether the institutional systems established after World War II are now adequate and sustainable, or should either be reformed or replaced by new arrangements.

Our own judgment is that the sense of community of the Atlantic nations needs to be consolidated by developing further the element of a joint identity overlying the separate regional and national identities. Institutions of cooperation play an important role in this, to the extent that they are able to embody, validate, and sustain a visible common identity.

The creation of a TAFTA, including those Central and East European states which met agreed criteria, would go a significant way to stimulate trade and to meet the economic aspirations of the new members, while giving new purpose to North America's European engagement. However, as the Report of the Trade and Economics Committee stresses this must be pursued without causing damage to the World Trade Organization.

We strongly favor the creation of a major U.S.-European initiative to liberalize world trade and investment through the WTO, but were this to be frustrated we would favor the creation of a TAFTA as a way of achieving the same objectives. We believe that the political rationale for both possible courses of action is even more compelling than the economic ones, and we believe that political leaders on both sides of the Atlantic should do more to raise consciousness about what is at stake.[2]

At present we believe that NATO is the only organization that expresses the transatlantic idea whose significance is widely understood by the public. It remains the best foundation for building the transatlantic future. In the light of the complex and sometimes obscure discussions about alternative defense arrangements it may be necessary to point out a truth that was formerly taken for granted:

13

that NATO could not long survive the absence of a strong U.S. commitment to Europe and that, as in the past, it is most likely to prosper under a leadership to which the United States makes a contribution commensurate with its size and power.

We recognize, however, that in order to meet its wider responsibilities NATO should be open to adaptation (for more detailed discussion of this see the report of the Security Policy Committee). Most importantly, we believe that the advantages of expanding to the east considerably outweigh possible costs, and that greater urgency be given to the processes of integrating new members. These should be sufficiently flexible to deal with the specifics of military and administrative integration on an individual basis. We are equally firm in our conviction that the Russian attempts to discourage the West from admitting the Central Europeans should be resisted. The accession of the Central European states does not represent a threat to the security interests of Russia; on the contrary, we regard their absorption by an expanded Atlantic community as a factor for regional security and therefore as an advantage to their eastern neighbors, including Russia. In our judgment it would therefore be a serious mistake to succumb to Russian pressures by making concessions of this kind in the hope that this will strengthen democratic forces within Russia; developments there reflect internal factors over which the West is likely to have strictly limited influence.

In the case of the EU we hope that the goals of enlargement and of renewing strong links with North America figure prominently in the agenda of the forthcoming IGC. We understand the fears of the Central European applicants that a further "deepening" of EU institutions will further delay their full accession. For that reason we believe that the discussion about the future development of the EU should take place in the context of enlargement. We also believe that the accession to the EU and NATO of the Central Europeans should be viewed as parallel processes, complementary but not made conditional upon one another.

With the accession to NATO of new members, a strong case can be made for enhancing the role of the North Atlantic Assembly, parliamentarians from the allied states who meet regularly to discuss Atlantic issues. While the Assembly at present has no direct policy role, its members are influential in their domestic legislatures. Its function as a consultative arm should be strengthened through the provision of an expanded secretariat able to prepare more developed independent analyses and recommendations for members to consider. This would enhance the ability of participants to play a more active role in influencing public opinion on issues of mutual concern within the Alliance. To further these aims, and to give the Assembly a stronger public presence, we suggest that it should hold its deliberations in the parliamentary buildings of members states on a rotating basis. We also suggest dropping "North" from its official title.

The political consultation role of the North Atlantic Council and its subsidiary Senior Political Committee and Political Committee has been sharply circumscribed in recent years, focusing mainly upon political developments in the Treaty area, narrowly construed, with a strong emphasis on East-West relations in general, arms control, and related matters. Lately, the consultations at council level and below have embraced significant developments in former Yugoslavia, as well as more detailed discussion of so-called out of area concerns. However, great latitude remains for intensified consultations on regional threats outside the Treaty area, for example global concerns such as instability in the Middle East, proliferation of weapons of mass destruction, terrorism, and drug traffic, which all represent dangers to members of the Alliance.

Against this background we propose:

- a decision by the Allies to pursue more vigorously consultations in NATO on developments out of area that impinge on their security, discarding former national inhibitions that previously hamstrung such consultations
- the addition to NATO's international staff of experts seconded from national capitals able to expand the processes of common analyses and development of policy based on national contributions
- invitations to the Eastern and Central European states deemed candidates to full NATO membership to participate as observers in these enhanced political consultations

We also believe that there may be a case for a new organization for cooperation at the political level. Like the Organization for Economic Cooperation and Development (OECD) it could constitute a modest but increasingly valuable agency, providing scholarly analyses, publishing relevant data and opinions in areas of expertise, and seeking areas for agreement where conventions for cooperation are possible—an Organization for Political Cooperation and Development, so to speak. In the long term the success of such a body would

15

be judged by the quality of its analyses and its influence on debate in member countries. Subjects on which a transatlantic perspective would be welcome might, for example, include movements of population, international trade in narcotics, and the challenge posed by Islamic fundamentalism.

Most importantly, we believe there is a very strong case for summit meetings of the prime ministers of all of the countries of the Atlantic community—as suggested by Margaret Thatcher in her lecture in Fulton, Missouri, of March this year. The EU-U.S. summit which took place in Madrid on December 3rd last year and *The New Transatlantic Agenda,* a 60 page action plan, which it approved, provide a possible basis on which to build. This made a welcome start, both in recognizing many of the problems described in these pages and in stressing the need for a common approach.

Lady Thatcher suggested in her lecture that the U.S. president should be the chairman on these occasions. We see the virtue of the proposal as reflecting the realities of power across the Atlantic. It is probably the most sensible approach.

But the experience of the European Union in giving its presidency to each member state in turn for six-monthly periods has both ensured the maximum public interest and given the president a real political incentive to advance his agenda in the limited time available. We see some advantage in the principle of rotation. But this principle is already running into difficulties as membership of the European Union grows. How can it best be expressed in an Atlantic context is something that requires further discussion. For instance, if the summit itself were to be rotated between capital cities, the local head of government might then join the U.S. president in the role of co-chairman. This would have the further advantage of encouraging close working political cooperation between the U.S. president and other heads of government in turn.

High-profile summits have the advantage of being able to highlight the need for the renewal of the Atlantic ethos, and of bringing home the dangers and costs of inaction. Their fundamental purpose must be to set broad strategic goals and to maintain the impetus behind the new Atlanticism. They might also be expected to offer valuable help in mobilizing the necessary investment of moral, intellectual and material resources by those outside government and in encouraging existing Atlanticist groups to reexamine their own roles and mutual relations: politics are too important to be left purely to politicians. The recent series of twice-yearly meetings between the U.S. president and the rotating EU presidency, which have already proved their practical worth, could be adapted to deal with questions of implementation. Whether the changes proposed here would require the creation of an entirely new body served by a permanent staff is something which we believe requires further thought.

In formulating the new transatlantic agenda great care will, of course, need to be taken to demonstrate that the creation of an enlarged and outward-looking Atlantic community will not be harmful to the interests of Japan and other increasingly important and dynamic Asian economies. We must also demonstrate that every attempt will be made to include them in any future program of economic integration.

Finally, we issue a call to individual citizens, interest groups, and those in commerce and industry to involve themselves in the creation of a new Atlanticism and a wider Atlantic community. To succeed, a network comprising new and rejuvenated institutions on the nongovernmental level needs to be created in order to sustain the Atlanticist idea, to keep it in the public mind, and to facilitate the discussion of its meaning and implications. We believe that the New Atlantic Initiative can—and should—continue beyond the Prague Congress in order to provide one of the foundations on which such a future can be built.

As we stated at the beginning of this report, there are rare occasions when history is unusually open and therefore susceptible to those who wish to influence its course. Such periods seldom last long and the opportunity only exists for those prepared to will the means, as well as the ends. We are strongly of the view that the future of our civilization—and the values which sustain it—depends very crucially upon just such an attempt being made.

Notes

1. In a speech at the College of Europe on September 15, 1994, King Juan Carlos of Spain argued that the successful political development and enlargement of an "outward-looking" Europe were conditional upon continued U.S. security guarantees; he also argued for closer European links with South America: "Above all Atlanticism means an open mentality for an open world."

2. One member of our committee, Luc de Nanteuil, expressed strong reservations both about a major U.S.-European initiative and the creation of a TAFTA, arguing that a more cautious step-by-step approach was required if the issue of trade liberalization was not to frustrate the aim of EU enlargement and the strengthening of transatlantic political and security links.

4

Security

New Threats for Old

The Atlantic Alliance, which finds its best expression in the North Atlantic Treaty Organization, is a trust of the sovereign liberal democracies of Europe and North America. Its purpose is to guarantee collective and individual security, to maintain peace, and uphold freedom. It provides the indispensable weight in the European balance, the vital institutional bond between Europe and America, and a barrier to the denationalization of Western defense. It is the only body capable of achieving these aims and the only one so constituted.

In order to survive, however, it will need to adapt and to act more decisively than during the war in former Yugoslavia.

The demise of the Soviet Union and the Warsaw Pact and the disintegration of communism are among the most profoundly important events to have occurred in modern times. They were bound to have wide implications for the security policies of NATO members since in large measure these were designed to deal with a single threat.

Although hugely welcome, it has been clear for some time that the collapse of the Soviet Empire would not be followed by a new world order in which a peaceful resolution of differences between states could be taken for granted. As we moved from a relatively stable bi-polar world to a multi-polar world new sources of instability and conflict emerged. This was inevitable since, quite suddenly, a major constraint on the spread of conflict—the fear that a minor flare-up might lead to a nuclear conflagration between the superpowers—had been removed. The new sources of conflict and instability included the reemergence of ultra-nationalism and irredentism and the reappearance of the kind of ethnic and religious wars which predate the nation state and the rise of ideology. To these must be added the future dangers arising from a nationalistic, unstable, and possibly resurgent Russia.

Despite this greatly altered security environment we believe that the North Atlantic Treaty Organization remains the best guarantee of security within Europe. The current operation in Bosnia provides a sign that it is capable of establishing a new and wider role; there has been some welcome progress in the creation of a consensus among members of the Alliance to allow this to happen.

One of the keys to NATO's strengths has been its ability to act collectively. This made it impossible for any potential aggressor to pick off the European democracies individually, and this proved a significant factor in the containment of Soviet power. The collective character of NATO, which reflects common values as well as common obligations (see the report of the Political Cooperation Committee for a fuller discussion of values) remains a great asset, one which must be preserved if it is to influence events and its spokesmen to speak with authority.

It is now widely accepted that many of the new challenges to the democratic order come from outside NATO's traditional area of operation. There are potential threats from tyrannical regimes and terrorist organizations motivated either by fanatical antidemocratic, antipluralist ideologies or by the more familiar age-old lust for power and territory. Those risks are enhanced by the disturbing fact of nuclear proliferation and the spread of other weapons of mass destruction, together with the means to deliver them. The proliferation of such weapons has the potential to upset regional power balances and to create fears of surprise attack. Even where there is no immediate military threat to the territory of NATO members such developments may present serious threats to their vital interests.

It should be borne in mind that the nuclear systems developed during the cold war may no longer have the same deterrent value as in the past. Deterrence assumes effective means of communication and sufficient knowledge of an adversary's politics and culture to predict how it will behave in particular circumstances. These conditions do not appear to be met in the case of a number of the new

19

missile states (during the Gulf War Iraq attacked Israel *despite* the latter's possession of a nuclear deterrent).

Early in the 21st century a growing number of third world states will have the capacity to target cities in Europe, America, and even Japan. This development could also pose a particular threat to expeditionary forces sent in response to regional crises, and indeed to those countries which had provided military contingents to those forces. For obvious reasons of geography this is a threat which could mature more quickly for Europe than for America. It is one which carries particular risks for France and Britain which, alone among contemporary European states, have been ready to consider the use of military force in response to aggression outside the NATO area.

Experience strongly suggests that the problems arising from the proliferation of weapons of mass destruction are unlikely to be resolved by a combination of antiproliferation regimes, measures, and diplomacy alone; there are no mysterious diplomatic means available to disarm states which do not wish to be disarmed and whose leaders, in some instances, depend upon the display of aggression or the exercise of force for their survival. In our view effective measures to counter this problem—in Margaret Thatcher's recent phrase, "the most awesome threat of modern times"—must necessarily include a global system of ballistic missile defense. This would include space-borne sensors and interceptors in order to target missiles in the early stages of their flight as well as ground-based systems. Its aim would be to provide protection against a limited, accidental, or unauthorized missile attack while strengthening deterrence against a major missile offensive. The development of ballistic missile defenses might also be expected to diminish the incentive to acquire ballistic missiles and to reduce the capacity of rogue states already in possession of them to coerce their neighbors and to launch surprise attacks. In a more unpredictable and complex world the potential contribution to stability of a global system of ballistic missile defenses may prove to be very great indeed. In our opinion NATO provides the best means for providing the organizational infrastructure which would enable America's allies to make a significant contribution in both economic and technological terms to the research, development, and deployment of a system answering common needs and concerns.

It is true that NATO was not designed to deal with the kind of developments briefly described above, but it is our judgment that they are likely to be best dealt with by a collective organization with moral and political authority as well as established methods of consultation and procedure. The key to progress lies in the development of a consensus among members states which would enable NATO to act outside its traditional area of operation and to adopt new modes of operation reflecting political and military developments.

It is important to recognize that a wider international role for NATO quite obviously assumes a continuing commitment to NATO by the one remaining superpower. Without the active engagement of the United States such ambitions cannot be seriously contemplated. As events in Bosnia have already demonstrated an American military presence is likely to be a necessary condition of conflict resolution even within Europe. In the words of President Chirac, ". . . the political commitment of the United States in Europe and its military presence on European soil are still an essential element of the stability and security of the continent, and indeed the world."

Europeans should not overlook the fact that they cannot begin to match what the United States makes available to the Alliance in respect of air-lift capability, command and control, surveillance, and sheer fire-power even at greatly increased levels of military expenditure—and no significant increase seems presently likely. Among Western states only the United States has the technological capacity to develop and deploy a global system of ballistic missile defense. Much discussion within Europe about the future of collective security falls to take account of these realities, even though defense expenditure in Europe, as in the United States, has been falling. Whether or not a purely European defense organization would display greater internal cohesion, or whether in the absence of the United States there would be greater wrangling over its direction and leadership, is open to question; the experience of the interwar squabbles between the Western European states may be instructive in this respect.

A formal widening of NATO's role might not be enthusiastically welcomed by those in the United States who have argued that Europe's contribution to collective defense has been inadequate. It is therefore important to stress that this would also entail wider responsibilities on the part of its European partners who, for the first time, would be committing themselves to participate in a mutual response to "out of area" threats. In return America's military commitment to Europe, including its nuclear guarantee, would be reaffirmed. Both parties, therefore, would be able to justify greater shared responsibilities by reference to the advantages from a revision of existing NATO arrangements.

The Case for Enlargement

Present circumstances provide a window of opportunity for NATO expansion which may close once Russia resumes its role as a great power. We believe that it is possible for NATO to reappraise its role and to admit new members as part of parallel processes. We do not accept that these aims are incompatible; on the contrary, the latter could serve as a catalyst for the former. In pursuing these twin objectives, however, great care should be taken not to erode any of NATO's current strengths.

Some of the arguments against enlargement have a measure of force and should certainly be treated with respect. The most important of these are (1) that the inclusion of new members would diminish NATO cohesion and (2) that by admitting some—but not all—of those seeking to accede, we would indicate that those excluded could be regarded as falling within a new Russian area of influence. We shall seek to deal with both arguments.

Providing strict entrance criteria are met and the obligations of membership are properly observed an increase in membership may be regarded as a source of strength, rather than weakness. At the most fundamental level cohesion depends on shared values and interests. Membership should only be open to those states which have demonstrated their commitment to democracy, the rule of law, and pluralism and are prepared to accept the obligations as well as benefits of membership. No applicant should be admitted if it appeared to be turning against the values which NATO has traditionally been committed to defend. While decision making in a large international organization can be more difficult or complex than in a small one NATO was not weakened by the inclusion of Greece and Turkey (1952), the Federal Republic of Germany (1955), or Spain (1982). In a large organization, as in a small one, the interests of cohesion are most likely to be served by a sense of clearly defined common purpose and the political will of members to achieve it. In present circumstances we believe that this requires the kind of reappraisal—a top-level strategic review—whose broad outlines and implications are set out in this report.

In our view the interest of unity would not be served by creating a new category of NATO member or, as has been suggested, by seeking to keep alive for an indefinite period the possibility or potentiality of membership for those wishing to join. On the contrary, we believe that for NATO to remain cohesive there must be only one kind of membership, one conferring equal rights and obligations. An attack on the territory of one must continue to be regarded absolutely and unambiguously as an attack on all.

We regard the idea of an indefinite postponement of the present applications for admittance as impractical; it would fail to provide an adequate basis for stability and certainty for the aspiring NATO members, while suggesting weakness and indecision on the part of existing ones.

It follows that new members must be willing to play a full part in NATO operations, including those outside of NATO's traditional ambit. It must be clear to them that membership is more than a symbol of their initiation into the club of Western democracies. This will require that NATO-dedicated forces be of sufficient standard to play a militarily significant role in joint operations. This requirement could initially apply to quite modest levels of forces, with existing NATO members giving new members full assistance in reaching appropriate standards.

Accordingly, the criteria for NATO membership would be as follows:

- a new member would have to demonstrate a fundamental commitment to democracy and political pluralism and to share the broad strategic interests of Alliance members
- a new member would accept the full obligations of membership including readiness to contribute directly to collective defense through participation in joint NATO operations
- the military units dedicated to NATO by a new member should reach an acceptable standard

In our view, however, the admission of new entrants does not require the immediate stationing of foreign troops on the territory of new members, a step which in present circumstances could send misleading signals about the nature and purpose of NATO expansion. However, this eventuality should not be ruled out since to do so would effectively create a two-tier membership. Moreover, we accept that a change in the security environment could require such a response.

NATO has always been a purely defensive organization; care will need to be taken to insure that the proposed changes do not in any way change the perception of its character. Given this proviso we do not believe that NATO expansion of this kind can be seen as

23

marking a new division of Europe, and therefore of giving Russia the right to intervene in those states currently denied membership. What we propose is not a matter of bringing the NATO frontline forward in order to prepare for a major land war in Europe, but of reappraisal and adaptation for the purpose of safeguarding the democratic order generally. The changes in the nature and composition of allied forces which will be required by this change of role can be stressed to reassure any other power about the underlying purposes of this change.

Defined in these terms expansion could prove to be the catalyst needed to give NATO a new impetus and purpose, without which it is likely to decline.

A New Role for NATO

Although some future challenges to security will come from Europe, as in the case of the conflict in Bosnia, others will come from further afield. In such instances the traditional NATO guarantee—i.e., that an attack upon one is an attack upon all—may have little immediate relevance. Many possible threats are unlikely to present themselves as a direct challenge to the territory of a member, but as a threat to its vital interests, or more generally to the liberal democratic order. New mechanisms are required to trigger responses to new situations. It is important to be clear, however, that any understanding or framework for new measures to be taken under NATO auspices is in addition to existing ones, and is not intended to replace them or dilute existing mutual defense guarantees.

One consequence of a wider role for NATO is that where the security interests of members are not directly challenged it may not be possible to enlist universal participation. Indeed, it should be recognized that a wider role for NATO cannot be contemplated if universal participation is regarded as a precondition of such operations. What is required in those circumstances are flexible arrangements which permit "coalitions of the willing" to act in response to particular crises.

As the term implies these would consist of NATO members wanting to act using NATO mechanisms—and NATO's military assets—with nonparticipants leaving their seats at the NATO Council vacant for the duration of the operation. Each member would preserve the right to opt out of any operation which was not undertaken as the result of mutual defense guarantees, but would not have the right of veto. For example a member state opposed to a military intervention of the kind which took place following the Iraqi invasion of Kuwait would not have the right to prevent it from taking place, but would have the right not to participate militarily.

The rules governing the terms under which such a coalition might take action need to be the subject of further consideration, but it seems clear that something in excess of a majority would be required. Anything less than that would not provide sufficient moral and political authority; insistence on something greatly in excess of a simple majority would make any such operation difficult to initiate. Nevertheless, the important decisions must remain with NATO: any tendency for it to become a mere subcontractor of the United Nations would prove fatal to its effectiveness and ultimately to its survival.

Two more factors need to be taken into account if NATO is to be effective in its wider role.

First, the hope that it will come to play a wider role will come to nothing if defense expenditures continue to be cut back. In the absence of a single potential adversary of roughly comparable strength there is a very real danger that research and development will be neglected and that Western technological superiority will diminish. This danger implies, far from any slackening of research, continuous and well-funded programs of research. It also implies Western practical development of such technology; otherwise we discover, and our possible foes develop our discoveries. It is therefore necessary to try harder to convey the message that defense is a permanent necessity rather than a cold war habit of little present relevance. Some savings can be made by avoiding the duplication of technology and equipment; the need to share technology and information has not been diminished by the demise of Soviet communism and the advent of a more diverse and complex security environment. Indeed, the reverse is probably true, even if this is a truth which carries difficult economic implications domestically. Cooperation is more likely to be achieved through the development of more open and reciprocal trading arrangements; the ideal of a "two-way street" permitting the U.S. government to purchase from European suppliers and European governments from American manufacturers is still worth pursuing.

Secondly, and rather more encouragingly, it needs to be understood more widely that new technology makes a wider NATO role somewhat easier in military terms as well as less costly. The newer generation of weaponry is more accurate and should thus dramatically reduce the casualties of war since there is likely to be less collateral damage. As a result it has become feasible to target those directly responsible for initiating conflict. As the human toll of military intervention is reduced it should be easier—in moral and political as well as economic terms—to confront the unacceptable conduct of the aggressor.

A wider role for NATO and expansion to the east in our view provide the best basis for renewing and redefining the Atlantic Alliance. We hope that others will join a growing debate about the means by which these goals can be achieved prior to their adoption in an intergovernmental declaration by NATO members held for this purpose.

The meeting held under the auspices of the New Atlantic Initiative at Karlovy Vary from November 24–26 provided a very welcome opportunity to discuss these and related issues. It also served to reinforce the conviction that any alternative response to emerging threats and dangers would be vastly inferior to that which might be achieved by building on NATO's existing foundations.

5

Trade and Economics

Members of the Trade and Economics Committee unanimously agree on three broad recommendations. They are:

- that the EU should remove all obstacles to accession of the countries of Central Europe (CCE) at the earliest possible date
- that the enlarged EU and the members of NAFTA should prepare a joint initiative for further liberalization in the World Trade Organization (WTO)
- that in the event that this initiative is rejected by other members of the WTO, the EU and NAFTA should proceed with liberalization of transatlantic trade and investment

Obstacles to Accession of the CCE

"Brussels keeps shut the gates to the east," said a headline in the *Financial Times* of November 16, 1995. It was followed by the subhead, "Enlarging the EU has taken a back seat as members grapple with problems closer to home."

Two principal problems for accession of the CCE lie within the EU. One is the Common Agricultural Policy (CAP) and the other is regional aid. These two policies together currently account for two-thirds of the EU's $100 billion annual budget.

Enlargement to the east, however, will hugely increase the budgetary cost of these policies. On some estimates, the additional cost will be $50 billion per annum—unless the policies are reformed. Few believe, however, that such a massive enlargement of the budget is feasible. Enlargement therefore implies reform. But reforms of the CAP and of regional aid designed to reduce the budgetary impact of enlargement face bitter opposition from the member states that currently benefit from those policies.

Some in Brussels and the capitals of some of the member states see a turning away from enlargement as a solution to this dilemma. If there is no enlargement, their argument runs, there is no need to reform the policies, and all the difficulties that reform entails can be avoided.

It will be an unhappy day for the EU if that argument is accepted. To fail to meet a historic challenge because proper response will create parochial difficulties is the way of the morally bankrupt.

Moreover, so far as the CAP is concerned, the argument is based on a false premise. Extension to the east is not the only source of pressure on the present structure of the CAP—and to delay extension will not remove pressures for reform of the CAP. Confronting the issue of reform, moreover, does not involve withdrawal of support from existing beneficiaries. As a technical matter, regional aid and support of the income of EU farmers can be restructured without harm to existing beneficiaries, without increased demands on the EU budget, and so that all markets of the CCE—including agricultural markets—are integrated with those of the EU.

We return to these issues in the section on the special role of the CAP.

WTO Commitments

Free trade between enlarged EU and NAFTA, embracing the free Atlantic countries and the newly free states of Central Europe, is an enormously attractive idea. It is, however, an idea in potential conflict with existing commitments of many of the countries involved. It is necessary to tread with caution.

All advocates of transatlantic liberalization express concern about the impact of the proposed arrangements on the multilateral trading system. Klaus Kinkel, the German foreign minister, for example, "saw TAFTA as the force behind a new round of trade liberalization which must in no circumstances be seen as block building" (*FT* of April 20, 1995). Roy MacLaren, speaking as the Canadian trade minister, saw it likewise: "As long as the goal is not to replace the multilateral system—still less to set up a defensive block—but to move beyond the commitments that we accepted in the WTO, then a new free-trade partnership of Europe and North America could set in motion a competitive dynamic to reduce barriers world-wide."[1]

Members of the Trade and Economics Committee believe that this concern is appropriate. The WTO provides an indispensable framework for dealing with broader trade relations—for example, between the West and Asia. For the Atlantic powers to act in such a way as to damage that fledgling organization would be short-sighted and foolish.

Concern about the impact of transatlantic liberalization on the WTO, however, implies that thought must be given to the relation between any proposed transatlantic arrangement and the relevant provisions of the WTO. It also implies that the question, "If liberalization across the Atlantic, why not liberalization in the WTO?" must be treated seriously.

A free-trade area (FTA) implies relaxed regulation of trade between members, but more discrimination against nonmembers. If a more general relaxation is possible, why should an FTA be preferred?

GATT Article XXIV. Any two WTO members can agree to reduce restrictions on imports from one another. Unless the agreement between them is accepted as a customs union or free-trade area under Article XXIV of the GATT, however, the most-favored-nation (MFN) clause on which the GATT is built obliges them to extend the concessions to all other WTO members.[2]

To be consistent with Article XXIV, an FTA must *inter alia* cover substantially all trade between the participants. The conditions present a problem for advocates of transatlantic liberalization. A number of speeches note the existence of sectors so sensitive that it would be difficult to include them in a transatlantic tariff-cutting exercise (agriculture and textiles and apparel being the sectors most frequently mentioned).[3] But a transatlantic free-trade area that failed to include trade in agriculture and in textiles and apparel (and possibly in other sensitive products—for example, steel, chemicals, and audio-visual) could hardly be represented as covering "substantially all" trade. If the EU cannot bring itself to liberalize agricultural trade nor the United States its treatment of imports of textile and apparel, then a WTO-consistent free-trade area between them is unlikely to be possible.

Taking WTO obligations seriously therefore implies that advocates of transatlantic trade liberalization must decide whether to:

- grasp the nettle and go for a full-blown transatlantic free-trade area that includes the sensitive areas; or
- use the combined weight of the United States and the EU to push through the WTO a free-trade area that is inconsistent with the WTO; or
- restrict the project to areas in which there is no WTO involvement and hence no MFN obligations to extend concessions to other WTO members

Grasping the Nettle. The "sensitive areas" are sensitive because they are highly vulnerable to transatlantic competition, but currently protected from it (and typically, from any other competition). Because they are heavily protected, much of the economic gain to be expected from transatlantic free trade would come from liberalization of trade in these sectors. But the heavy protection implies muscle, which in turn suggests that proposals to thrust competition upon them will from the start face powerful political opposition.

That might not matter if other members of the affected economies perceived major economic gains from transatlantic free trade. But that seems unlikely. There are certainly problems in transatlantic trade, but, outside the sensitive sectors, they do not seem so serious and so widespread that elimination of them would produce large net gains.

Pushing a GATT-Inconsistent Free-Trade Area through the WTO. This alternative implies conflict between the transatlantic initiative and the legal structure of the multilateral trading system, represented in institutional form by the WTO.

The EU-NAFTA attempt might or might not succeed. In neither case, though, would the outcome be good for the WTO. If the attempt failed, prospective members of the transatlantic free-trade area would either have to abandon the free-trade area or leave the WTO (which would be tantamount to wrecking it). If the attempt succeeded, the WTO would appear as an EU-NAFTA puppet, with ill consequences for the allegiance of other members. Moreover, such an EU-NAFTA "success" would open the way for other partial preferential schemes at grave cost to the most-favored-nation clause on which the WTO is founded.

Restricting the Scope of the Project. The constraint represented by the requirement that a free-trade area cover "substantially all trade" probably explains the frequent mention of projects on a smaller scale than a full-blown FTA. These include a comprehensive investment regime and an open-skies agreement for civil aviation (Christopher); EU-NAFTA cooperation on environment, crime, and terrorism (Brittan: *FT* of April 28, 1995); EU-NAFTA cooperation on crime, weapons, drug trafficking, and foreign aid (Christopher); an "Atlantic Community" (Malcolm Rifkind: *FT* of July 7, 1995).

Some of the projects suggested are in fact covered by the WTO—for example, the elimination of nontariff barriers to trade in goods and services (mentioned by Christopher, Hurd,[4] Helistrom, and MacLaren). Nontariff barriers to trade in goods and services are already the subject of WTO agreements. In the absence of an Article XXIV-consistent free-trade area, therefore, the EU and NAFTA would not be able to exclude other WTO members from obtaining any improved conditions that the EU and NAFTA offer to one another.

Others are not within WTO competence, and are unlikely ever to be (crime and terrorism, for example). Transatlantic projects in such areas have no direct effect on the WTO, nor the WTO on them.

But the possibility is also mooted that the EU and NAFTA might negotiate codes for foreign investment, or coordination of competition policy. No current WTO agreement applies in these areas (though both are candidates for future negotiation in the WTO), so the EU and NAFTA can make arrangements between themselves without any WTO obligation.

Bilateral versus Multilateral Liberalization. Consistency with Article XXIV, however, is not the only problem that preexisting commitments in the WTO create for transatlantic liberalization of trade. Whatever trade-related transatlantic agenda is proposed, the question arises—why not do it in the WTO?

A good answer to that question would be that further liberalization is not immediately possible in the WTO—that WTO members outside the EU and NAFTA refuse to contemplate further liberalization in the near future. That answer, though, is not currently available—those WTO members have not been asked.

Members of the Trade and Economics Committee propose that they should be asked. The EU and the NAFTA countries should jointly prepare an initiative to liberalize trade and investment to be presented to other WTO members.[5] If the initiative succeeds, the value of the Atlantic partnership will be reaffirmed. If it is rejected by other WTO members, the EU and the members of NAFTA will have done valuable spade work for further liberalization between themselves, and can proceed with transatlantic liberalization secure in the knowledge that they have treated seriously all of their obligations to the multilateral trading system.

The Joint Initiative

The proposed joint initiative has a double function. It is a true initiative in the WTO. The Uruguay Round is not a satisfactory stopping place on the road to liberalization.[6]

The joint initiative should be an honest attempt to move things forward.

But it would also prepare the ground for transatlantic liberalization. If there is to be transatlantic liberalization rather than more general liberalization in the WTO, members of the Trade and Economics Committee would prefer to grasp the nettle and aim for a WTO-consistent free-trade area, or even a customs union. Whether or not that course is followed, agriculture, textiles and apparel, steel and audio-visual—the so-called sensitive sectors—must be discussed to see how far liberalization can go, either in the WTO or across the Atlantic. Discussions, moreover, should cover all areas of mutual concern—for example, foreign investment, competition policy, labor standards, and environmental concerns.

These discussions need not be secret or opaque—nor, indeed, should they be secret or opaque. Other countries should be encouraged to proceed with their own initiatives or to contribute to the transatlantic initiative.

The intent to proceed with transatlantic liberalization if the initiative is blocked in the WTO should be open. So long as it is made clear that the EU and NAFTA will abide by WTO rules, transatlantic liberalization poses no serious threat to other WTO members. Article XXIV(5)(b) of the GATT requires that:

> with respect to a free-trade area . . . the duties and other regulations of commerce maintained in each of the constituent territories and applicable at the time of the formation of such free-trade area . . . shall not be higher or more restrictive than the corresponding duties and other regulations of commerce existing in the same constituent territories prior to the formation of the free-trade area . . . .

The threat that a WTO-consistent free-trade area poses to non-members is therefore limited.

Special Role of the CAP

The CAP in its present form is a barrier both to enlargement of the EU to the east and to any proposal for genuine transatlantic liberalization of trade and investment. The CAP is also a very expensive policy, but that is not the issue here. An expensive policy is one thing—an expensive policy that cripples desirable foreign policy initiatives is quite another.

It is important to be clear, moreover, that the problem to be faced is not that of removing state support from farmers. Desirable as that might be, neither enlargement nor transatlantic free trade makes it necessary.

What either enlargement or transatlantic free trade does make necessary is integration of EU agricultural markets with those of the new member states and North America. The CAP stands in the way of these initiatives because the CAP, in its present form, does not support farmers' incomes directly, but rather the prices of agricultural products. Food mountains and wine lakes, set-asides, border measures, and export subsidies derive from that fact. It is that fact, moreover, that puts the CAP at loggerheads with trade initiatives—ince farm incomes depend on the prices of agricultural products, anything that threatens to reduce prices becomes an enemy of the CAP and the farmers.

But there is no necessary connection between state support for farm incomes and farm prices. If the objective of the policy is to support farm incomes, there is a great deal to be said for tackling that objective directly, for supporting farm incomes directly, rather than interfering with prices. As a technical matter, support for farmers can easily be detached from production—for example, by paying them amounts based solely on past production, which are not affected by current or future production (or by whether they produce at all). EU farmers will then be free to produce and sell whatever amounts of whatever crops they choose, wherever they can, for whatever prices they can get.

Separating support for agricultural incomes from agricultural prices does not solve all problems. The economic cost of supporting farmers would fall, but the cost to the EU budget might rise. Agricultural income cannot be detached from agricultural prices, and EU farmers will still want to erect barriers against imports of cheap produce. In that, though, they are no different from any group hitherto protected from competition, and raise the same problems for liberalization of trade as any other pressure group.

With the CAP in its present form, integration of the EU and CCE agricultural sectors entails EU support prices for CCE produce—hence the budgetary cost, and the inclination to avoid integration. Integration on those terms, though, would distort the economies of the CCE and would give a misplaced boost to their agricultural sectors. Some of the CCE may have a comparative advantage in agriculture. If so, they should be allowed to exploit it at world prices, not at artificially inflated EU prices.

Moreover, there is no reason—economic, strategic, or moral—for existing members of the EU to support the incomes of farmers in the CCE. Detaching support for farm incomes in the existing member states from current production will allow agricultural markets to be integrated without any implicit requirement that the EU should provide such support.

Conclusion

All great projects call for difficulties to be overcome. EU-NAFTA cooperation to move the world toward free trade, whether in the WTO or across the Atlantic, is a great project. It faces difficulties that are real, but that are also parochial. What is the Western world to think of itself if it allows such difficulties to stifle fitting responses to a historic challenge?

Notes

1. Address by Roy MacLaren to the Royal Institute of International Affairs, London, May 22, 1995. Douglas Hurd credits MacLaren with initiating the current round of debate on TAFTA in a speech MacLaren delivered in October 1994.

2. Participants in either a customs union or an FTA remove tariffs on trade between themselves. Members of a customs union, however, also harmonize their tariffs on imports from nonparticipants while each member of an FTA maintains its own tariffs on imports from nonparticipants. The different tariffs of members of a FTA make "rules of origin" a central issue in the negotiation of such arrangements. The rules of origin determine whether goods crossing internal borders (e.g., from Canada to the United States in NAFTA) are deemed to originate in the partner country, and so to be entitled to duty-free entry; or to

originate outside the free-trade area and therefore to be subject to duty. Without rules of origin—and customs posts at internal borders to enforce them—goods will be imported into an FTA through the member with the lowest duty, and the FTA will become a *de facto* customs union, with tariffs harmonized at the lowest rate charged among the partners.

A country can be a member of several FTAs. The United States, for example, has a free-trade agreement with Israel and is a member of NAFTA even though its NAFTA partners do not have free-trade agreements with Israel. So long as the rules of origin are enforced, goods imported duty-free under the rules of one FTA will pay duty on entering a partner in another FTA.

3. For example, by Sir Leon Brittan (April 28, 1995); Mats Helistrom, the Swedish minister of trade (May 3, 1995); and Warren Christopher (June 3, 1995).

4. Speech by Douglas Hurd to the Economic Club of Chicago, May 18, 1995.

5. This part of our suggestions has already been put into effect. In Madrid, on December 3, 1995, the EU and the United States signed a *New Transatlantic Agenda*. It is accompanied by a *Joint EU-US Action Plan,* which sets out areas for cooperation and joint action.

Among these is a promise that "We will work to ensure a successful and substantive outcome for the Singapore Ministerial meeting" [of the WTO in December, 1996]; and an ambitious program to that end (pp. 28–29). In particular, the United States and the EU agreed to:

- "work for the completion of the unfinished business...[in the WTO]...with regard to goods and services";
- "explore the possibility of agreeing on a mutually satisfactory package of tariff reductions on industrial products";
- "promote the launching by Ministers in Singapore of negotiations within the WTO aimed at covering substantially all government procurement by WTO members";
- "work to develop a comprehensive agenda for future TRIPs (trade-related intellectual property) negotiations within the WTO";
- "work together in the WTO and/or other appropriate fora" [on new issues]. New issues expressly mentioned are environment; investment; competition policy; and labor standards.

6. Hindley, "Two Cheers for the Uruguay Round," *Trade Policy Review,* 1994 (London: Centre for Policy Studies, 1994), pp. 5–28.

6

Culture and Art

The common culture of Western Europe must necessarily play a large part in any discussion about a New Atlantic Initiative. That culture is deeply rooted in the European past—from Shakespeare to Valery, from Newton to Einstein—in the countries and the languages from which it spread to North America and Latin America. By its means there has been established a canon, by which cultural activity can be judged, nonsense rooted out, and vulgarity combated. The criteria which are contained in it can be applied to contemporary cultural manifestations, of which new forms have been produced by the technological advances over the past century. The cinema and the television screen have developed sophisticated techniques through which artifacts of real artistic value can be fabricated and other cultural forms be communicated. Yet the basis for all this new activity remains the traditional cultural canon developed in Western Europe.

It is this that must be studied if the culture of the present and future is to have the richness it has known in the past. This is true whether we give the word *culture* its narrower sense of the high cultural achievement we have inherited or the wider (and perhaps undefinable) anthropological meaning of "the general behavior of man in society." In the latter sense, the spread of sport around the world is one example of the predominance of Western values and habits. Others are the spread of what we call "modern, industrial civilization" with all the consequences that this entails for daily living habits and standards of living, epi-phenomena of this such as tourism, the motor car, the telephone. In all these fields the pattern of diffusion has been from America or Western European countries to the rest of the world. The cultural initiative still remains with the Atlantic geographical region, to which should be added English-speaking countries such as Australia and New Zealand.

This inheritance of culture has been carried down the centuries by the medium of language, which at the same time introduces an element of disunity. During the ages in which it was dominated by an aristocracy, the knowledge of the principal European languages was widespread among the governing classes, sometimes to the point of replacing their own mother tongues (e.g., the Russian nobility being largely French-speaking). With the spread of education, however, culture became familiar to the middle classes, and these no longer shared the *lingua franca* (French) in which communication of a cultural nature had largely been carried on. Now, the transmission of great literature or philosophy had to be carried on in translations or with a knowledge of the original language gained from schools or universities. Neither of these were effective means of communication as had been the almost universal knowledge of French in the aristocratic circles of the 18th century. Though music and the visual arts were unaffected by this, it was an important feature of European civilization that the transmission of ideas was effected through the medium of one national language which had made itself the unique instrument of cultural discourse.

In the 19th and 20th centuries English replaced French in this role. But the function was no longer the same. Not only did English become especially the medium of science, to a point where French scientists, in the late 20th century, often drafted their papers in English, but it was English which became the medium of popular entertainment in addition to its function in the transmission of technological information (English as the language of air-controllers, etc.). All of this was largely due to the part played by the United States in the diffusion of popular culture, as well as the so-called "youth culture." This extended role for English also has had an effect on the language itself. There has been a sort of inner-rusting of language leading to a simplification of syntax and vocabulary. Thus English is not only more used for utilitarian reasons, but also often robbed of its ambiguities and subtleties to ensure the rapid communication of information necessary to communities needing the help of modern technology. A basic English has become the *lingua franca* of the late 20th century.

The position of culture in the late 20th century has been complicated by what amounts to a planned attack on its role, which, in much that is written under the influence of "deconstruction" goes as far as denying the traditional canon any role at all. This attack began with a number of mostly French intellectuals who were determined to deny works of art or literature any more than purely relative worth. Their thesis was that since literature exists through its audience, it cannot be said that, say, Shakespearean works have any greater value than the latest thriller. Both of them aim at audience satisfaction and, provided that this is achieved, it cannot be said that one contains more "value" than another. This idea, transferred to the U.S. campus, took on a life of its own, with professors using it to lay claim to some form of moral superiority over their colleagues and students from various minorities coming to believe that a culture which they invented for themselves could replace the inheritance of the last three centuries. For political reasons, ranging from hostility to elite culture to a false application of the principles of political democracy to cultural affairs, these views spread, and have prospered. A combination of a populist yearning after equality and a false appreciation of the nature of education, together with bullying tactics on the campus which make teachers reluctant to stand up for their beliefs, has spread an anticultural frame of mind; if it prevails it would rob the Atlantic community of both its moral principles and its links with the past.

It follows that these ideas—or heresies—must be strongly resisted by proponents of a new Atlantic initiative. Although we may believe in political equality and the granting to all men, whatever their race or creed, equal rights as citizens we cannot accept an extension of this political belief to one in the equivalence of all cultures, whether of historic importance or not. To speak of Dante or Milton as "dead white males" merely demonstrates the vulgarity and Philistinism of those who use such phrases. It resembles the National-Socialists' expulsion of Jewish writers, musicians, and so on from the national community. There is no excuse for this type of barbarism—still less for letting oneself be dragooned into accepting it. It is totalitarian in its desire to impose one form of belief, in the violence with which such ideas are put forward, in the intolerance which admits no discussion and stifles freedom of debate, in the superficiality of an approach that eliminates the past and throws overboard what has been won, over the years, by past generations. It is hard to know where more wickedness resides: in the scholars and intellectuals who have betrayed the cause of intellect or among students who have turned themselves into political fanatics in order to follow fashion or to lay claim to an unwarranted notoriety.

Wrong-headed though we believe those who have espoused such ideas to be, they must be met and confuted by free discussion, not by any attempt to deny them their rights to be heard. Those with whom we disagree must be granted the freedom they deny others, but, if they turn to physical violence or intellectual blackmail, then believers in traditional cultural values must defend themselves by words or other means available to them. "We must believe," R. A. Butler once said, "that even the very youngest among us may be mistaken." Students have no standing except in as far as they submit themselves to the processes of education. To educate anyone is necessarily an "elitist" procedure.

Unfortunately it is a fact that what is called "a multicultural society" easily becomes a society where relativism goes so far as to leave it without values. If we believe the civilization of the Aztecs to be the equal of the West's we cannot avoid stating what we believe about the human sacrifice which formed a part of its religion and hallowed its festivals. Do we grant that feature of Aztec society the beneficent results which presumably the Aztecs themselves expected of it? Or do we simply dismiss as inhumane the accumulation of prisoners of war with the object of eventually cutting out their hearts or flaying them? If we do the latter, then we are judging by the light of our own present-day views. But are we not bound to judge? And do not such judgments undermine the whole idea of a multicultural society? But it is those cultural liberal ideas which cause us to reject the Aztecs which also provided the basis of our rejection of the slave trade. It was a great 19th century liberal, Macaulay, who claimed that the English language was better adapted than Hindi for the education of the Indian people. A multicultural society must challenge us to establish a real hierarchy between the cultures concerned. Only confusion will result from any attempt to produce a morality based on a pick'n'mix from different cultures. The change in the United States, from melting-pot to salad bowl, has created very great problems for which no answer is yet in sight. The idea of a multicultural society, though originally, no doubt, idealistic in its motivation, can be developed in directions that are highly damaging to that society's homogeneity, particularly where this is motivated by political considerations. If carried through to its logical conclusion of denying its cultural identity from European sources this would imply a profound cultural divide between America and Europe. A new Atlantic initiative must, therefore, point out the dangers in this concept.

Thus, while those in favor of such an initiative must devote themselves to a democratic society which permits no exclusion on the grounds of race, sex, or religion they must also defend their own cultural inheritance against any attempt to downgrade or dissolve it. This is primordial to the whole concept of Atlantic unity. This is why we considered this point at such length. No question is more important. If the culture of the Atlantic community is fragmented, it is hard to see how it can be united politically.

Patronage and the Arts

That being said, we must not forget the lesser questions that are at issue between the two sides of the Atlantic. These concern such matters as the financing of the arts, the economic foundation that enables them to continue to exist, the cultural rivalry that is present between America and Europe (with a large role being assigned to France, a country that was once culturally predominant in Europe but presently feels itself invaded and to some degree violated by American popular culture through the medium of cinema and television).

To appreciate these differences we must look backwards in history. Traditionally in continental Europe culture has been financed by the state or else by the monarch. In France a centralizing monarchy bequeathed its traditions to the Republic and to Napoleon. Some cultural institutions continued unchanged through different political regimes. The Comédie Française is only one example, but it was joined by the Académie Française, which exercised control over the French language, conservative in nature, but usually unswayed by political considerations. In Germany the existence of many small kingdoms (the *Kleinstaaterei*) produced a multiplication of sources of patronage, to which Germany owes the existence of opera houses in all major cities. Italy too shared this court culture. What should be emphasized is that most cultural institutions owed their existence to the state or a state, tiny though this might be.

On the other hand, in Britain and later in America culture has to make its own way, helped perhaps, but never dominated by the state. In Britain the royal family did indeed act as patrons of culture, as the royal collections bear witness. But, even in the 18th century, the acquisition of works of art, for instance, was largely the work of an aristocracy a good deal richer than the monarchy. In the United States, during the 20th century, cultural institutions were founded by men who had made their money from the vast expansion of American industry in the 19th century. Today private encouragement has led to a huge development of museums and galleries, quite largely due to tax arrangements which encourage charity more than is the case in Europe. Meanwhile, Britain has had to rely on a national lottery to raise admittedly large quantities of money for the arts. The British theater, however, seems to manage to exist on its own earnings, whereas Broadway has fallen on evil days. In this game the name of Shakespeare is a trump card.

There are, therefore, in the Atlantic area two strongly differentiated traditions of the way in which culture is sustained financially. In the one case there is state subsidy, often with a dignified patina inherited from the princedoms of the past. In the other, culture has to earn its own living by selling itself on the market. In that case it is subject to the same temptations as other goods—the exclusion of competitors and protectionism in fact, if not in name. At present, both the EU and the United States are liable to succumb to cultural protectionism, often disguised by some cultural imperative. On the European side there has been an attempt to restrict the flow of American films and TV programs into European countries. The excuse for this has been the need to keep national cinema and TV alive. Indeed, these media have recently known difficult times, with the expense of films rising and the audience for non-English speaking productions going down, because of both the restrictions imposed by language and the themes necessarily different from those of Hollywood. This issue surfaced during the negotiations for the recent GATT round, and intermittently, with the efforts made by the European Commission in Brussels to evolve a cultural policy. These have been marked by a scarcely veiled protectionism, including attempts to forbid certain types of advertising, which were they successful, might erode the financial basis of privately operated television networks.

On the American side protectionism expresses itself through a refusal to admit dubbed European films—a prohibition that denies them the possibility of large audiences across the United States. The reason given for this is that American audiences will never go to see dubbed films, the European response being that the intention is that

Americans never *shall* go to see dubbed films. However this may be, it is certainly the case that American film companies do exercise protectionism through their control of distribution networks.

Consumers, therefore, on both sides of the Atlantic are deprived of certain films and television programs which they might have enjoyed. The solution to this problem does not lie in protectionism but through fiscal measures designed to encourage new artistic enterprises. The same means could be used to aid publishers, organizers of art exhibitions, and patrons of music and contemporary art. The principle needs to be accepted that culture can be helped, not by keeping out foreign works, but easing artistic production at home. Particularly important here will be assistance for translations and translators. The latter are very badly paid, but their work is essential if communication between the different branches of European culture is to be maintained and also to be transmitted to the English-speaking civilizations of North America. Such institutions as the Bollingen Foundation do good work in this respect, but not enough is done and very often what passes for a translation is badly executed simply because the translator lacks time. Similar means are needed to facilitate important cultural contacts between the two sides of the Atlantic in the worlds of art and music; orchestras should be able to travel and exhibitions to be created as a result of tax concessions to those providing patronage.

It should be noted that, in cases where private patronage is invoked to provide resources for cultural projects, there are two advantages over state patronage dispensed by committees of the great and the good. In the first place such committees will usually tend to recommend "safe" projects, except in cases where they consciously turn their attention to avant-garde artists. In that case, their bias may well be toward the fraudulent and those who represent the most questionable aspects of modern art, literature, and music. It would seem that the muddle which ensues when committees try to have a discussion on artistic values naturally militates against sensible decisions. To do away with such committees, "animals with four hind legs," as the saying goes, in favor of a single enlightened patron or else patrons who are, in any case, accessible to ideas from outside the fashionable cliques of government appointees would be a great advantage. And the ranks of patronage would be considerably enlarged, were the necessary tax arrangements made to ensure that rich people obtain some alleviation of their tax burden through their benevolent interest in culture.

Secondly, government-appointed committees are naturally subjected to political influence. This is not necessarily exercised in favor of fashionable avant-garde art, but is subject to influence by the nonsense that goes under the name of political correctness. In all sorts of ways—by journalists, by broadcasters, by members of Parliament—influence is brought to bear, often in the name of pseudo-conceptions of democracy, to make it appear that "high culture" has no relevance for the vast mass of the population (which may be true) and should not, therefore, be supported by public money (which is untrue) though it is a point of view often advanced by those who would lose their audience were the cultural standards of that audience to be improved. The advantage of private patronage is that it takes the argument out of the hands of Philistine politicians and illiterate journalists. The state and elected politicians meddle enough these days under the pretext of furthering "democracy." At the moment culture would probably find it hard to do without some government support, but we must strive to ensure that its resources come from elsewhere. In Britain the present arguments about the national lottery, including the ludicrous remarks from church leaders and attacks from those who dislike a successful company, should not disguise the fact it has done much to find a solution for the problem of funding arts. We should not allow ourselves to be diverted from this by unanswerable questions about whether it is better to rebuild Covent Garden or give money for research on cancer.

As will be readily apparent we are strongly opposed to measures that ban or restrict access to culture in all and any of its forms, but we are also greatly concerned at the vast outpouring of pornography. Pornography dehumanizes and degrades both its participants and its audience. Without advocating censorship we believe that problem could be diminished if cultural elites on both sides of the Atlantic do more to promote standards which reflect respect for the person, a principle which is deeply rooted in the religious and cultural traditions of the West.

This important stricture notwithstanding the key word in the debate on culture within the Atlantic region is availability. Citizens on both sides of the Atlantic need to be able to lay hands on the books they need, view the pictures they like, see the films and plays which entertain them, increase the breadth of their culture by learning the languages of their neighbors, have access to as many television chan-

43

nels as they wish without finding political obstacles in their way. The *gleichschltung* of world culture that is now appearing under the cover of the gradual emergence of English as a *lingua franca*—convenient, but mutilated— should not mean an impoverishment of cultural experience. It should not eliminate the past or prejudice the future.

Nor should a new mechanized Internet civilization lead us to imagine that the previous concept of culture is out of date. *The Times* of London may appear on the Internet but this quite obviously represents no particular improvement in its content.

In effect, as to its dealing with the human personality, culture can be described as an atmosphere within which man may find the possibility of solitude, repose, meditation, thought, and perhaps the possibility of excelling oneself by producing artifacts—a poem or a symphony—which conveys to one's fellow or to posterity the possibility for them too of contemplating such achievements.

Culture is also an educative process, by means of which we can convey to the young the fascination of the past and the opportunities of the future. For the old it is a never-ending excitement through which life may be lived "under the angle of eternity," as Conrad put it, and death encountered with dignity and a sense of meaningfulness. Culture is what makes the difference; it ensures that we do not live like slobs or die like dogs. We conquer the painful facts of human life by understanding them. In doing this, we impart meaning to our course on earth. This is why culture must not be allowed to succumb to an idolization of modernity as such. Any future Atlantic community which abandoned its cultural inheritance or ceased to seek to improve on it would be a poor thing indeed, an unworthy descendant of Athens or Rome. We should recognize that the cultural tone of such a community will matter at least as much as its institutions or its economic arrangements.

Summary of Conclusions

We assert our attachment to Western culture, not as a view of the world to be imposed by whatever means upon other peoples, but as a heritage to be preserved and studied as a continuing source of inspiration for new generations, as well as for the modernization of other parts of the world.

We wish to expose the contradictions of those who demand, in the name of the principles of intellectual freedom, the voice that they would deny to us in the name of their ideological or religious principles.

We consider beyond compromise our commitment to multiracial, color-blind society, but we consider extremely dangerous the idea of multicultural society, where important human values are being trivialized by their being different for each person or group.

We should be prepared to accept a "clash of civilizations" if that is the price for defending the right of every human being—irrespective of civilization of origin—to life, liberty, and respect.

We reject cultural protectionism even when it is intended to defend traditional values and high culture. We are convinced that cultural policies have to be reformed through the reduction of political and bureaucratic intervention in the arts and their encouragement through an atmosphere and social environment favorable to private patronage.

We seek favorable conditions for market-orientated initiatives in the field of art and entertainment, so that the choices of the public may find their fullest expression, without ever accepting that commercial success may be directly equated with great artistic achievement.

We favor the transfrontier diffusion of television, and we are opposed to the proposed banning of advertising to children.

Without advocating a system of censorship we suggest that attention on both sides of the Atlantic be given to the problem of pornography through the promotion of standards in accordance with the principles of respect for the human person, a principle which can be considered a basic characteristic of Western society.

We object to the *de facto* protection of the U.S. film market, resulting in barriers to free circulation of European products, barriers that are created at the initiative of organized interest groups, through obstacles to translations and dubbing; we are similarly opposed to barriers to the import of U.S. films to European countries, normally on the grounds of their presumed threat to national cinema and television.

We favor a mixed regime for television, with public and commercial broadcasters on an equal footing and with spontaneously identified complementary roles. And we object to the growing drift toward a European cultural policy operating through quotas and subsidies. Such a policy not only represents an unhealthy degree of bureaucratic supervision, it is likely to foster conformist and Philistine qualities in the arts.

PART TWO

The Common Crisis

7

The Common Crisis: Is There Any?

Václav Klaus

Being known as a passive and almost submissive person who always accepts somebody else's suggestions, a few months ago I accepted the suggested title of my speech for today: *The Common Crisis*. But several days ago, when I started to think seriously about what to say, I modified the title slightly as compared with the printed version of the program, adding the question, *Is There Any?* The reason is that I am the last person who would call our situation—either at home, in Europe, or in the world—a crisis. Such a pessimistic label seems to me not appropriate. To call our current situation a crisis implies that we consider some other period of human history to be a noncrisis. I cannot find, however, any moment in the past for which I would use such a term.

I prefer to start today's discussion with different assumptions. We live in a real, not a hypothetical, world, with real, which means imperfect, people, with imperfect social institutions, with many issues that remain to be solved—but with tangible results, with visible improvements, and with innovative solutions to many difficult problems. For me the term *crisis* means a situation in which everything goes down, not up, where there are questions without answers, where there are problems without solutions, where there is a lack of elementary social cohesion and mutual understanding, where there are no dynamics, just a stationary state. This is not what I see when I look around.

The post-Communist and post–cold war era demonstrates, for me, a visible movement forward. To interpret it differently means to be disappointed with what has happened since 1989. For me, we are moving, we are "on the road" to a better world, to a world without totalitarian regimes (at least when we talk about Europe and America, about our common Atlantic region), without threatening military structures, without totally inefficient economic systems, without overideologized thinking. We have not yet entered heaven, and we never will, but I am confident that we are on the right track. I know there are people among us who see crisis in any moment when there is no central authority in full control of events, when there is no *dirigisme* from above, when we witness more spontaneity in human behavior than conforms with somebody's intentions whenever there is anything new, unknown, unplanned, and unprepared, when the old clichés are lost or forgotten. I do not belong to that group.

We have probably entered a new period, but I see it as an opportunity, not as a problem.

I know, of course, that human society is very fragile and vulnerable to all kinds of disturbances. To think that we will be able to move forward without a permanent effort, without the daily involvement of all of us in a never-ending fight for freedom, would be a fatal mistake—a fatal conceit—and would take us on the road to serfdom, which some of us know too well. To think that the collapse of communism and its probable definitive end is a final victory, the "end of history," would be very costly. We all see around us new dangers, new blind alleys, new attempts to create brave new worlds based on very promising rhetoric, on more sincere or less sincere intentions, but on wrong ambitions and false assumptions about human behavior.

Even though I expressed my strong disagreement with the term *crisis* in the title of my presentation, I accept the adjective *common*. With all the historic and cultural differences, human society is more homogeneous than some of us assume. I agree with those who say that there are common answers to our problems. In addition, I believe that the answers are simple, more or less known and old-fashioned, and realizable. I am optimistic, and I agree with one of the heroes of the Atlantic movement, Ronald Reagan, who many years ago said: "The experts tell us there are no simple answers to our difficulties. They are wrong. There are simple answers, just not easy ones." It is our task to look for them and to find them. I hope the Congress of Prague will help us in this respect.

The ambition of the congress, of course, is not so general. We are interested in a closer issue, in transatlantic relations. The idea of transatlantic cooperation between Europe and North America was born at the end of World War II. The tragic experience of our fathers and grandfathers with fascist dictatorships, with communism, and with the devastating war and their resolution not to go through it again led to many postwar activities and to the formation of several international organizations, especially NATO.

The transatlantic cooperation was—for decades—kept together by an imminent Communist threat, and we subconsciously accepted the idea of NATO as an anti-Communist bloc and nothing else. With the end of communism the common enemy disappeared, and some of us seem to be at a loss about what to fight for.

I am not. For me, the transatlantic community was never connected solely with one enemy. It has deeper roots and a stronger basis. It is based on ideas, not on enemies. It is connected with the traditions of freedom, democracy, and the market economy. European and American liberalism (in its original, European meaning) represents our common cultural heritage, which we try to keep alive for future generations on both sides of the Atlantic Ocean. We are committed to such a duty, and we have to guard it in all spheres, including the security one.

I am aware of existing dangers and know that for the time being they are more in the field of ideas than in the field of security. Some of them are "domestic" and are connected with new attempts to corporatize and syndicalize our societies, with legislative attempts to support organizations and associations. These attempts serve to partialize us, filling the space between individuals and the state at the expense of both, denying the elementary principles of a liberal society. Such approaches are erroneously justified by well-intended people who, instead of advocating further liberalization, deregulation, and privatization (not just in the economic sphere), advocate not freedom but new versions of collectivism; advocate not overall healthy competition, but more and more areas controlled by experts, professionals, and "better" people; advocate not the acceptance of incrementalism and Pareto improvements but isolated, absolutist "solutions" to partial problems; advocate not a coherent society but new "feudalities," to borrow Ludwig Erhard's term.

Such tendencies, if they prevail, will have enormous influence on international relations and on the whole transatlantic cooperation, and we should not underestimate them. Our foreign policy reactions and initiatives are less autonomous than is often assumed, and their roots in domestic ideological tenets are very deep.

I see the danger of the increase of isolationist tendencies in both Europe and America, even if for different reasons. In Europe it is because of more deepening than widening in its integration philosophy, because of less vigorous market forces and less vigorous individualist traditions. In America it is because of the prevalence of new, less liberal ideologies and because of traditional self-centeredness in world affairs. I see external dangers as well, but I consider them less dangerous than our own deficiencies.

At the beginning of my presentation I rejected the assumption of the existence of a common crisis. I can, however, imagine the arrival of such a crisis at the moment of closing ourselves, instead of opening ourselves in the field of both ideas and trade. For several decades, we in Czechoslovakia lived in a closed society, and we know what it means. We know what it means to stress differences and hatred instead of searching for commonalities and friendship. I believe the original postwar transatlantic idea arose as a reaction to our prewar insularity, and we should not repeat our mistakes. The disappearance of one common enemy should not demotivate us. We know that the slippery road to serfdom is not far away and that some parts of the road may offer seductive views of the natural beauties around.

8

Are There Common Answers?

Discussion

Irwin M. Stelzer (United States): The question we have been asked to discuss is, "Are there common answers?" As Prime Minister Klaus has pointed out, this refers not necessarily to a crisis, but to problems that many countries confront. So let me briefly sketch what the common problems are, even though they may not constitute a crisis, for which we seek common answers.

All governments in the Atlantic community as we broadly define it are wrestling with the question of the proper role of the welfare state in the next century. All governments are under pressure to reduce employment costs and to lower taxes. All governments have the problem of an aging population, with fewer workers to support more and longer-lived pensioners. All governments face the problem of a fraying social fabric, with criminality at unacceptable levels, and with the vague feeling that popular culture is somehow debasing society. And all governments face pressure to do something that we in America call *downsizing* and Europeans simply call *unemployment*.

These are some of our common problems. And each country has a stake in having other countries solve these problems and prosper, because the creation of prosperity is not a zero-sum game. We have a stake in each other's prosperity.

Perhaps fortunately, we have not had common solutions to these problems. Fortunately, because a variety of models are available for us to consider, America has relied on flexible labor markets to provide full employment, but real family incomes have risen at a rate slow enough to qualify as a problem. Britain has followed the American model, more or less, while Europe has rejected this approach in favor of a high labor-cost, high-unemployment model, with high transfer payments to maintain social cohesion. America has opted for a relatively low tax regime, Britain for a somewhat higher one, and Europe for a higher one still. America has what the Europeans consider to be a cruelly deficient welfare system. Europe has one that seems to Americans to be extravagantly costly.

The risk in these differences is that a sclerotic Europe, unable to lower its employment costs, might lurch toward protectionism. A restless America, writing Europe off as terminally ill in economic terms, might focus not only its economic but also its diplomatic and its political attention on the more vibrant Asian economies. Some of the participants in the Prague Congress have said that this danger is already a reality. Fortunately, we have a distinguished panel to solve these common problems, and they address them below.

PAUL FABRA (France): I will speak especially about fiscal policy, and especially in France. As everybody knows, the French are very proud of their cooking, which is supposed to be one of the best, if not the very best, in the world. But also, in our language the word *cuisine* has a pejorative connotation. Alongside the cooking itself, the word refers to what is done in the kitchen generally.

I would like to demonstrate what is happening today behind the curtain in different states of the community. In order to cope with the Maastricht conditions on monetary union, those attempts are giving way to a sort of cuisine that is neither politically, financially, nor economically very appetizing. It is not just that the attempts to cope with the criteria are not genuine; it is also the case that the criteria of Maastricht are inadequate. The single reason why they are inadequate is that they are entrenched in the mythology of the gross national product. To follow the track of a free Europe and a more effective economy, as Prime Minister Klaus has said, we have to stop the misuse of national accounting, which leads to the mismanagement of the political economy.

So let us consider how these member states are doing. Luxembourg, for example, is considered the best alumnus of the community in terms of equilibrium. But if you take into account the cost of funding retirement payments to the civil servants of Luxembourg, you will discover that Luxembourg is probably in one of the worst situations in the community. Even the illusion that we have even one good small country that is financially solvent is probably false.

In Germany, you will discover that the actual deficit as a proportion of GNP is probably 10 percent rather than 4 percent. But let us consider the gross errors of judgment, the mismanagement of public affairs that is encouraged by the misuse of national accounting. According to the Maastricht Treaty, supposedly, the deficit cannot be allowed to go higher than 3 percent. Well, that is not exactly so. A spectrum is implied for what is called *fine tuning*. Forget the most important feature we know about deficits—that they are intractable—and allow me to pronounce the very simple rule that should be at the center of any financial public policy. Because it is so simple, I shall probably be discredited as an economist. The rule is that we have to solve problems in public affairs, as in private affairs, as they arise. If we do not master them at the moment the problems are arising, we shall not be able to master them at all.

In France, the destructive power of the Maastrict Treaty has been more destructive than in other countries. Why? Because French elites, even today, do not have the faintest idea of how the market economy should function. The idea that government intervention is necessary in almost every field is still with us.

The contradiction between the market economy and national accounting can be summarized in a few sentences. According to national accounting, public-sector spending is considered to be a contributing factor to GNP growth. Consequently, the idea that public spending is contributing to growth collides with the imperative to squeeze the deficit. To promote growth becomes contradictory with squeezing the deficit. Another approach is to deny that public spending is a contributor to growth; the problem can be posed in different terms.

In my view, the deficit is not to be compared with the GNP. The deficit has to be considered in absolute terms—this is the approach we follow at the Center for the New Europe in Brussels. We think that we have to have a realistic, in contrast to a nominalistic, approach to the deficit.

WILFRIED PREWO (Germany): Having a German speak about the welfare state, which I am going to do now, might make you wonder. Let me say that I am not here to resurrect Bismarck, but to bury him.

Irwin Stelzer started the discussion by naming some differences between the United States and Europe. Here is another one: between

1970 and 1995, jobs rose by 60 percent in the United States and only by a meager 10 percent in Western Europe. Since 1960, unemployment in Western Europe has been moving gradually upward. In every recession, unemployment went up; and in the ensuing upswing, unemployment was hardly brought down. In the subsequent recession, unemployment went up further.

Until the 1980s, we could afford—or politicians could afford—to close our eyes and forget about this phenomenon. Everybody thought it might just disappear someday. Until the end of the 1980s, Western European countries were competing mostly within the triad of Western Europe-North America-Japan, where labor cost differences of 35 percent or so could be compensated by locational or productivity advantages.

But with the end of the cold war and the onset of the information age, the situation has changed completely. The labor-cost benchmark is no longer set within the triad. It is now set by Central and Eastern Europe and by Southeast Asia, where we not only have low wages, but also low wages with good labor quality and, therefore, low unit-labor costs. And this is producing a production exodus from Western Europe, particularly Germany, from which even mid-sized countries can take advantage, given the proximity of Central and Eastern European markets.

Germany does not lose from this—Germany benefits. German unemployment is lessened by this and will recede because of this fact. The labor-cost problem is the first major problem of the welfare state because in post–cold war Europe, the labor-cost problem is melting the financial pillars of the welfare state.

In the Bismarckian variety, the welfare state is financed by payroll taxes. Payroll taxes for unemployment and pensions in Germany now exceed 40 percent of the gross wage, paid half by the employer, half by the employee.

In addition, we have an investment problem. As we move from the machine age into the information age, we need new investment to grow. We do not have that. In 1970, in most countries of Western Europe, welfare, or social, expenditures were below investment outlays. Now the typical picture is that welfare expenditures are twice as high as investment outlays. We do not have the money to set aside to save and to invest for the information age.

The most pressing problem arises from our demographic trends. In Western Europe in 1960, the typical age tree had a pyramidical shape—with many young people, with mid-lifers in the middle, and with fewer old people. By now our age tree has become a pumpkin, or an American football standing on one tip: fewer young people, many mid-lifers still, and a growing number of retirees living longer than they did before. By about 2030, we will have a mushroom—a thin stem of young and active people supporting many old people.

By about 2030, in Germany we will have one pensioner per one active person in the labor force, implying that the average pension payroll tax in Germany will have to be exactly equal to the average pension. No jobs will be able to support that, and no young people will be willing to pay for that. The pension payroll tax would have to rise today from 19.2 percent up to 34 percent in order to provide the same benefits. Add to that health payroll tax and unemployment payroll tax and we are at 50 percent. And our current marginal tax rate is 57 percent. So where does that lead us?

We speak of security, or social security, or old age provision, as if they were insurance. They are not. With the pension payroll tax, a pay-as-you-go system, we do not set money aside for our own future pensions. All we do is support the pensions of our parents. Insurance means to set aside something for ourselves, either by building up financial capital, creating a fully funded pension plan, or raising children and educating them, that is, investing in human capital. The latter we are not doing any more. We have broken the generational contract. We have broken this chain letter, just as any chain letter is broken.

The systemic fault of our social system is that it is a uniform plan that disenfranchises the individual. We give him no options. Benefit packages are standardized; one size fits all. One cannot buy a lesser plan for a lower premium. There are no deductibles and no copayments, or if there are, they are the same for everybody.

Now this diagnosis points to the therapy. We cannot just throw out our aim of social security; we have to preserve that. Also, especially in the European environment, we have to address not only efficiency issues but also equity issues. We have to empower the individual to act with responsibility.

Empowering the individual means first giving him the money he needs to finance social safety and social insurance products. To this end, I suggest—and to Americans this may bear some resemblance to medical savings accounts or IRAs—that we put all the current employer and employee contributions into individual social savings accounts. The social savings accounts would be vested in the individuals; they would control them.

If we put all the current money into such accounts, everybody can buy the current benefits. Nobody loses, everybody is taken care of. Social safety is preserved.

But the individual is not obliged to buy current benefits. All we do is oblige him to buy a mandatory minimum package, because as a society we would not gain if an individual did not insure himself; indeed, in the worst case, he would again become a burden to society. So there has to be mandatory minimum insurance.

If the individual buys less than the current full plan, if he stays with the minimum plan or buys something between the minimum and the optional 100 percent benefit package, he keeps the savings. Those savings will be his. They will stay, however, in a social savings account. They will stay there and he can draw on them to cover himself for contingencies he has not covered, and he can use them to buy other social insurance products.

To be practical, allow me to give some examples of what this would look like. In health, it would mean copayments and deductibles. This would reduce excessive spending, especially in ambulatory care. The plan would enable individuals to have a full choice of providers. It would allow people to opt with their money for fee-paying care or for managed care. Competition on the supply side would unlock a tremendous efficiency potential, especially on the European scene, with publicly run hospitals.

Another feature is sick leave. In Germany, currently, we talk about lowering the sick leave compensation from 100 percent to 80 percent. Why not, in compensation, give the remaining 20 percent to the social savings account of the employee? He can then insure himself with the remaining 20 percent, or he can just save it and keep it in his social savings account.

One consequence would be a tremendous incentive to cut down on absenteeism. Two-thirds of the first two days of sickness in Germany are weekend related: they fall on Mondays or Fridays. Only 6 percent of the first days of illness fall on Wednesdays.

Also consider unemployment. Here, again, we currently have the same benefits for all. Why not differentiate according to risk classes? Somebody who undergoes training has a lower unemployment risk. Why not give him an incentive by means of a lower unemployment premium? Again, the savings from that will augment the balances in the social savings account.

Now, what do we need all this money for? For pension reform where we have to complement the current pay-as-you-go system by building up a fully funded pension plan.

TOMÁŠ HALÍK (Czech Republic): My contribution could be called *the ecology of freedom*. I wish to speak about the necessity of supporting and protecting the moral climate that forms the biosphere of a free society for the development of values on which the identity of the Atlantic culture is based.

Václav Klaus expressed an important idea when he observed that "the transatlantic community is based on ideas, not on enemies." The main common enemy has departed, and now his departure compels us, once again, to seek our own identity, our common values and ideas.

Are the most important things that bring us together liberal institutions? Liberal institutions are immensely valuable. We who were deprived of them for so long know this very well. And yet, in the words of Lord Dahrendorf, they are cold. They do not give the feeling of being at home, of being rooted; they do not provide the means of being conscious of our identity. To lead a happy life man also needs warm institutions—traditional structures such as the family, the community, the church, and a homeland. These are the mediating structures, wherein one learns to discern what is of value, where one acquires the basic customs and traditions that lay the foundations of our moral and social lives.

Certainly, at the time of the cold war, NATO was primarily a cold institution, even though in these lands it was warmly valued by democratically thinking people, above all, as an expression of the resolution to protect the security of those warm structures. Its mission was seen as one of protecting the freedom of nations, protecting their cultures and their spiritual life, and guaranteeing the security of family life. The Atlantic community is now facing the task of seeking its positive identity: that is, not only defending democracy and peace but positively stimulating the political culture as well as the internal peace of societies.

A free society, political and economic democracy, the legal state, respect for human rights, and the dignity of the individual did not simply fall from heaven; nor are they the product of some sort of universal human experience. They have arisen only where there exists the centuries-old cultural influence of Western Christianity, the catholic synthesis of Jewish religion, Greek philosophy, Roman law, and the Protestant ethic. The ideals of the Enlightenment are a predominantly secularized version of these Christian values. Such values form the biosphere of a free society and the roots of Atlantic identity. Since respect for the freedom of conscience of each being is a part of these values, it is evident that such values themselves cannot be forced with aggression upon a person.

The natural means whereby a person acquires these values are precisely in the mediating structures. The state and the communities of states must remain ideologically neutral. It is, however, in the interests of a democratic state to give its full support also to those institutions that seek to broaden the values on which political and economic democracy stands.

It is just these mediating structures, particularly the family but also religious and other communities, that have helped many people in a number of countries, even during the reign of communism, to maintain basic moral values. They did not permit the totalitarian regime to destroy the culture entirely.

Under favorable conditions a stable democratic society may develop, although in several countries (especially in some of the countries of the former Soviet Union) the tradition of Western Christianity did not exist before the Communist era, nor was there any tradition of a democratic political culture before the Communist era. This lack, followed by the long-term destructive effect of a totalitarian regime, has greatly harmed natural structures and values, such as family life, neighborhood communities, religious life, moral values in the workplace, initiative, and creativity. In these places, adversity to communism was a matter for a few courageous individuals, but it did not create any sort of parallel structures, such as the Solidarity movement in Poland or Charter 77 in Czechoslovakia. It is understandable that what is happening in those countries is fundamentally different from the way that, for example, the Czech Republic and some of the other Central European countries are evolving. Here, the majority of citizens never doubted that their country belonged to the West.

It is understandable that among those countries of the so-called post-Communist world there are enormous differences. The prospects of a stable democracy and a prospering economy differ sharply where cultural traditions and the moral climate of individual societies are concerned. Political, economic, and moral transformations all mutually condition each other. But the moral ground provides the key. Wherever the basic values of Atlantic culture have not been incorporated into the living culture and have not become the motifs for human conduct, the political and economic structures of a free society are unable to establish themselves and to carry on for any length of time. Instead of a mature, prospering society, chaos settles there. Or the little hatchways to democracy again lead back, through the agency of free elections, to the devotees of old totalitarian ideology or their successors.

The vision of a united Europe, from the Atlantic to the Urals, was inspiring and has played an important, positive role in the overthrow of communism. But I am afraid that it will remain a wish for some considerable time. It is absolutely necessary to strengthen the Atlantic community and extend it to include those countries that belong to the culture of the West. It is vital that the Atlantic community not be limited merely to military, political, and commercial cooperation, but that it also support cultural interchange. It is necessary to support educational and research programs that would be directed at recognizing and broadening values. Such programs create the basis of Western culture's identity.

One cannot respond to the challenge of the times simply through the mechanical addition of a few states to NATO. One must overcome the mentality of the cold war and the thinking that makes categories of hostile groupings, no matter how low the danger from the east is today estimated to be.

The disappearance of the common enemy once again forces us to recognize our own identity. Analytical psychology teaches that the enemy makes it easy for us to define our identity. The enemy often serves as a projection screen onto which we cast our own shady side. We then identify our bright side more easily and do not focus quite so much on our negative side. The demise of the enemy offers both a painful and a useful possibility to encounter that which we have for so long not wanted to admit.

After the fall of communism there was a moment when even we in the West came to recognize how much we had departed from the moral values of Atlantic civilization. The welfare state, too, contributed to the weakening of people's capacity to work well and bear personal responsibility for themselves and for others. And that responsibility is the basis of the social ethic. The West also could not resist its own hedonistic inclinations, which are unfavorable to family life and to bringing up children. The West finds it difficult to guard against terrorism and the drug trade. And it seems that it cannot respond to the emptiness, loneliness, and anxiety in people's hearts from which these phenomena take their source.

A new Atlantic initiative must result in something greater than the mere extension of NATO. To mediate dialogue and cultural exchange is an essential concern of Atlantic culture. This includes giving, especially to young people, the opportunity to know other nations within the community, and further, it includes taking responsibility to overcome prejudice and misunderstanding.

In the era of mass-media culture, we have an enormous responsibility to ensure that the media provide educational programs to help people understand other cultures. Programs directed at understanding diverse cultures help to solve conflicts and to weaken assertions of xenophobia, racism, nationalism, and the destructive response to the problems of migration from the east and the south. Programs to uncover our own spiritual traditions of Atlantic culture may serve to prevent the effects of destructive religious sects, which by analogy work like a drug in the area of spirituality and consequently expand, especially in those places where man has become uprooted in his own culture.

The Atlantic civilization cannot cease to export its technology and its products. We must also, however, feel some responsibility for the ideas, the culture, way of life, and values we offer and for the kind of moral message we are sending to the rest of the world. We must also think about and discuss these matters together. Perhaps it is really we who are particularly sensitive to such questions: we, whom communism forced to look at the edifice of Western civilization after such a long time, and who feel from the outside that the West is where our natural home lies.

Our contest with the Communist Utopia taught us that the strongest thing in life is hope. Are not such large social problems as terrorism, migration, and chemical and spiritual drugs brought on by a loss of hope? And so all partial attempts at a reply and a solution must once again lead to the question: what is the nature of the hope that Atlantic culture offers the world?

EBERHARD VON KOERBER (Germany): The changing geopolitical landscape of the past few years has certainly brought with it new problems, both internal and external, but it has also brought great new opportunities, as Mr. Klaus mentioned earlier. It would be, however, most unwise to be complacent about the problems that, if not properly managed, have significant potential to create crisis. Equally we must be careful not to fall into the trap of "crying wolf" and risking a loss of credibility and an absence of response, or even worse, risking the destruction of the hopes of societies in transformation. Instead, we must strive to ensure that good and prudent management of key political, security, and economic issues promotes new opportunities and helps to solve both internal and external problems.

Now is the time to consider new initiatives to strengthen the transatlantic relationship in all its dimensions—political, economic, and security. In particular, it is important to forge a modern and renewed conceptual understanding of the foundations and realities of the relationship among the current generation of opinion formers on both sides of the Atlantic.

The governments of both Western Europe and North America can take a series of mutually reinforcing actions that could improve governance of globalization and provide more effective leadership on key economic and trade issues. This is particularly the case on trade and employment questions.

The European Union can do more to reduce regulation and thus assist competitiveness and promote greater employment opportunities. Both the EU and the United States should continue long-term efforts to reduce public deficits and safeguard price stability in their domestic markets. Sustainable growth and low inflation are necessary to ensure domestic economic strength and effective external leadership.

Leaders in both Western Europe and North America could and should do more to counter many of the current media myths and angst that suggest economic insecurity is an inevitable consequence of globalization. Trade, which in 1995 grew by 8 percent—three times faster than economic output—continues to be a key driver of economic growth and job creation. Higher growth in emerging markets creates new consumers, who in turn buy large quantities of higher-value-added goods and services from the more mature markets. This is a fabulous win-win situation. While structural change can be a difficult adjustment for those immediately affected, the long-term economic benefits clearly outweigh short-term dislocation. In the information technology age, our people are more ready than some would have us believe to adapt to the economic and cultural changes required to generate new jobs and to take advantage of trade opportunities. Concepts of decentralization, mobility, and empowerment through responsibility correspond more closely to the fundamental human desire for freedom than do inefficient centralization, large static organizations, or jobs unrealistically guaranteed for life.

The EU and the United States can mutually reinforce sound domestic strategies through an ambitious program of transatlantic cooperation. Business should be closely associated with formulation of and implementation of this program and the Transatlantic Business Dialogue is an excellent example of such business involvement. For example, a major priority in the economic and trade area should be application of the mutual recognition principle: that is, once a product is accepted on one side of the Atlantic in either the EU or NAFTA area, it should be possible to offer it for sale in the other without further regulatory permits. A good start was made at the EU-U.S. Madrid Summit in December 1995, but the agreements made there must be followed up actively. An important feature of transatlantic cooperation is that it should remain open and not closed to the rest of the world. It should not be seen as an exclusive process but rather as one of providing effective global leadership. Transatlantic agreements on new issues should be offered on a most-favored-nation basis to other WTO members through the WTO negotiating process. In other words, we have to keep multilateralism on track.

Given their weight in the global economy, both the United States and the EU have a particular responsibility to demonstrate effective leadership on international economic and trade issues. In particular, they could implement their Uruguay Round commitments on an accelerated basis and seek to reduce the permitted transition periods for liberalization of agriculture and textiles. They could seek to abstain from short-term protectionist policies on trade in steel and other basic materials.

The governments of Western Europe and North America have to give particular attention and support to the process of economic reform in Russia, in the other states in the Commonwealth of Independent States, and in Central and Eastern Europe.

Business has been one of the early risk takers, with Western European and U.S. foreign direct investment here running close to $30 billion. My own company, ABB, over the past five years has expanded its activities in thirteen countries, creating 30,000 jobs, generating more than $2 billion in new orders, and making selective acquisitions worth about $300 million in Central and Eastern Europe.

The governments of Western Europe and North America should also be prepared to take calculated risks to promote trade and economic reform. They could make special efforts to avoid protectionism against the products of Russia and other Eastern European economies and ensure that they enjoy effective market access. They could aim to underpin political democracy and stability in security through more and more trade and mutual interdependence. They could work in a focused manner to encourage these countries to accede to the obligations and rights of WTO membership. In return, they should expect that these countries will establish more secure and predictable investment regimes, hasten the process of privatization, implement the necessary financial reforms, and take steps for better environmental protection.

Institutions are necessary to underpin more effective transatlantic cooperation, but it is not necessary to invent new bureaucracies. Instead, there should be regular senior political review of developments in these areas and verification that existing institutions are carrying out their mandates in a coordinated manner and with the necessary degree of coherence and interaction to achieve concrete results within an agreed timetable. In this context, regular transatlantic EU-U.S. meetings at political and senior official levels can drive the process forward, as can meetings of the G-7. Business should be closely associated with such reviews. I am convinced that all the steps and efforts mentioned will contribute to more international trade and, accordingly, to higher employment.

Questions and Comments

JEFFREY GEDMIN (United States): I would like to direct my question to Wilfried Prewo, who gave an eloquent exposition of some of the economic problems facing the welfare state in Germany. Mr. Prewo, perhaps you could respond to a political question. What do you see as feasible? What is likely, and what is less likely, to actually happen?

MR. PREWO: If you look at the environment, you become pessimistic about what our governments are doing. They do not open up the system along the lines that I have suggested. They are still caught in their old, machine-age thinking. They try to operate on the welfare state as one would operate on a monolithic system. You reduce some

65

benefits, try to open a valve here and there. For example, you try to help the system by raising the retirement age for women, as has recently happened in Germany.

This is typical machine-age thinking: social engineering, top-down tinkering. This will, if it succeeds, help for just a few years. But the problem will come back in a more serious form later, and it will still haunt us. I am presently doubtful whether we will see developments that will allow people more freedom of choice about their own social safety. I believe we will hear more thoughts along these lines, as possibly in the United States such reform will take place, and this will spill over into our political debate five or ten years later. At the moment, it is not happening. So at the moment I am pessimistic, but I am optimistic that in a few years' time the voices will increase.

ROBERT D. HORMATS (United States): I have one comment to make, inspired by Eberhard von Koerber's interesting presentation. The requirement now is for economic and cultural change. The culture of the economy is extremely important.

One of the points frequently made in Europe is that the United States is creating poor, low-income jobs. That is one of the myths that has to be dispelled—not just because it is a myth but because it goes to the heart of what is happening in the United States. What is occurring in the United States is not just an economic revolution, but a huge change in entrepreneurship.

What is required to make the economy run effectively is a rebirth of the entrepreneurial spirit. This requires a series of changes that encourage people to take risks and give them economic benefits, the returns of taking risks successfully. And that involves a reduction in the role of government. It certainly involves a reduction in the degree of regulation. But it also involves a cultural change that comes not just from the top but from all levels, that enables people to understand the benefits of risk, that encourages risk taking and entrepreneurialism.

My worry is that Europe is still too protective of the old order. The economies do not have the necessary agility. The notion of economic safety is built into the governance process and into the regulating process, so that risk taking is not encouraged and profitability is not supported. When we discuss these institutional changes, that cultural dimension, as well as the economic side of entrepreneurialism, has to be addressed directly if we are going to improve the creation of jobs in Europe and the profitability of environment in Europe. That seems to be the big risk: that Europe will not take risks, because it continues to sit in an old era and, therefore, does not benefit from the changes in the global economy.

MR. VON KOERBER: You have really hit the nail on the head. In Europe, we have the paradox that we have developed a high degree of individualism and liberalism; but at the same time, this individualism is not applied in the correct way. Its consequence is to create high expectations about the contribution of the state while discouraging risk taking.

And if we do not come back to entrepreneurial individualism, self-initiative, and self-development, then the adrenaline that our European system requires will not flow. I think this is the key element of cultural change, and it is very sad that the achievements in the United States in creating new jobs are discounted by the media, which minimize them by saying, "These are McDonald's jobs." We know statistically that more than 50 percent of those jobs created are medium-to-high income, good, strong, quality jobs. And it is important that this is properly communicated as an example of how to invigorate economic change and how to invigorate the economic system in terms of growth and employment.

R. F. M. LUBBERS (Netherlands): First, I fully agree with the need to make it clear in Europe that the successes of the American economy are very much related to entrepreneurship. The dynamics in American society of that job creation are a success.

Having said that, though, I cannot agree fully with Mr. Prewo, talking about Europe as if it is homogeneous in this respect. It is not. In the Netherlands, unemployment is too high—7 percent—but it is steadily going down. So in fact, that economy is creating more or less the same proportional number of jobs as is the American economy. I cite this as one of the proofs that it is very dangerous to talk about Europe as one entity.

In the United Kingdom, as a result of the leadership of Margaret Thatcher, the economy was energized. That has happened not only in the United Kingdom. In the Czech Republic and Poland, there is a lot of entrepreneurship, growth, and perspective. So it is a little dangerous to start this discussion with the assumption, "Everything is fine in the United States and everything is tragic in Europe."

Second, I wish to respond to Eberhard von Koerber. Germany is an important country, but for some time it has been so busy with reunification that Germans forgot about globalization and the need to invigorate the economy. But I am a little more optimistic. I think that under the leadership of Helmut Kohl, we will see them start that process—maybe a little late, but it will come.

I do see the strengths of the American economy. But twelve years ago in the United States, in the pre-Reagan period, there was a lot of pessimism. There was gloom and doom, and people no longer believed in their future. They were afraid of the Japanese and so forth. And then they started to change. Don't be that pessimistic.

MAX BELOFF (United Kingdom): As Mr. Lubbers has pointed out, there are considerable differences among the European countries. And as Irwin Stelzer pointed out, the United Kingdom is, in many respects, closer to the American than to the continental model. Why, then, should Britain accept having its advantages diminished by accepting pressure from the European Union to add to its labor costs on the European Union's favored German model?

MR. STELZER: Has anyone in the room the nerve to propose that? The answer is that they should not, if you want it from me. Michael Spicer wishes to respond. He could perhaps defend the desire to push the social chapter down Britain's throat, but I doubt it.

MICHAEL SPICER (United Kingdom): Mr. Stelzer, I am going to do just the opposite. I was delighted to hear Mr. Lubbers say that there were several different countries in Europe. The problem, as was pointed out by Lord Beloff, is that there is a move toward abolishing the different countries and creating a single country. In the process of doing that and indulging in centralized and protectionist measures, the European average unemployment, if there is such a thing, has been going up to around 10 percent. The American level has also been going up, but it is at a considerably lower level. And there are some implications to be drawn from that.

I would like to ask a question of the panel. One of the strongest protectionist arguments is based on the idea that low labor costs and ready access to capital in Eastern European countries give them such an unfair advantage that it is almost impossible to trade with them. I wonder if the panel—or someone on the panel—could address the fallacy in the argument.

MR. VON KOERBER: I would like to comment on that as an investor in Central and Eastern Europe and in many locations in Western Europe. We have created and secured some 30,000 jobs in Central and Eastern Europe, and what I call the win-win relationship is really clarifying the fallacy of one-sided advantages. Growth in the emerging market in Central and Eastern Europe is also creating new markets for Western European goods and exporters. And we have seen, so far, exports from Western Europe growing faster than exports from Eastern Europe to Western Europe.

And so, for the time being, as numerous politicians can confirm, the beneficiaries are not the countries of Central and Eastern Europe; they are the locations in Western Europe that are increasing their exports to these new emerging markets more than the new markets are exporting to the West.

At the same time, Western European companies have the advantage of low-cost sourcing from Eastern Europe and of making their own locations more competitive through a new division of labor between Eastern and Western Europe. This is another advantage for Western investors and manufacturers particularly in hard-currency, high-wage countries. And therefore the fallacy lies in believing that low-cost competition from Eastern Europe is destructive for Western locations.

MR. STELZER: Could you expand on one point? Robert Hormats mentioned that, as a key ingredient to stimulating entrepreneurship, a lower tax regime is vital so that people can keep the benefits of their entrepreneurial efforts. Wilfried mentioned a 57 percent marginal tax rate. Are you as optimistic that the tax rates in Europe can be lowered to accommodate this new entrepreneurship as you are about other things?

MR. VON KOERBER: A few specific and technical remarks. First, overmatured, wealthier states in Europe are now diminishing their deficits. This is one of the convergence criteria for the single currency. After this step, they will be able to lower taxes.

Belgium, for example, has to pay enormous interest on its debts of the past. So it has a balanced budget, in a sense, but it still has to pay this enormous interest bill. It takes time before a country can lower taxes. But the process will go on, with budget cuts and possibilities to lower taxes.

Second, in a globalized economy, we will see shifts in the tax system. We will see reforms from what we call direct to indirect taxes on end consumption. And we will see income taxes, taxes on labor, and taxes on entrepreneurship all go down in Europe.

I am optimistic. But, because of our excessive burdens of the past, we have to pay our debts. It is a slow process. But we will see it through; we will convince politicians to reduce taxes. And we will convince them that taxes must be shifted to consumption rather than labor and entrepreneurship; but that was the traditional, old-fashioned way.

MR. PREWO: I fully agree that we have to reduce our taxes and shift them toward indirect taxation. I do not quite agree that we can afford to wait until we have fulfilled all the criteria. For me, the 3 percent Maastricht criterion is a quotient. And a quotient has a numerator and a denominator, and the denominator is GDP. If we work on the budget deficit, as we have for the past couple of years, by raising taxes and not just lowering government consumption, we may lower the numerator, the government deficit. But we may also lower, or stifle, the growth in the denominator, the GDP. So we need growth policies now, as painful as they are. Although this implies a double burden on the government and an extra reduction in consumption spending, we cannot wait until later on.

MR. LUBBERS: Let me respond to the first question. Because I had to be brief, I had to be blunt, and I want my position to be understood. It is quite consistent with what I said, that Holland is an exception. Holland is a small country. A small country always has to adapt. A small country has to be open. Germany will also adapt; I think it will take longer. The small countries are the champions of free trade in Europe, of antiprotectionism, of going into the information age.

9

What Role for International Institutions?

Discussion

Géza Jeszenszky (Hungary): Nineteen eighty-nine marked the beginning of a new historical era in Eastern Europe in which the intellectuals played a permanent role. Intellectualism dominated that revolution, perhaps more than in 1848.

Nevertheless, the intellectuals had to give room to the so-called experts, or they had to become experts and politicians themselves. While the role of the individual has not declined, and great charismatic leaders played a very important role in the twentieth century, they could not have achieved much without help from professional staffs.

International organizations were practically nonexistent in the nineteenth century. The first one was a Socialist organization built on solidarity: the Socialist International. It had a Utopian vision of the disappearance of the nation-state. Under the Communist version, Lenin and Stalin tried, rather, to obliterate the nation-state by crushing other nations.

But nations are still alive today and very unlikely to be subsumed by a bureaucratic superstate. States and nations are not identical, however. Unlike most West European countries, most other countries are multinational. Whether we call them "international institutions" or "interstate institutions," what is evident is that after World War II a number of important institutions emerged to deal with international and national problems by using a supranational

71

and international approach. The people of Central and Eastern Europe, who against their will had been under Communist dictatorship for decades, came to see the very influential and supportive role of such institutions as NATO, the emerging Common Market, and also to a lesser extent the European Union. So, in that sense, citizens of formerly Communist countries are really strong believers in international institutions.

MAX M. KAMPELMAN (United States): *Globalization* is a word that is frequently used and increasingly being disparaged by some. The total globalization of science and technology has many consequences that support the development of democracies. Authoritarian governments, for example, require a monopoly on information. With the ability to communicate by satellite, however, no government can have a monopoly on information. That technological change undermines the fundamental principle that permits authoritarian governments to flourish. Border police, who can prevent vaccines from being shipped from one country to another, cannot keep out the germs, nor can they bar the broadcasts and ideas, both of which are vital to the concept of globalization.

A recent *Wall Street Journal* article about what constituted an American-made automobile pointed out that the automobile consisted of parts made in twelve to fifteen different countries—a reality of our economics and industry. Moreover, one cannot fully understand the New York Stock Exchange without knowing what is happening on the Tokyo and London Stock Exchanges, because of the global interrelationships involved.

Not long ago, the *New York Times* printed an article about all the Nobel science winners. My recollection is that the team of scientists who won included somebody from the United States and others from outside of the United States. The individuals involved had evidently found it possible in the information age to conduct joint research, even though they are in different parts of the world.

Science, technology, communications, and economics enable globalization to govern our lives effectively. But in the world of politics, we have a long way to go, and that is our current challenge. How do we apply the concept of globalization, which has in those other fields enhanced welfare? How do we apply that principle to the political realm? If we can meet that challenge, we shall have made a very significant contribution to the welfare of the human race.

LANE KIRKLAND (United States): The longer we delay NATO expansion, the worse off we shall be. Far from risking revival of the cold war by expanding NATO, failing to do so carries cold war overtones suggesting an implicit or explicit veto by the Commonwealth of Independent States over the sovereign decisions of free states. We need to focus first on the future role of NATO. The Central European countries in particular should be in a position as members to participate in and contribute to that debate. We can safely assume that there will continue to be common problems that will require a military or police response.

Second, we need to attend to the potential value of the Organization for Economic Cooperation and Development in pursuing common economic and political objectives and policies more than we have in the past. We have too often bypassed and neglected the OECD in designing assistance programs for developing democracies in the East, or we have largely limited the organization's role to underfunded sectoral analysis.

The OECD is a living souvenir of the Marshall Plan, the last really successful economic undertaking of the Atlantic powers. It has the membership, structure, and historical memory to do much more than it has been funded or allowed to do. Among its positive attributes are its active, competent trade union committee and its business advisory committee, which participate vitally in the processes of civic society.

I had the honor to chair the trade union committee for some years, and I am familiar with its work. That trade union committee is the instrument through which the democratic trade unions reach common ground on economic and social issues and prepare representations for the annual G-7 summits.

I do not mean to suggest that trade unions at large embrace all formulas and prescriptions of the OECD secretariat, for we do not. We have hotly debated and resisted many of them, particularly in the macroeconomic and labor market fields. I am distressed to see some of those formulations replicated in the mission statement here. But the OECD enables us to take an active and effective part in the debate on the future role of NATO, which is not the case with many other government-dominated international bodies.

Third, a comparison of the International Labor Organization with the United Nations is instructive. I have been both a critic and a supporter of the ILO and have influenced the U.S. decision both to withdraw and to rejoin that body. As a public delegate to the fiftieth anniversary of the UN General Assembly, I had my first in-depth exposure to the UN proper.

That experience gave me a new and heightened respect for the International Labor Organization. By comparison with the UN, that organization now seems to me a model of efficiency, organization, and dispatch. Resolutions on everything under the sun, mostly repetitions of previous actions, flood the UN General Assembly, which considers and acts on all of them.

I kept a casual count of how many politically charged, repetitious, and otherwise foolish resolutions were passed by overwhelming margins in the UN. Less than half of those would have survived the ILO's rules and procedures. If the UN were tripartite, as is the ILO, that number would have been further reduced to the vanishing point.

Three of the ILO's rules and procedures would make good sense in any reform of the United Nations. First, the UN should have a limited conference agenda defined by the director general and a relatively strong governing body. Second, the organization should establish a resolutions committee, which would act as a safety valve for political pressures, limit consideration of resolutions to those that make the top of a priority vote, and ensure that only one or two reach the conference floor. Third, the UN should adopt a quorum rule, under which the yes and no votes must constitute a majority of the delegates to pass, because the preferred tactic to defeat a proposal is abstention.

If the UN adopted those procedures, the organization would save large sums of money and the General Assembly could complete the useful or at least the relevant work in weeks, as is the case with the ILO's annual conference, instead of in the months now required.

Finally, when my organization was being accused of protectionism during the NAFTA debate, I published a proposal that fell on deaf ears. I proposed that instead of merging America's future marketplace with the fate of the peso and the ethical and labor standards that applied in Mexico, the United States should try to elbow its way into the European Common Market. I proposed a North Atlantic free-trade agreement, creating the largest free-trade area in the history of the world. I now urge, as I did then, that its border to the east in Europe be further extended as soon as possible.

I have grown a bit weary of the mindless and pejorative use of the term *protectionist*. Regardless of its other logical virtues, my proposal serves the purpose of at least clarifying who the protectionists really are.

ADRIAN KARATNYCKY (United States): Both President Václav Havel and Karel Schwartzenberg expressed concerns about reversals in the direction of Central and East European countries in their moves toward democracy and an open society. Prime Minister Václav Klaus, however, rejected the idea of a common crisis. I believe that, in the end, the prime minister is right. There is no common crisis but rather a set of very different crises. In Central and Eastern Europe, we see a growing differentiation, and we may be at the point where some of those diversions, digressions, and partings are of a more permanent nature. Therefore, in considering the role of international institutions, we should focus attention on the countries' making their transitions from the old totalitarian and authoritarian orders.

In Central and Eastern Europe, we now see BMWs traversing ancient cobbled streets. We see stock markets in many countries booming in quick spurts and generally trending very comfortably and impressively upward. We see the high degree of prosperity that benefits a large segment of the populations of those countries but bypasses others. Many of those countries enjoy open, vigorous free media that are privately held and impervious to any possible predations by the state. At the same time, however, we see the rise of revisionist Communist ideas in Europe further to the east of where we sit today. We see scandals—serious charges of potential treason and espionage against sitting prime ministers. We see, in Belarus, the beating and bloodying of journalists and peaceful protesters on the day commemorating the Chernobyl disaster. And we see in a candidate for NATO membership an important government official who was, in effect, a bag man for the Communist Party of the Soviet Union, seeking to concentrate within a single ministry the functions of the internal revenue service, the census, the ministry of the interior, and all security structures. We also see a Europe in which a major European, if not Eurasian, power is engaged in a campaign of carnage that has left more than 40,000 people dead.

It is fitting, therefore, to look at this Europe as we attempt to assess what kind of institutions are appropriate to serving its needs and making it more integrated. Not all the news is bad: of the seven-

75

teen Central and East European countries, excluding the former Yugoslavia, fourteen, including Russia, had relatively free and fair elections. Of those, only six could be said to have vigorous civic institutions—with a balance of power among the state, the individual, mediating institutions, and civic associations—that truly enable us to regard them as free societies. So there is a long, long path to go.

Discussion about the kinds of institutions appropriate to Central and Eastern Europe should also take into account another set of international institutions that are being created. They may seem feckless to some, but they seem threatening to others. Those are the institutions such as the Commonwealth of Independent States and the Soviet Socialist Republic, which currently comprises two states, Belarus and Russia. Therefore, when we speak of extending or enlarging NATO, we should also keep in mind those other institutions that affect a number of countries that are to a great degree geographically and culturally part of Europe.

Our discussions and documents should consider those institutions as well as the optimistic "do good" side of Western institutions in trying to help the transition from the totalitarian old order. In fact, between those two types of structured institutions, we have a political no-man's land—a no-man's land of opportunity for the transformation of those countries into normal, democratic, and stable societies. That no-man's land includes the Baltic states, Ukraine, and Moldova. These countries are not in the front ranks of NATO integration; they are not in the front ranks of European Union integration. But this conference and policy makers should give great thought to those countries, for as we try to satisfy the problems of the security vacuum in one part of Central Europe or Eastern Europe, we simply displace the vacuum to another part. Unless we adequately and thoughtfully address the world that is shaped by expanding NATO and other institutions, we shall not adequately address the longer-term needs of a stable Europe from the Urals to the Atlantic.

What types of institutions, general trends, and values should inform our thinking? It is extremely important to keep in mind the broad diversity of those states and to rid ourselves of the tendency to consider those countries simply as emerging democracies. A number of those countries are emerging tyrannies or emerging dictatorships, and we should speak forthrightly about that. We should think in a coordinated fashion to help the civil societies that are resisting such a political tightening, particularly in the East European states.

To facilitate that coordination, it is important for the United States to continue to maintain a substantial role in Europe and to be anchored in a set of institutions. In addition, we need a permanent common forum on which the countries supporting the growth of democratic institutions could meet on a regular, systematic basis to plan more thoughtfully and in a more coordinated fashion how to support democratic transitions.

It is also important to strengthen the defensive security of the countries in the no-man's land. As NATO expands eastward, we should consider creating a secure community of neutral states in Europe. Such neutral states, which were not, for example, part of the Commonwealth of Independent States or a military part of the Tashkent Treaty, might participate in whichever trading bloc welcomed them or in whichever bloc they felt comfortable. Such action by neutral states could help, eventually, in opening the door to the creation of a common Europe. Thus, we should consider giving countries beyond Austria and Finland—the long-shot candidates—a special treaty with NATO resembling the 1955 Austrian State Treaty. But some new impetus to acknowledge the neutrality of those states might be very valuable.

As we think about expanding European institutions, we ought to recognize that the offer of participating in a community of property, civility, and democracy is tantalizing. We should keep open that door even to Russia. The guiding principle ought to be that we oppose an artificial division of Europe into east and west, but we should acknowledge an existing divide: the division between open societies and those that, by the choices of their own leaders, seek to plunge their people once again into darkness and tyranny.

MR. JESZENSZKY: Your analysis shows that you do not fully subscribe to what you once wrote, "How the East Was Lost." You also believe like all of us that it is not yet lost. But that is one of the reasons why we are here—to make sure that that is not the case.

International institutions constitute a vast subject. I am pleased that our analysis could deal with the problems and hopes of existing, well-functioning Western institutions, as well as with how those institutions could be expanded and the relevance to Central and Eastern Europe. We have to agree with Adrian Karatnycky that not all those countries are emerging democracies.

MICHAEL SPICER (United Kingdom): I have two brief comments on the excellent mission statement. The first is that the European Union and free trade are becoming mutually contradictory. Any move toward free Atlantic trade should not be left as the sole responsibility of discussions between the European Union and NAFTA, for instance. A strengthened WTO should be responsible.

Second, in this context the term *Atlantic* is not so much geographical as one based on common Western values. At the very least, we should consider including South America as those countries become more and more attuned to Western values in trade and security matters. Perhaps we should consider dropping the *N* from NATO.

ROGER ROBINSON (United States): I thought Adrian Karatnycky made a number of sobering points that are worth building on in the NATO context. Although the policy papers are very fine documents, I could not help but notice that there is no mention of economics in the security report and no mention of security in the trade and economics report.

That is regrettable, as the nexus between those two that is embodied in the concept of international security could well emerge as the leading policy portfolio for the next decade and for the twenty-first century. Having attended many such conferences in both a public- and a private-sector capacity, I am not at all surprised by the seeming fire wall separating those two portfolios of the congress. As a former banker and one in the international field, I know very well that taking action to advance our common security concerns is viewed as sometimes disruptive to normal trade and to financial, energy, and technology flows.

For those in the political-military field, many elements of the international economic portfolio seem hopelessly arcane and not suited to security-oriented policy making, for example, access of national borrowers to our bond and interbank deposit markets, official exports programs, and other trading institutions. Fortunately, on the security side, matters have been better understood.

From this point forward, however, the fire wall between security and markets will inevitably be breached with greater frequency and violence. A lack of allied unity continuously dilutes or undermines economic and political sanctions against proliferators and other important strategic trade offenders. Such was the case in the U.S. administration's seeming unwillingness to impose sanctions on the recent Chinese sale to Pakistan. Although I am an ardent free trader,

I believe that we must strengthen and identify more creative policy tools if we are to be able genuinely to deter weapons of mass destruction and ballistic missile threats. We simply cannot permit our nations' needs for exports and jobs to supersede our common security concerns, or the ultimate violence to the international markets will inflict potentially debilitating costs on our populations. Therefore, we no longer can afford to separate those issues as in the past, just as we cannot afford to eschew strengthened multilateral export controls and other essential economic security measures. Accordingly, I think a major upgrading of NATO's economic secretariat and operations is in order as soon as practical.

KENNETH MINOGUE (United Kingdom): My question for Mr. Kampelman is about globalization. It arises from the tensions in our deliberations in general, as to whether we are asking, What is necessary to protect our civilization? or What is necessary to protect a political tendency within that civilization?

When Charles Martel defended Christian civilization in 732, he did not hold a seminar to decide what he was defending; he simply got up a collection of stout-hearted Frankish knights and went down and won the battle of Tours. But when we faced a Nazi and Communist threat, we had to turn a civilization into an idea. And the problem is always whether one can identify a civilization with an idea.

Speakers in this particular session have suggested that there is a universal tendency called globalization and that the politicians are behind in the process. Do we really want to politicize globalization? Globalization enables international organizations to control and override sovereign democracies. Today, whenever two or three people are gathered together, a politician will usually spring up among them and say, "I will be your leader." When I see such a desire to politicize, I want to draw back.

MR. KAMPELMAN: There is obviously in this world and in our societies resistance to any kind of globalization, though I did not go into any detail. People who have power do not want to give up that power. Globalization does, in a sense, impinge on that power. People feel threatened by Westernization, which is an element of globalization. They do not like their children to dance or wear jeans; they feel their values being threatened. We must understand that a lot of people like their flag, their language, land, national identification. They do not want to give those up. All those elements of resistance exist within the globalization process.

I am not worried about politicizing. Politicizing could be a healthy process. It allows for debate and provides for differences to be expressed. If we are going to express differences, we need a cohesive idea that motivates and binds. For me, no globalization that we envisage in this meeting can work without a fundamental principle. For me, that very important principle would be "no profit from aggression." That is part of the United Nations Charter; it is part of the Helsinki Final Act. Until now, in Europe we have failed to live up to that principle. The Yugoslav experience is the first challenge to that principle, and I think we failed.

I like the idea of having an idea that binds us. Fundamentally, in the security area that idea must be "no profit from aggression." And of course that is in addition to "human dignity," which is an element of political democracy. But I am not overly concerned by the political process.

György Granasztói (Hungary): Enlargement of NATO is important for those of us in Central Europe. We are now, however, facing a completely new situation, because up until now, enlargement was easy: it involved like-minded countries with practically the same level of development. Now a new era begins as nations with different historical and sociological backgrounds try to join the rest. Is it possible for international organizations taking special measures in Central Europe to monitor and sanction potential crisis situations to prevent actual crises if the participating countries abandon a part of their sovereignty and autonomy?

Mr. Jeszenszky: It will be very difficult to give a full answer unless Adrian Karatnycky is willing to say something.

Mr. Karatnycky: If I believed the premise and had deep concerns about ethnic bloodshed among the early candidates for NATO membership, I think that any wise person would urge that we not enlarge NATO by admitting such countries. There is no need to create special kinds of institutions, because the transformations that are occurring in Central Europe are irreversible and are bringing about societies that can reasonably and peacefully handle ethnic tensions. I point that out because NATO went through a period—the cold war—when the alliance was driven by another logic, the imperative of balance of power, and it included states within it that had less than perfect democratic credentials.

More important, if you look at the incipient interethnic and social conflicts in the United States, or the problem of the Kurds in Turkey, just to give two examples of NATO states, I believe that the standards should not be so pristine as you seem to imply.

JAN NOWAK (United States): Adrian Karatnycky mentioned some negative considerations, which, of course, are a legitimate source of concern: for example, the Polish prime minister's being suspected of spying for Russia. Those problems are typical of the transition period. After every revolution one has excessive expectations that are followed by disappointment, frustration, and nostalgia. We had the same symptoms after World War II—after all, the Communist votes were only an inch away from winning in France and Italy, and the Communists penetrated everything. The West's quick integration of economic and military structures frustrated the process. If, however, those symptoms do become dangerous, if there is an indefinite waiting period, if the opponents of democracy undermine pro-Western orientation, which is fortunately still very strong, the situation may become really dangerous.

In the process of enlarging NATO, we have to solve two problems. One is to be more precise in our standing offer to Russia, not in the sense of giving membership, but of developing strategic cooperation between an enlarged NATO and Russia. Second, when we come to enlarging NATO, we should avoid dividing East-Central Europe into protected and unprotected countries. If we do not apply Article 5 to all of those countries, then in some way we must raise the perception of the cost of aggression against those countries.

MR. KARATNYCKY: I fully agree with what Jan Nowak has said. While I favor early integration for the first tranche, we should not drop our standards. As we move toward integration, we should insist that those countries deal with some of the problems. I am not necessarily seeking to retard the integration of some of those countries into NATO, but I understand that we should press them to come clean, to have structures, and to examine questions that may arise about the loyalties of government officials.

MR. JESZENSZKY: We are assured now that Oswald Spengler was not really right when he said that the decline of the West was at hand. But I am reminded that Reginald Dale—writing for the *International Herald Tribune*—speaks about "The Crisis of Western Leadership." His statement is worth considering. It is a good contribution to our discussion.

Let me conclude by citing a nineteenth-century Hungarian statesman who said that democracy should not simply be proclaimed; it should be organized. I think interstate cooperation between like-minded countries in the European Community should not simply be proclaimed, as we are going to do, at this Congress of Prague; it should be organized.

PART THREE
Common Solutions

10

The Common Crisis: Atlantic Solutions

Margaret Thatcher

This glittering Congress of Prague, of course, is not the first European congress. And in the past, I must admit, such congresses have achieved mixed results. The Congress of Vienna in 1815 was called to restore order in Europe after the Napoleonic Wars; it began a series of such gatherings designed to achieve a Concert of Europe. But, as is usually the case in European affairs, the concert was distinctly discordant. The style was too rigid and inflexible. And finally, amid Europe-wide upheaval, Austria's Chancellor Metternich, who had orchestrated the system, had to flee to England.

The Congress of Berlin in 1878 was called to resolve the Eastern Question, this time with Germany's Chancellor Bismarck holding court as an "honest broker." Again, great power politics was relied on to manage awkward national aspirations, particularly in the Balkans. But the Eastern Question stayed unresolved, the Balkans became more Balkan, the shaky empires staggered on and, with fateful consequences, Germany emerged as the arbiter in Europe.

Here at our Congress of Prague, however, we have a very different purpose: the defense, entrenchment, and extension of our Western inheritance of freedom. And the only concert we shall be hearing from is that performed this evening by the excellent Prague Symphony Orchestra.

The British, indeed, have a special fondness for Czech music: Dvorák and Janácek both spent some time in England. And although the phrase has since been used to rather different effect, it was Janáček who memorably remarked—on a visit to London—that the Czech nation was "the heart of Europe, and Europe needs to be aware of its heart." Magnificent buildings, superb art galleries, in fact on every side the accumulated evidence of a continuously rich intellectual life—anyone visiting this most beautiful of the cities of Central Europe needs no persuading of the justice of Janáček's observation.

Moreover, here in Prague we are surrounded not just by beauty, but by beauty that was paid for by business success. In the last century, Bohemia was the industrial heartland of the Hapsburg Empire. And before the Second World War, Czechoslovakia was one of the world's leading economies, enjoying an income per capita equal to that of France. It is in keeping with that tradition of industrial prowess that the Czech Republic today is the outstanding economic success story of Central Europe: where others have flinched under the pressures of free enterprise reform, Václav Klaus—my other favorite prime minister—has kept going along the right track. And the results are internationally recognized and admired.

Yet, we know also the darker side of Central European history, whose shadows in successive generations fell over Prague. That too makes our meeting here appropriate. We dare not forget that the freedom of this cultured, enterprising people was snuffed out by each of the two monstrous, totalitarian systems of our century—intimidated, dismembered, and absorbed by Nazi Germany; subverted, betrayed, and enslaved by Communist Russia; and each time with the West standing impotently aside. These are blots on the history of the civilized world. They came about because the West was selfish and unprepared. And they confirm an important truth about international affairs. In the language of Thomas Hobbes: "Covenants without the sword are but words." No amount of promises by world leaders, no amount of guarantees by international bodies without firepower, mattered when the tanks rolled in. Such experience provides a poignant lesson for today's multilateralists, who retain a naive conviction that international institutions, rather than alliances of powerful nation-states, can be relied on to preserve the peace.

The Post–Cold War Crisis

The fact that now the Czech and Slovak peoples—and the Hungarians, the Poles, and other former captives of the Evil Empire—are free to express their nationhood, rebuild their economies, and rejoin the international community as sovereign states is, therefore, a cause not just for rejoicing but for deep reflection.

We should reflect that it was not the United Nations, or the World Bank, let alone the European Community, that overthrew communism. It was a united West, under American leadership, enjoying the support of brave dissident patriots in the lands of the Eastern bloc: together we applied irresistible pressures on the Soviet system. And it was the inherent and cumulative failures of that system that caused it to collapse in the face of our challenge. Had we waited for international consensus and its diplomatic practitioners to win the cold war for freedom, we would be waiting still.

But, as so often, with victory also came complacency. And it was not long before signs emerged that all was not well with the so-called New World Order. Even the expression *New World Order,* with its echoes of Utopian euphoria from the League of Nations, should have sounded the alarm, for the post–cold war Western leaders had made a fatal confusion between two quite distinct propositions. The first—true—proposition was that international institutions, above all the United Nations, could at last begin to work as originally designed in a world free from Soviet obstruction and aggression. The second— untrue—proposition was that these institutions could themselves perform all the essential functions required to uphold global peace, prosperity, and justice.

There was a counterpart to this post–cold war confusion in the domestic policies of our own nation-states. Again, the release of tension induced a slackness of political muscle. With the lifting of the forty-year threat to our very existence, the general cry was for governments to cultivate the arts of peace. The demand was for a peace dividend—and politicians were too timid to explain that the only true peace dividend is simply the dividend of peace itself. Furthermore, the dividend is yielded only if sufficient capital is first invested in defense. But, in any case, the resulting—often imprudent—reductions in defense spending did not lead to governments spending less overall: quite the contrary. The state-welfare complex proved more rapacious than the Left's favorite ogre, the defense-industrial complex, ever was. To pay for increased welfare, governments weakened their own financial disciplines, ran deficits, and hiked taxes. And all these actions in turn worsened deep-seated social problems like welfare dependency, family breakdown, and juvenile crime.

These tendencies, as the experts have explained, are so general—and their results so deleterious—that we can without exaggeration talk of a "common crisis." But it is not, of course, a crisis of capitalism.

Indeed, outside the hefty, unreadable tomes of the Marxist pseudo-economists, there was no crisis of capitalism, only a crisis of socialism—wherever and whenever it has been applied. Its sour fruits are still with us.

Where socialism has left its deepest impression—in most of the former Soviet Union—we see not Western-style democracy and free economies but corruption, cartels, and gangsterism. There is a pervasive lack of trust and civility, the breakdown of civil society in matters large and small. A dour Russian parable on the history of Soviet communism says it all:

> That's how it is with a man. He makes a bad start in his youth by murdering his parents. After that he goes downhill. He takes to robbing people in the streets. Soon he sinks to telling lies and spreading gossip. Finally, he loses all shame, descends to the depths of depravity, and enters a room without knocking at the door first.

That's how it was with communism. It began in terror and mass murder and it ended in petty corruption, inefficiency, bad service, ill manners, the loss of every social grace, and a society pervaded by rampant egoism. And the social desert thus created was unpromising ground for the economic transition to a market economy.

All the more credit, then, to our hosts here in Prague, and to the democratic reformers in other Central European countries that they succeeded so well in their market revolution.

Alas, in some countries we have seen a reversion. There is a progressive disillusionment among ordinary people with pseudocapitalism and—worse—a growing nostalgia for the false security of socialism. Former Communists, sometimes in disguise, are returning to power in ex-Communist countries. In Russia itself, there is the possibility of a government that combines Communist economics with an imperialistic foreign policy.

Such a reversion is not uncommon. Rudyard Kipling wrote about this as a sort of natural law:

> As it will be in the future, it was at the birth of Man—
> There are only four things certain since Social Progress began:

That the Dog returns to his Vomit and the Sow returns to the
    Mire,
And the burnt Fool's bandaged finger goes wabbling back to
    the Fire . . .
As surely as Water will wet us, as surely as Fire will burn,
The Gods of the Copybook Headings with terror and
    slaughter return!

We can and must provide against the dangers—the "terror and
slaughter"—that this reversion threatens. To do so effectively, we
must turn to those Atlantic solutions that our distinguished panels
will be debating at this conference.

Security Challenges

The world is today a freer, and in many ways better, place than it
was when the two superpowers—America supported by its European allies and the Soviet Union conscripting its European satellites—
confronted each other. But the world is also more complex, more
volatile, and more dangerous. Let me give you three reasons why.

First, there was a kind of unholy symmetry in international affairs created by a balance of terror. Deterrence—above all nuclear
deterrence—worked as it was designed to do. Neither the West nor
the Soviets could afford to let any regional crisis so destabilize the
system that either side was pushed to the brink; for beyond that brink
lay the abyss of mutual destruction.

This does not, of course, mean that the Soviet ideological
commitment to global revolution in those years was mere bra-
vado. Had they been able to achieve their goals at a sustainable
cost, they would undoubtedly have done just that. But, accepting
that attrition was the only possible strategy, and regarding their
client states as pawns and not players, they kept those client states
under firm control. The breakdown of Soviet power, however,
brought that discipline to an end: it allowed rogue states, often
connected with terrorist movements, to emerge and set their own
violent agendas.

Second, with the collapse of the Soviet Union there was also a
dispersal of weapons of mass destruction and of the technologies to
produce them. This has gone much further than we envisaged; and
it now constitutes quite simply the most dangerous threat of our
times. Yet there is still a conspiracy of silence among Western governments and analysts about it. We have, of course, known for some

time about the danger of the so-called back-pack nuclear weapon. The ability of rogue states to produce chemical and biological weapons, without detection, is a constant worry.

But it is the proliferation of advanced missiles and missile technology that has fundamentally altered the threat over the past few years. The North Koreans have developed (and continue to develop) a range of missiles that are even available for sale in a catalog to all comers. The mail-order missile business is no fantasy of science fiction: it is a fact.

There are many imponderables in precisely assessing the time-scale of the threat; but they should increase our vigilance. On present trends, it is likely that the United States will be threatened by such missiles early in the next century. And, once they are available in the Middle East and North Africa, all the capitals of Europe will be within target range. We thus face the appalling possibility—for which we are at present unprepared—of an attack on a Western city involving thousands of deaths.

It is not only the terrible consequences of their actual use, but the implications of their threatened use, that should disturb us. For that threat casts doubt on the ability of the West to project its power beyond our shores. The North Korean missiles are, for example, a threat to American defense of its allies in the Pacific. And would we have taken the punitive action we did against Libya in 1986, if Gaddafi had been able to strike with his missiles at the heart of our cities? Gaddafi himself has no doubt of the answer. And I quote him:

> If [the Americans] know that you have a deterrent force capable of hitting the United States, they would not be able to hit you. Consequently, we should build this force so that they and others will no longer think about an attack.

Of course, the Gaddafis may be wrong. We must maintain all possible diplomatic pressure against proliferation. And we should not forswear the possibility of preemptive strikes. But, in the face of all this, our response must also urgently include ballistic missile defense.

Third, we are seeing today a fundamental shift of economic power—which will certainly have political consequences—away from the West to Asia and the Pacific Rim. Unlike the first two challenges—the emergence of rogue states and the proliferation of weaponry—this should not be regarded in itself as a threat to us. Although Asian countries may initially grow wealthier at the expense of our industries by capturing our markets, they will increasingly themselves offer new markets for our goods. All the classic arguments for free trade and against protection remain valid.

The danger, though, lies in the fact that these Asian countries that are making such rapid economic advances generally lack the liberal traditions that we in the West take for granted. America is worthy of its superpower status because it has been not only economically but politically liberal. Therefore the advance of American interests in particular, and the West's in general, has been more or less synonymous with the advance of liberty. By contrast, China's extraordinary economic progress is occurring despite, not because of, its political tradition—which has always been one of tyranny. China's behavior toward Taiwan demonstrates that the economic challenge from the Far East could easily become a security challenge too.

So the task we face now is to devise a framework of international cooperation that allows these and future threats to be met successfully. It is one that requires principle and shrewdness, tenacity and flexibility, resolve to apply our strength but prudence in conserving it. Above all, it requires the unity of the West under American leadership.

The West

This state of affairs, however, is far from universally recognized. Irving Kristol once wrote that "no modern nation has ever constructed a foreign policy that was acceptable to its intellectuals." This was true during the cold war years. It is true now. And in recent years we have heard repeated suggestions that the West was essentially a cold war construct, rendered irrelevant by the end of a bipolar world.

In fact, it was—and is—nothing of the sort. The distinctive features of the Western political, judicial, social, and economic system existed before communism and will continue after it. Those features are: the long-standing historic commitment to human rights, the rule of law, representative democracy, limited government, private property, and tolerance.

Attempts today to suggest that American civilization is antithetical and antipathetic to European civilization, which itself is portrayed by contrast as some homogeneous whole, are bad history and worse politics. American civilization began its life as a branch of the English oak. It has since had the cultures and traditions of other European countries grafted onto it. It is today the center of an English-speaking civilization with cultural and ethnic links to every European country. And in our present age, in which communications increasingly obliterate distance, culture is a more important fact of life than geography.

In truth America is a European power—and must remain one. And even if we could overlook our common history and cultural ties, we dare not ignore the politics of Atlantic cooperation. Any ideology that threatens Atlantic unity is one that ultimately imperils our collective security.

Europe—Dreams and Nightmares

And here I must touch on the relationship between the Atlantic countries and the European Union. I realize that there are some among us here, and among supporters of Atlanticism, who are strong devotees of European integration.

Now, I take it as a sign of the strength of the Atlantic idea—and as a sign of its broad political appeal—that it has captured the imagination of many people who differ on other political questions. But imagination must also be complemented by clear thinking.

Of course, some of the lesser dreams that went into Europeanism are by no means ignoble. There is the dream of peace in Europe by permanent reconciliation of the old enemies, France and Germany; the dream of reuniting a continent divided by the iron curtain, so that nations like the Czechs' could rejoin the free West; the dream—of a less inspirational kind—of a single European market, without barriers to trade.

But the overarching European federalist project, which was envisaged by some from the start but which has only in recent years come out into the open, is in truth a nightmare. For the drive toward a European superstate—with its own government, its own laws, its own currency, and its own citizenship—would achieve none of the goals that enthusiasts on either side of the Atlantic claim for it.

Were it to come about, another great power would have been born—equal or nearly equal in economic strength to the United States. Does anyone suppose that such a power would not soon become a rival to America? That it would not gradually discover different interests from those of the United States? That it would not by degrees move toward a different public philosophy—one less liberal, more statist? And that it would not eventually seek to establish its own military forces, separate from those of the United States?

If this new Europe were not to follow the path to separate great power status, it would be the first such power in history to renounce its independent role. It would have pioneered a new course in self-abnegation. It would have chosen moral influence over political power. The history of Europe—bloodstained, as well as idealistic—should not encourage us in these fantasies.

Europe separated from the United States would in my view be an unequivocally bad thing—bad for America, bad for Europe, and bad for the world at large. For America, it would transform an ally into a rival—or, at the very least, would permanently threaten to do so. For the world at large, it would increase instability by dividing the West and so would hasten the move to a multipolar world. And for Europe itself, it would remove from our continent the one power that has kept the peace for fifty years—and that no European really fears.

How quickly lessons are forgotten and deductions from events distorted! Two world wars have flowed from American disengagement from Europe. By contrast, the cold war was won because America defended Western Europe's security as its own. So talk by some continental political leaders of the possibility of war unless Europe moves toward political unity is profoundly misguided—as well as unbelievably insensitive. Only if America, as a global superpower, remains directly engaged in Europe is there a guarantee against any continental European power's asserting dominance.

The shortcomings of a common European foreign and security policy have been shown by Europe's feebleness in the former Yugoslavia. There is no reason to believe that attempts to apply a common European defense policy would be any less risible or chaotic—though they could do untold harm to the Atlantic Alliance.

All this means that our energies must be directed toward strengthening NATO, which is as important in the post–cold war world as it was under the circumstances of its creation. NATO's role should be expanded. It must be prepared to go out of area, where so many of today's threats lie. It must be prepared to accept the Czech Republic and other Central European countries as full members, giving them much needed reassurance in a time of growing fear about future instability to the east. NATO can also coordinate support for the construction of that system of global ballistic missile defense that is now an imperative requirement. And if, as I hope, there is a renewed enthusiasm for such a system in the United States, Britain and other European countries must make a fair contribution.

Atlanticism

Economic integration on an Atlantic basis can nurture this vital Atlantic relationship in defense and foreign policy. It will also help to counter some unwelcome trends in European economics. For Europe today is far from being synonymous with free enterprise and open trade: it too often also stands for burdensome controls. In fact, that classic victim of Austro-Hungarian bureaucracy, the Good Soldier Sweik, might have felt gloomily at home in today's highly regulated Europe, where like then, "every day brought new instructions, directives, questions and orders."

The most practical way forward, I believe, is to merge the North American Free Trade Area with the European Community, including the countries of Central and perhaps in time Eastern Europe. Of course, in terms of pure economic analysis, global free trade is the ideal. But trade cannot be divorced from politics, no matter how hard we try: it is politically realistic as well as economically beneficial to concentrate now on creating a transatlantic free-trade area. Such a bloc would be able to push effectively toward global trade liberalization. It would prevent transatlantic trade wars from jeopardizing wider transatlantic links. It would bring our Atlantic civilization closer together.

Finally, as part of this endeavor, we must try to develop a real Atlantic political consciousness and public opinion. Of course, this will take time to emerge. Such transformations come about organically and subtly or not at all. So, I am not talking here about cultural politics. The stupidities of attempts to remold old national identities into new artificial forms—whether ruthlessly, in the Soviet Union, or absurdly, in the European Union—should not be repeated. But the Atlantic political consciousness is different—for three reasons:

- It reflects the realities of recent history.
- It does not seek to eliminate national identity; it respects it.
- And it makes excellent strategic and economic sense.

For that we may need new institutions; we may need revived ones; but we certainly need more contact. This will follow our Atlantic initiative, and it is not the least of its advantages—and pleasures.

11

The Expansion of NATO, Part One

Discussion

RICHARD N. PERLE (United States): The purpose of this discussion is to give an opportunity to the participants to comment on controversial issues concerning security policy.

CHARLES GATI (United States): One of the consequences of the enlargement of NATO is that some countries will be left out. They may be left out at the beginning or at the end. This is an argument against NATO enlargement, and those of us who are in favor of enlargement should not dismiss it. But might not some intermediate steps be taken at the beginning for those who will not be admitted right away? If, for instance, Hungary, Poland, and the Czech Republic are admitted in a year or two to NATO, as I hope will be the case, and perhaps also the Baltics and Romania, and maybe Slovenia, then NATO should treat these countries very carefully.

MR. PERLE: Brian Beedham and I cochaired the security committee that met in late 1996 in Karlovy Vary. We spent a couple of days discussing this issue, and then Gerald Frost and his team produced a study reflecting the notes that were taken during the discussion. Charles Gati has raised an important problem.

MAX BELOFF (United Kingdom): The study reflecting the Karlovy Vary views says that the Russians will raise objections and that these objections are ill founded. One may agree that they are ill founded, but that they will not necessarily prevent the Russians from using their objections as an excuse for future pressure on some other countries not admitted. That fact may carry the conviction to those in Western countries that it is a dangerous thing to do. It seems to me that the study does not tackle the Russian side of the debate quite as deeply as it should.

MR. PERLE: Lord Beloff, can I urge you to suggest one or two ways in which you would tackle those objections? I agree that the study could well have said more about that.

You cannot persuade the Russians, as you well know, of anything; they will do what they like, when they like. The important aspect must be to set matters out in greater detail. Having listened to discussions in England over this matter I find there is an element in public opinion that might prefer not to go forward, on the grounds that it might provoke. I think this attitude is foolish, but I do not think enough has been done to persuade people of the fact.

BRIAN BEEDHAM (United Kingdom): When we were at Karlovy Vary, we did have a considerable discussion on the position of Russia. We thought that it should be handled in quite a separate way from the issue of NATO enlargement. In other words, the concern about Russian reaction should not prevent us from enlarging membership and thus providing security to Europe.

Nevertheless, there ought to be arrangements drawn throughout the whole process to show what we are trying to achieve with respect to Russia. There is a strong case for taking into consideration the Russians' likely reaction to enlargement, but not for allowing it to prevent us from enlarging. We have to investigate ways to reassure the Russians that we do not represent a threat to their security.

MR. PERLE: The current Russian position on enlargement seems to be that enlargement would be tolerable if it did not entail either an eastward movement of NATO's infrastructure or nuclear weapons. Now others may have encountered different views, and happily we have a Russian with us, so it would be a good time to invite him to comment.

SERGEI A. KARAGANOV (Russia): The problem is, we understand that, in spite of all you ladies and gentlemen willing to expand NATO, there will be a lot of problems along the road. We could use every problem along the road to defeat the decision or to make it so horribly expensive as to be virtually counterproductive.

The problem in our eyes—and I am speaking not on behalf of a probable future Russian government headed by Gennadi Zyuganov, who would love NATO expansion, but rather on behalf of a future Russian government led by President Boris Yeltsin, or someone like him—is that we believe we cannot afford to defeat NATO expansion. We have to look for a grand compromise. But the grand compromise, like most others, has so far been restricted to a very narrow road. That road is nondeployment of troops and nondeployment of nuclear weapons.

The starting point of Russian thinking is that it is time to think big and create a real structure for cooperation within Europe—between Russia and Europe, and among Russia, Ukraine, Europe, and other countries—that transcends security. Security is the lesser issue we are facing now. But because we have been trained in security matters for so long, we are still fighting on this very narrow road. We are thinking now about a possible grand transatlantic bargain, including Russia, Ukraine, and some of the other former Soviet republics, which would mean a new security structure for Europe, maybe a new treaty. We envision the military part of the new European security structure built around NATO, for clearly this is an organization that must return to the real world. In the real world, the European energy charter, which has been strangely left out, is far more important for Russians and for Europeans than NATO is or will be in the twenty-first century, with its global-system communications. These things are the essence of security in the twenty-first century.

I am sorry for speaking in Gorbachev lingo. I know that the new political thinking has effectively died, but we are returning to it, because we are now living in a different world, a capitalist world, and we are not necessarily seeing NATO as the main problem. Now NATO is a hindrance in the building up of Europe, along the lines I have mentioned. Even in this study, you get a hint that NATO could expand in Spanish or French style. You say at this Congress of Prague that there should not be a two-tiered NATO; but you already have a two-tiered or three-tiered NATO, and that does not impede the effectiveness of the organization. What the three countries of Central Europe need is a strengthening of democratic institutions. The study is brilliant, but it is very narrow.

ARRIGO LEVI (Italy): In this very building a few years ago, we heard

Mr. Arbatov speak on the occasion when the native Czech flag flew over Cernin Palace for the first time. The Czech delegation and the Polish delegation were asking for NATO protection, saying that it was the only security organization existing in Europe. And of course, the Russian delegation said, "Careful, you are endangering Mr. Gorbachev." Well, now we are being told, "You are endangering Mr. Yeltsin." I assume that in a few years' time, supposing Mr. Zyuganov wins, we will be told, "Careful, you are endangering Zyuganov." That is the first observation to be made: let us be careful, because what happens in Russia does not depend only on what we do but on many other factors.

Second, we had a two-year-long discussion at the Western European Union in Paris involving a European delegation and a Russian delegation. Whatever subject was raised, the Russian delegate present would say, "Yes, but above all don't enlarge NATO." It was so repetitive that in the end somebody said, "When something is repeated too many times, it begins to be doubtful whether the speaker is really serious." On the last day, an hour before the end of the meeting, one member of the Russian delegation—the only one who really was a general, and the most authoritative member of the delegation—suddenly made a list of "We might consider if " items. It was a long but reasonable list of reassurances that Russia might ask for, in order to accept NATO enlargement. So suddenly, at the end of the discussion, there was no time to proceed, and we were left not knowing what to think.

OWEN HARRIES (United States): In a way, we have all become super-realists in the sense that changes of regime, changes of ideology count for nothing. It is worth remembering that NATO was created not as an alliance against Russia, but as an alliance against the Soviet Union. Certainly it was not intended to be against a Russia making its first attempt at becoming democratic. Yet suddenly the Soviet Union has been disbanded and there is no longer a Communist ideology there—people speak of Russia as if it were naturally and inevitably, under whatever character it assumes internally, an enemy. Russia's existence is seen as the justification not only for the continued existence of NATO, but for its enlargement.

As an exercise, it is worth imagining what would have happened if, in 1989, the West had been offered the following deal by Moscow: they would give up the Warsaw Pact and dismantle the

Soviet Union, give up communism as an ideology, and take a stab at becoming democratic. In return all they would ask is for the West not to take advantage of them by advancing strategically into what historically has been their sphere of influence. Everybody would have accepted this as a done deal in five seconds. We propose to press for much more, and in fact to advance into that sphere at a time when there is no convincing threat. But this is a measure that might create, or help create, such a threat.

In addition to there being no convincing threat, there is no commitment on the part of Western countries to such an extension. Are the countries of the West really committing themselves to guaranteeing the security of countries that they were not even prepared to guarantee even in the coldest time of the cold war? Or is this another example of a Locarno Treaty, which the British entered only with a strict understanding that they would never have to honor it? It is worth thinking about these problems, given the synergy between the demands of leading politicians in Central Europe and the political fortunes of the more extreme elements in Russia. As John Stuart Mill said, unless you have understood your opponent's case at its strongest, you have not understood it at all.

CHARLES POWELL (United Kingdom): The Karlovy Vary report is comprehensive and reflects enormous credit on its drafters. But the issue of enlargement is of concern. What worries me is the use of the phrase *advancing NATO toward Russia,* or into Central Europe. It is not a question of advancing, it is a question of responding to the wish of a number of countries to be considered for membership. It is their right to ask to be considered for membership, and it is our duty to respond positively. Indeed, I would argue that we have been too slow in responding to their request, just as the European Union is being far too slow in responding to the request for membership in its institutions. Had we moved more rapidly and more decisively, this issue could have been settled far more easily. Instead we have invented concepts such as "partnership for peace," which sounds great but means nothing.

I have more sympathy with Mr. Harries on the question of our guarantee; this has always worried me in two respects. First, as he has quite rightly pointed out, the historical record of West Europeans, including Britain, in responding to or honoring guarantees they have given is not exactly brilliant. Second, I have often wondered to what degree American public and political opinion has absorbed the implications of extending NATO and the nuclear guarantee to this part of the world. I rather suspect it has gone straight over their heads, because enlarging NATO sounds great. What it might involve has not exactly been drawn to their attention in large capital letters. There is a danger here. But all I would say is this: if some future crisis were to develop, it would at the very least be harder for the Europeans, and harder for the United States, to respond adequately and properly if the Central European countries were outside NATO than if they were in it. So the argument must come down firmly in favor of going ahead with enlargement, and going ahead rapidly with it.

I have three other brief observations to make about the Karlovy Vary study. First, at a quick glance I cannot spot the initials *WEU*. Now, some of us might think that a blessing, but it is very much an issue, much discussed in the European Union. There is a debate looming over whether the practical European contribution would be more effective if grouped within the Western European Union—provided, of course, that it is set up as a genuine part of NATO and not as a rival or an alternative to it, or as something that would sap the vital forces of NATO by making it a subsidiary organization. As a subject we will have to address at some point, we should be aware of it in the context of this report.

My second additional point concerns the call to maintain defense spending. Everyone present at this discussion would certainly agree with that, but everyone present would equally disbelieve it. I see no signs of willingness on the side of most countries to maintain defense spending; most of them are finding every reason to diminish it. How we get this message across in political terms is one of the most difficult issues facing us. There is little constituency for defense spending nowadays. Recreating one is something this conference can help with, but our help certainly will not be decisive.

Last, I note the reference toward the end of the report suggesting that new technology eases the burden of defense spending, because all these marvelous new weapons can stand on their heads and turn corners and follow traffic lights and so on. I am always a bit skeptical about that: one has seen some very good footage from the Gulf War—mostly shot by the manufacturers, rather than the television stations—showing how marvelous this technology is. But alongside weapons that take out military targets and spare people, there is another development: as the degree of military coverage provided by CNN and other television stations is increasing, the tolerance of casualties is equally declining rapidly, indeed. So we should not find any solace in technology as somehow making war easier to get involved in—as if there won't be the nasty side effects, and boys won't be shipped home in coffins. The reality is that public tolerance of any level of casualties is decreasing, at least as fast as technology develops.

MR. PERLE: The last point is one of particular interest. The evolution of technology carries some promise. The risks to which properly equipped troops will be subjected will also decline over time—one hopes they will decline as fast as will the lack of willingness to stand up when necessary and go in harm's way.

GÉZA JESZENSZKY (Hungary): This debate should not be focused on enlargement and on Russian reactions. That is not our mandate, and this is not the place to convince the Russians about the need for enlargement. But I have one or two points to make on this. From personal experience, back in 1992–1993 I saw no visible Russian rejection of the idea of NATO enlargement. In 1993, the Russians listened with some interest to the Central European arguments about our wish to join NATO. They listened to the argument that in fact it is in the Russian interest to see enlargement, because it would stabilize their Western neighborhood. But ever since then, Russian opposition has increased, rather than decreased. So I certainly agree with those who think that this decision ought to have been made earlier, and that attending to these rather insincere Russian arguments about the dangers and the threats to Russia is leading nowhere.

It is a legitimate right of sovereign nations to join alliances. In 1990–1991, the Soviet Union, still existing, objected to the conclusion of a treaty where Hungary would have retained the right to join any association, including the European Community.

I suppose that we could certainly find many arguments that it is not endangering Russia; but the Karlovy Vary report rightly concentrates on how to convince Western opinion about the need for enlargement. In my view that is the major aim of this meeting. The enlargement of NATO would provide stability for a strategically important space, and certainly the present action in Bosnia shows the importance of Central Europe. Enlargement would also provide a link with the southern wing of NATO.

But it is important to return to the issue that Charles Gati raised: how to avoid creating a bad impression on those who will not be admitted in the first wave. It is important to hold out the hope of future enlargement, but the process of enlargement should be only gradual. The prospect of further gradual enlargement provides important leverage with respect to the countries where the democratic commitment is not strong enough, or where the economy underperforms.

The issue of Russia is also handled in the report on political cooperation, and there is a very good answer to the argument that NATO expansion will provoke Russia. The argument is that it is in the Russian interest to ensure stability. It is Russian propaganda to suggest the opposite; the Russians have always resorted to this type of argument. They say there is a danger, but in fact they invented the danger, and for internal consumption the argument works very well.

JOSHUA MURAVCHIK (United States): In response to the point that Owen Harries raised, NATO was an alliance against the Soviet Union, and there is no reason to say that in a new era NATO is or ought to be an alliance against Russia. Rather it should be something else—an instrument of collective security, which proved its effectiveness during the cold war period. One of its goals now ought to be to develop as an association of the Western democracies against any threat or enemy that nominates itself for that role, and to try to keep the environment generally peaceful.

This is going to be a constant job to develop, or evolve toward, as we have seen in the case of Bosnia and also in the policy toward Iran. We need to encourage all the Western democracies and the members of NATO to take a far-seeing view of the requirements to keep the environment peaceful. This effort should include upholding the basic principles of international law against aggression, as in the case of Bosnia, when many of the NATO members were unwilling to recognize the importance of resisting aggression. Indeed, there was a strong tendency to make things easier for the aggressors. This holds true with respect to Iran, the sponsor of substantial threats to the security of the West; there has been a tendency among the European members of NATO to wish the threats away or to ignore the dangers.

I hope that the spirit of appeasement is less a constant problem for the East and Central Europeans than it is for the Western Europeans. Although the physical, military contributions of some of the East and Central Europeans can be regarded as not very substantial, their political and spiritual contributions to NATO might be very salutary.

PETER CORTERIER (Germany): It strikes me as a good idea not to bring in the new members immediately. The Partnership for Peace (PFP) was altogether a good step for NATO, for a number of reasons. First, it helps us to organize cooperation, not only for the candidates for membership but also for many others who gain a measure of reassurance. It has also helped to get a clearer view of whether some countries that originally seemed to be serious candidates for memberships really are good candidates. In the past you always talked about four candidates. We now know that Slovakia, given its internal situation, does not seem to be a serious candidate right now. Then there is Bulgaria, which originally put in a very strong demand for membership, and now that is no longer the case. The concept of PFP has helped sort out the candidacies and has clarified which are serious and which are less serious.

But the time has come to act, basically for two reasons. First, the serious countries—Hungary, the Czech Republic, and Poland—have put so much political capital into their candidacies that it would be dangerous to keep them waiting any longer. We have seen in two of those countries a fundamental change in government: neo-Socialists—former Communists—have come into power. So far, both Hungary and Poland are still equally strongly in favor of NATO membership. It was quite impressive to see a large Polish delegation visit Brussels, where they had members of the government but also members of the opposition, including the former foreign minister and the former defense minister, to demonstrate how united they were in their desire to become members. If we keep them waiting any longer, these political forces both in government and in opposition are bound to lose credibility, and dangerous nationalistic reactions might then occur.

The second good reason why we should act now concerns Russia. In Russia there are really two groups, and Sergei Karaganov has hinted at that. One group is realistic, and it is ready to look for ways and means to make NATO enlargement acceptable to Russia. The second group hopes to be able to defeat the whole concept. To convince Russia that we are serious about NATO enlargement, we have to move now and bring in the first new members. I am convinced that Russia will be ready to deal, to look for serious ways to make this move acceptable to themselves.

MR. KARAGANOV (Russia): It is a bad mistake you are hinting at. First, 99 percent of the Russian elite are against NATO expansion. Second, 65 percent of the others would love to have a good relationship with NATO. If you expand without taking into consideration our interests, then it will be extremely hard to deal with NATO, extremely hard. And let me remind you that NATO is a big organization, but it deals only with narrow security issues that are now pushed to the back burner of European new world politics. I believe that Russia would win eventually if it had a fruitful relationship with NATO. But it would be extremely hard, and many people believe unnecessary, to have a relationship with NATO, even if Russia moves in the way you are advising it to move.

MR. PERLE: I cannot resist observing here that in retrospect, one could only wish that Soviet espionage had been more effective as it was directed against NATO. Had the Soviet intelligence penetrated NATO effectively, it would have understood how totally and completely defensive NATO was—not only in terms of its planning and organization but also psychologically. I know, because I tried. You could not get NATO officials to take seriously even counteroffensive operations. You could discuss military operations in NATO only after the presentation of a scenario in which the West had been viciously attacked and was on the verge of collapse, and then you could talk only about how we might respond from our own territory. If it were understood how totally defensive we were, you would not have been in the least concerned about NATO, even an expanded NATO.

MR. KARAGANOV: I was in the group that knew. I was betting with generals, saying that even if we attacked, NATO would not respond. But here we are again. We are not talking about military issues here. When we look at NATO, only a very few people in Russia think about military matters. What we think about is political influence, the direction of Russian policies, and social orientation.

VERONIKA SMIGOLOVÁ (Czech Republic): I would like to address the objections to NATO enlargement that were raised here. It was said that it was "superrealistic" to see Russia as a threat, but NATO enlargement is not meant as a threat against Russia, and a democratic Russia does not have to be afraid of an enlarged NATO. The sooner NATO is enlarged, the sooner the democratic forces in Russia will have the opportunity to see this, and to realize that NATO is not a danger to them.

But something was said here that I would call very unrealistic. It was said that NATO should not press for advantages that arise from the failure of the Soviet Union. That is dangerous thinking that encourages the imperial trends that might occur in Russia. As to the Karlovy Vary report, it is a well-balanced document that addresses all the important questions.

Mr. Powell: Two themes run through the conversation, and they can be linked to bring us toward something that perhaps may not be sufficiently addressed in the report. One of the themes is technology and the advantages it will give us. Of course we have to remember that the same technology that offers cheap, adaptable material has the same advantages and attractions to our potential enemies. An example, I suppose, is the global positioning system (GPS), which we all will have piloting our cars, so we will not need to use a map any more. That same little device can be put on a Silkworm missle by the Iranians, and the insurance rates in the Persian Gulf will go up the wall vertically. So technology is not necessarily going to work toward our interest.

Second, several people have implied that the biggest obstacles to NATO's future role are the internal objections, dissents, fears, and divisions among the Allies themselves. No matter how well Bosnia turns out, even if the experience eases NATO enlargement, that will surely not settle the kinds of problems that inhibited allied unity so badly for the first years of that conflict.

These two issues—technology driving us toward the need for a closer unity and, at the same time, the absence of a new cohesive factor in the alliance—suggest that the United States may have to offer its European allies new ways to perceive the alliance as reliable, useful, and credible. Particularly with regard to satellite surveillance and other forms of intelligence sharing, U.S. intelligence and its cooperation with the Allies remain largely unchanged from what they were during the cold war.

Yet the circumstances that required sharp compartmentalization at that time no longer prevail. In Bosnia, for example, the breakdown of intelligence sharing between the United States and the Europeans was really quite traumatic. So we need to think not just about what the Europeans can do, but a little too about how the United States can show its allies that leadership and new technology from the United States are going to help everybody to identify targets and enemies and to convince public opinion that the threat is there. That will produce cohesion, rather than doubts, concerning Iran, Bosnia, or some other future problem.

MR. PERLE: Let me suggest that other points addressed in the Karlovy Vary report be commented on, including proliferation and missile defenses.

HENRY SOKOLSKI (United States): With regard to using proliferation as a possible focus for collective security in NATO, it was quite useful to see in the report the prominence you gave to the strategic weapons proliferation issue. Missile defense, as distinct from ballistic missile defense, is an issue that we could usefully work on together. There is no reason, for that matter, even to exclude better air defense—a more catholic use of the words *missile defense* would be useful. The report says a great deal about the risks to NATO from proliferation, but it says little or nothing about one point raised by other speakers already, and that is the proliferation risks from NATO. That might be something NATO could usefully reinforce, because it has a military security mission. The problem is the technology and money that come from Western nations to the future Iraqs. That is something that ought to be of greater concern. There is no reason why NATO cannot be used as a means to do better in this regard, simply because the nonproliferation measures need all the help they can get.

Finally, the report says nothing at all about the proliferation from weapons states generally. These risks are growing, and they are of two forms. First, there is a growing amount of dismantled material in the U.S. and Russian stockpiles—literally, we are going to be living with materials from hundreds of thousands of weapons piling up. To add insult to injury, the civil production of materials that can be used for weapons will exceed that. NATO—and Russia should be involved in this—is a good place to talk about these things. It is perhaps better than some of the places where it is being talked about.

ALUN CHALFONT (United Kingdom): I will concentrate on the question of proliferation and possible defenses against it. But I would like to offer an afterthought on the earlier debate, especially on the exchange between Owen Harries and Charles Powell. Mr. Harries implied that the dismantling of the Soviet Union, the disbanding of the Warsaw Pact, and the rejection of communism were some kind of gesture or initiative on the part of Russia. I hope that it is not too triumphalist to suggest that the West actually won the cold war—and that one of the instruments of winning it was the Atlantic Alliance. It would seem very strange now if, in the current situation, we allowed Russia to exercise a veto on the future development of that alliance.

Having said that, I will shift my focus to the issue of proliferation. I was the British negotiator in the negotiation and signing of the nonproliferation treaty. I remember a neutral country at the conference saying that we who were advancing it and endorsing it were like a crowd of drunks trying to persuade other people toward total abstinence. Although I thought at the time that it was an unkind remark, it is true, of course, to say that the nonproliferation strategy has not been an outstanding success. It was a good treaty to achieve at the time. Now it seems to a large extent to have failed, in that a number of countries who at that time were not nuclear-weapons countries now are, whether declared or not. There is the danger of technological transfer, especially from dismantled stockpiles. And there is the phenomenon that was well covered in a paper that Gerald Frost published at the Institute for European Defence and Strategic Studies (IEDSS) on the proliferation of weapons of mass destruction and the means of delivering them, through ballistic and other missiles, over long ranges.

Indeed, the author of that report suggested that by the end of the twentieth century, a number of Western capitals would be within range of a number of other states possessing weapons of mass destruction, either nuclear, chemical, or biological, and the means to deliver them. Therefore, the emphasis that this report places on proliferation as a threat, and the need to investigate some form of missile defense such as the Global Protection against Limited Strike (GPALS), is well placed.

Two statements in the report go to the heart of the matter. The first is that "only the United States has the technological capacity to develop and deploy a global system of ballistic missile defense." That seems to me to be true. Second, the report claims that NATO provides the best means for providing the organizational infrastructure that would enable America's allies to make a significant contribution to this. Is the United States in fact sympathetic toward this idea now? And is an American administration likely to fund such an initiative? I remember the uproar that greeted President Reagan's Strategic Defense Initiative, which seemed to be opposed mainly by people who were against massive retaliation. This seemed to me never to make a great deal of sense. But is there now sympathy in the United States for ballistic missile defense? Is it likely to be funded? Bearing in mind what Charles Powell said quite rightly about the extreme unlikelihood of any European country increasing its defense budget, do the European countries of NATO have any desire or intention to participate in such a system?

A final question is this: is this not one area in which we could go forward without offending and upsetting the Soviet Union? If we even asked them to collaborate in it, would not GPALS or some such system make an extremely effective defense against the outstanding threat to global stability today?

MR. PERLE: The key part of that question ought to be posed to an American. And who can better speak for the Clinton administration than Frank Gaffney?

FRANK J. GAFFNEY, JR. (United States): I will rise to the challenge. To those of you who may not have gotten that inside joke, I do not share the view of the Clinton administration, which I regret to say in response to Lord Chalfont's question, is abidingly uninterested in what is described as national missile defense. There has been some secret talk about a concept involving the modification of a small number of Minuteman missiles, the existing intercontinental ballistic missiles based in North Dakota. The concept is to give them some minimal capability to defend against an accidental or very small attack. But it is phrased in a way that reinforces my earlier point. The administration describes it as a program that would take three years of future development, at the end of which time there might be another three years before something could be deployed. That is a rather long time when you think of the kinds of threats emerging here.

I would like to second the observations both previous speakers made. It is enormously important that this issue has been addressed, and in the very forthright way that it has been addressed, coming on the heels of Lady Thatcher's strong statements on the subject and Edward Streator's statement in the *Wall Street Journal*.

What is required now is global missile defenses. Much is being made in the American debate at the moment of the idea that long-range missiles capable of threatening the United States do not exist in the hands of anybody other than the Russians and the Chinese. There is some concern about those two nations holding such weapons. But there are other nations, too, that are bent on acquiring both the weapons and the means of delivering weapons of mass destruction. We know they are building them, and making sure that in due course their weapons will have sufficient range to attack not only Europe but also Japan and the United States. This fact means that there is a multinational need to address this threat.

One further point is that, clearly, the most efficient way to acquire over the long term a global capability to defeat ballistic missiles is from space. That point is well made in the text of the report. There is, however, another point that needs to be shared with this congress and with the audience that will follow its findings: a nearer-term, and exceedingly cost-effective, means of acquiring a global antimissile defense is one that will allow the U.S. Navy to build upon its air defense system, known as the Aegis program, so as to intercept not only cruise missiles and aircraft but also ballistic missiles.

An estimate prepared by a blue-ribbon group sponsored by the Heritage Foundation in the United States estimates that thanks to the roughly $35 billion the United States has already invested in ships and launchers and other equipment deployed today around the world, it would cost roughly $2 billion to $3 billion further, spent over the next five years, to achieve this shortcut, with the first ships coming on line in as little time as three years. The navy would then be able to start protecting our friends in Europe and Japan, as well as the American people against some of these emerging threats. I also wanted to point out that former Senator Bob Dole explicitly endorsed this initiative and urged its deployment. So I hope that the impetus given by this conference to the idea of missile defense will be propitious, coming as it does at a time when the issue seems really to be joined in the United States.

CHRISTOPH BERTRAM (Germany): I am intrigued when American delegations come from the other side of the Atlantic and teach us all about missile defense. But a number of us have been through that experience. I would like to make two remarks. First, Lord Chalfont, the nonproliferation treaty has not been a failure. It has really been quite successful so far—more successful than you and others expected at the time it was established. It is not perfect, but basically it has allowed us to identify the rogues, and their number is smaller than we expected. Now that does not mean that there is no case for missile defense, but two questions must be answered. One is, of course, the technical feasibility question. It may well be that technical feasibility is no longer a problem, that it can be fixed, as Mr. Gaffney says, with $3 billion here or there. Then we have a global system of missile defense. But the real issue is, how do you operate a global missile defense system that is not an American missile defense system? How do you avoid the political consequences that would arise if there is one country in the world that can, at its whim, impose missile defense? What are the political consequences for all others? Unless you have fixed not only the technical aspects but the political ones as well, many people throughout the world would have to be convinced that this a good idea.

Robert H. Malott (United States): My comments address several issues that have been discussed here. First is an issue brought up by Charles Powell: the procurement part of NATO. To address procurement at all, we must address the efficiency of the procurement and the mechanism for NATO. The current system was designed appropriately for the late 1940s, but a lot has changed. At some point, as you revise the charter and the mission of NATO, it ought to be addressed. There is no question about the fact that defense expenditures are going to go down. The fact of life is that we have to be as effective and efficient as we can be with the funds available to us.

12

The Expansion of NATO, Part Two

Discussion

RICHARD N. PERLE (United States): We should not be solicitous about Russian political concerns at the expense of democracies that are eager to associate themselves with the West. Most important of all is the question of the identity of countries such as the Czech Republic and Hungary. We should not leave the question of their identity open. That vacuum will only encourage the belief that as long as matters remain unsettled, there may be opportunities for others to exert influence.

Lady Thatcher spoke of the need to come to grips with the proliferation of weapons of mass destruction; and the same point has been made in the report of the Security Committee of the New Atlantic Initiative. Lady Thatcher strongly urged that we proceed with ballistic missile defense. She is entirely right in that suggestion. What she proposes will not happen, however, without a great deal of political pressure, because the only country in the position to bring to fruition a ballistic missile defense—by converting technology that has been developed to an impressive degree over the years as a result of the Strategic Defense Initiative program—is the United States. And the United States is presently governed by those who are fundamentally opposed to ballistic missile defense. They have carried on only a modest program.

We should proceed with theater defenses as well as strategic defenses. We also have to face the reality that sooner rather than later the Anti-Ballistic Missile Defense Treaty will be an unwarranted inhibition on the freedom to deploy defenses in a timely and effective

111

manner. That treaty is part of history. It has no fundamental relevance to the situation we now face and are likely to face in the near future. The nostalgia with which that agreement is treated seems extraordinary. Under the present circumstances, there are new threats—no longer the kind of East-West dangers that would cause us to regard the ABM Treaty as the centerpiece of the world. In this new world, the tolerance for casualties is much lower than it was in the cold war. We in the West therefore need to work hard to maintain effective military forces and, at the same time, to minimize the risks to the men and women in uniform in our countries.

That goal can be accomplished by the skillful exploitation of technology. Even in a period of shrinking budgets, new technologies offer opportunities to fight beyond the range of the enemy, for example, to maintain an awareness of the battlefield based on information technology never before possible. Far from wringing our hands about the decline of Western defenses, we should be thinking about ways to exploit potential advantages at reasonable costs and at reasonable risks. There have been references to the United States as the remaining superpower. That designation of superpower entails something more than an army and a nation; it surely entails judgments about political will. I am not at all sure that we have emerged as a superpower, if one regards the matter in such terms.

The example that causes me such concern is the handling of the war in Bosnia by the United States and its European allies. Bosnia was a test—and a test that we failed despite the appearance that we saved the situation at the last minute in Dayton. The United States and its allies stood by and watched unspeakable crimes take place. We did little or nothing even though we could have. We would have been able to bring the conflict to a conclusion had we acted decisively. I draw one lesson from that: force should not always be the last resort—sometimes it should be the first resort. We must not always try the diplomatic path first, especially when that diplomacy evaporates into a failure of will. In this instance, the blind have been leading the blind: the Europeans first leading the United States, then the United States leading the Europeans. Before we comfort ourselves on the superior performance of the NATO force in Bosnia compared with the United Nations force—whose performance was truly dismal—we should ask whether the formidable force now there is performing an honorable mission. In the failure to escort refugees wishing to return to their homes, the failure to arrest war criminals, and the obsessive concern with defending itself, we are once again failing in the fundamental way, as we failed earlier in Bosnia. I hope that this policy will change and that, at the end of the day, the West will acquit itself honorably.

HANNA SUCHOCKA (Poland): Sometimes we hear that those of us living in Central Europe are obsessed with having no roof after the collapse of the Warsaw Pact and, for that reason, we are forever discussing our future membership in NATO and the EU. That is not the problem. We made our choice to be a member of NATO; this choice is obvious.

I feel prompted to make some pessimistic remarks. After the collapse of the Berlin Wall—forever the symbol of the collapse of the artificial division of Europe and the collapse of the bipolar world—the question is, What will constitute the new security order? How should we organize to guarantee the security of states?

With the collapse of the Communist system, we envisioned peace in Europe. It has not happened. The common perception of the societies living on both sides of the former border is that the end result may be a growing number of conflicts and civil wars. This situation creates a specific kind of nostalgia for the divided world. My approach is pessimistic because I sometimes feel this type of nostalgia. The cold war for many was seen as the guarantor of peace and security, as a system that was preventing another war in Europe. A feeling of common security in Western Europe contrasts with the loss of security because of the fall of the iron curtain. Thus, nowadays, one would speak of a sort of confusion in international affairs.

This state of confusion particularly manifests itself in the West. During the period of confrontation, Western countries had a more coherent concept of their interest and objectives. Providing security vis-à-vis the Soviet bloc was the common binding factor. After the fall of the Communists, the situation changed dramatically. The feeling of a common threat disappeared. But a new real vision did not take hold.

For us, the societies of Central and Eastern Europe, the end of the cold war was the unique chance to be included in the Western European system of security. Membership in NATO was and remains our strategic goal. We see NATO as the principal guarantor of European security and all security. We intend to extend the area of European security. From the beginning, we put the question, Would it be possible for NATO countries, taking into account our thoughts on a global Atlantic security area, to acknowledge officially that, in the longer run, the inclusion of Central European countries in NATO is in the interest of international stability and security? The question has not been answered or has been answered in a negative way.

We are convinced that an effective system of security must contain an Atlantic dimension, just as the alliance should also respect the need for closer European cooperation. The extension of Western security guarantees to our countries should prevent possible crises; this certainly is in the best interest of all democratic nations. The interests of European security are not served by keeping Central European countries in a vacuum. The Central European countries are not seeking another substitute for security based on regional cooperation. It is not the solution for a common security system, and if this formula became an alternative to NATO, this would be a bleak scenario.

This direction would mark the collapse of all our efforts toward the creation of a common European security system. When we discuss security policy, Russia must be seen as one of the elements of the system, but the ties with Russia must be built on different foundations. We do not envision our membership in NATO as hostile toward Russia. We should not leave Russia outside a new European security system. The greater enlargement of NATO should be accompanied by a comprehensive alliance including Russia to work out permanent forms of cooperation, possibly expanding existing institutions and organizations.

The future of Russia is still unknown. Building a new democratic Russia is a complex process, fraught with possible slips and reversals, and it is of profound importance to the world. Any long-term policy should be based on the assumption that Russia, regardless of the gravity of her present problems, will remain an important country and will continue to influence events in our region. A fellow countryman wrote, "The most convincing reason to offer NATO membership to countries like Poland is to send a clear warning signal to those in Russia who still feel nostalgia for Moscow's empire." A clear declaration recognizing the future NATO membership of countries like Poland will, no doubt, influence the course of Russia's discussion. Excluding the possibility of such expansionist scenarios could help to enforce those tendencies and the political direction in Russia by helping it to reject its imperial past and working toward cooperation and democracy based on partnership. Even after six years

114

of discussion, we begin and end all our speeches by declaring that Poland, like all other Eastern European countries, must be a member of NATO and that NATO remains one of the crucial pillars of European security.

CHRISTOPH BERTRAM (Germany): I must specifically warn against a push for ballistic missile defense. I am, in principle, against it. To talk about ballistic missile defense requires a discussion of the kind of world that we are going to have tomorrow, the kind of dangers that we are now facing, and the means that we have at our disposal, of which ballistic missile defense is perhaps one. Unless we do that first, it would appear as if the afficionados in the Republican Party are using this congress to push their favorite subject, as the Euro-skeptics in the British Tory Party are using expansion of the EU to weaken European integration. That would be an unfortunate impression. If that is the case, this congress will not achieve what it set out to do.

I strongly endorse Richard Perle's comments on Bosnia. We are going to see in 1997 another real test for NATO of its ability to deal with dangers outside its own membership—problems of security and morality. I am worried that we may not meet that test; the record so far is not encouraging. It is essential that we meet that test because clearly without NATO there will be no European stability.

Further, NATO's primary role will be to sustain stability on the European continent. The idea that NATO should act as some kind of fire brigade outside the European theater is idealistic; NATO will not become involved in that. Coalitions of the willing may appear—but not NATO as such.

Stabilizing the European continent is as much in the interest of the United States as in the interest of the European Union. Imagine what could happen in July 1997 if someone other than Mr. Yeltsin is elected. The election is not that far away, after all. Are we going to say, Well, Russia is becoming Russia again, not the Soviet Union; now is the time to enlarge NATO to protect ourselves against that type of Russia? We would be kicking ourselves against that kind of Russia—and that would be the totally wrong reaction.

Why is NATO in the business of enlargement? For its own sake, for its own purpose, to enhance stability in Europe. Of this, enlargement can be only one aspect; a relationship with Russia, which can last and can influence events in Russia, is another, but Western policy has not concentrated sufficiently on that. Many would hope for a

Communist victory in Russia, because it confirms our nice prejudices about Russia.

The process of Russian democratization will not take one election or two; it will take ten and twenty and fifty elections. It will take a long time. Even if Mr. Zyuganov ends up on top, that is not the end of the story. This long process of democratization is fraught with instability, against which we have to guard.

To do that, we need NATO enlargement; that is part of this stability. We also need an institutional arrangement with Russia so that we can have a day-to-day dialogue, consultation, and cooperation with Russia, so that we are not dependent on occasional summit meetings, G-7 and G-8 meetings, so that we are not dependent on other people's hotlines, so that we can influence what goes on in Russia, so that we can not only talk with presidents, who change, but reach more deeply into Russian society and the Russian bureaucracy.

We need to concentrate on these matters as a matter of urgency, because the first steps to enlargement will take place next year. We have until then to build up a relationship with Russia that is not just a compensation for enlargement but involves taking Russia seriously as an element of major stability and responsibility in Europe. We cannot do this short of a formal institution that includes Russia.

Another instrument for creating order is at our disposal—the European Union. NATO cannot provide stability all by itself; the EU has a role, too. The EU itself must enlarge; there is no question about it. But there is a contradiction, a tension between widening and deepening. Many people may think that merely widening will prevent any problem. An EU that is designed for six member-states but accepts thirty cannot function.

Some think that such expansion is a good idea. In fact, it is a rotten idea as far as EU stability is concerned. The idea that the EU does not have to prepare to get its own house in order before it enlarges is either naive or mischievous. The unfortunate implication is that opening the EU to all the countries, including the Baltic states already invited in principle to join, is not possible in the near future. Thus, we need to think about partial membership, which may be anathema to many, especially those in Eastern and Central Europe. Let us get the East Europeans, as quickly as possible, into those activities in the EU in which they can be involved.

Next, the real problem resulting from NATO enlargement is not

Russia's reaction or that Polish and Hungarian and Czech membership in NATO will pose major new instabilities. The real problem has to do with the signal that the first wave of enlargement will send to the others. How can we avoid the danger that the first wave will be regarded as a signal that all the others are to be allowed to fall under Russia's influence? We must start thinking harder than we have done so far.

This is where the EU comes in. We must convince the EU to say, "Let us get all those countries with an association agreement with the union into the union as quickly as possible—not yet into the Common Market, not yet into the structural funds, but into the club." Once they are in it, they will have a feeling of being part of it. They will be able to influence events inside the club. This ability would be a gain in security for those states that might feel left out when the first wave of NATO enlargement takes place.

MICHAL LOBKOWICZ (Czech Republic): NATO should continue its role in the security of Europe. NATO should enlarge into Central Europe. Mrs. Suchocka and Margaret Thatcher have advanced strong arguments in favor of NATO enlargement. Searching for a security model for the next millennium is not only a major responsibility but also a great opportunity for all of us. In this respect, we see two or three main cornerstones of European security. First, we feel the need for a transatlantic link; we feel the necessity for the strong presence of the United States in Europe, which includes a military presence as physical proof that the relationship exists and that responsibilities are shared. Second, we need a Europe that is strong and that will carry its part of the responsibility. There is no contradiction between those two points. Third, there is the need to establish the correct relationship between Russia and NATO. Security risks have survived the cold war. The fundamental political changes that began in 1989 have meant just the disappearance of the main enemy, which was totalitarian communism, not the disappearance of risk.

Two basic risks exist today: the proliferation of weapons of mass destruction and regional ethnic conflict. The interests of individual states and forces have not disappeared. They exist today in Europe; in some areas, they are compatible, but in other areas they are in conflict. It is, therefore, highly positive that the West was able to define and proclaim its interests in Central and Eastern Europe by saying that NATO will enlarge, that enlargement is on track. I quote

117

Secretary of State Warren Christopher and NATO Secretary-General Javier Solana, who were recently in Prague: "We welcome the NATO answer to two basic questions—why and how NATO will enlarge—and we expect the two other remaining questions will be answered as soon as possible, by the end of this year or the beginning of next year."

The two remaining questions are who and when. But we do not want to take the advantages of NATO in a passive way; we want to share the responsibilities for the security and stability of the area. We want to participate actively in the building of the security of Europe, and therefore we absolutely reject any type of membership other than full membership.

To answer the challenges, NATO must first be open to adaptation in order to work outside its territory and, second, must expand to the east to strengthen Eastern Europe. We sense a new opportunity to enhance European security. We have another reason for supporting NATO enlargement: the widening of the space is in the interests of our Czech Republic and also in the interests of the security and stability of the whole of Europe.

We do not see NATO as an umbrella that somebody will hold over us. For us, it is an opportunity to put on our raincoat and go with others through the rain; in other words, to cooperate with others in the interests of European security and stability in preparation for the day we will need it, the day it will rain.

WILLIAM E. ODOM (United States): The possible resurgence of Russia is not a troublesome threat, at least in the next decades. But there is a newer threat: trouble-making Russian diplomacy. We have already seen evidence of it in Bosnia, and we will see it in more forms than one can think of in the future. Sometimes we pretend that it is not happening. The counterpart of this trouble-making diplomacy is Western European trouble-making diplomacy. Europeans in Eastern Europe respond to this in an equally competitive fashion.

I am struck by the similarity of today's diplomacy with that during the interwar period in the 1930s; there is an inchoate resurfacing of those same patterns. Although the reason for enlargement is internal, we have not fully explored the degree to which it is an internal problem. Let me go a bit further on the Russian front and express some sympathy for, but also some candid realities about, Russia. Russia is in a traumatic transformation. And this period must be extraordinarily difficult for Russians—especially Russian liberals who helped bring this off without reaping the rewards from a transition as rapidly as they expected. At the same time, the less liberal forces are using the circumstances of our dallying in NATO to create problems there.

We can talk about Russia as if it is a government, a single state. Someone warned the Americans about the dangers of talking too much about the EU and coming under the illusion that the United States could just call up Europe and get an answer about Europe from the EU. It is not too much of an exaggeration to say that you can try to make a single call to Moscow but you really cannot get a single answer. For Russia, that is a real problem. You see evidence of the problem when Russia complains about the abuse Russian minorities suffer in Estonia, when they are forced to learn a few words of Estonian to vote. At the same time, the Russian government is killing thousands of Russian citizens in the south and suggesting an analogy with the American Civil War. Regrettably, my president was there to endorse such rhetorical nonsense.

But I would not blame Russia so much: this predicament arises from the collapse of the old regime. We will indeed have a difficult problem in the future, and timidity before these forces is the worst approach to take.

I have researched the reasons for the creation of NATO in 1948–1949. I have been struck with the complete absence of reference to the Soviet Union and the Soviet threat in France and in most other places on the Continent. Germany was the issue. If one explores why Robert Schuman and Jean Monnet supported the creation of NATO, it was because they wanted a security context that would allow old adversaries to get on cooperatively, economically. In other words, what Europe could not provide for itself, it looked to NATO to provide.

In Central Europe, the same arguments of 1948–1949 are compelling today. It is important for the U.S. audience to have a fuller understanding of this. Senator Sam Nunn, well known for his support of NATO, said recently in a panel that we should not expand NATO at all, that he is worried about taking on the additional military burdens of the east. He was overlooking the arguments advanced in 1948–1949 about why we went into NATO in the first place and failing to see the compelling relevance today.

We do agree that we need to include Russia, and let me be explicit on how we should include it. We will never buy Russia off through deals with NATO or by representation in NATO. There is a bigger problem than NATO enlargement that has to do with European security to the Urals. There we should take the existing Organization for Security and Cooperation in Europe, which looks like the United Nations General Assembly—it is a great discussion place incapable of action—and create within that organization a security committee, with membership for Russia, Ukraine, Germany, France, Britain, and the United States. When those members reach a consensus, they should be empowered to act militarily to establish peace or to prevent the outbreak of war in Europe.

Now that would put some teeth in an otherwise toothless organization, and it would be quite a challenge to Russian participation in Europe. Russia already has partial membership in the G-7. Russia should be given full membership, if it stays on the road toward a market economy. My own government is remiss in not engaging Russia in a four-power group to oversee the problems that we will face in the not-so-distant future and are already seeing in the Korean Peninsula. I favor a group of Russia, China, Japan, and the United States. There are specific tasks with an enormous need for Russia's participation.

OWEN HARRIES (United States): Surely, if one looks at the facts of the next generation, the West faces two major realities: a declining superpower and a rising superpower. The declining superpower is Russia; the rising superpower is China, which has hardly been mentioned. It is difficult to say which will provide the most serious problems. Decline can be as dangerous as, if not more dangerous than, emergence in some circumstances. Both these countries occupy the heartland. Insofar as there will be any containment of the rising superpower in that heartland, it is Russia that is in the position to do that containing or contesting. That factor alone makes Russia extremely relevant to Western calculations, if the West is thinking globally and not simply in local European terms. The world is ultimately larger than Bosnia, and the fact that Bosnia has been such a dramatic and dismaying event should not lead us to ignore that larger framework.

COMMENT: We are beset by some quite serious external problems. Nuclear proliferation is not just something to be discussed, it is a fact of life. Whether we have the Nuclear Nonproliferation Treaty or not, that horse is already out of the stable. And all around Europe, especially around the borders of Africa and the Middle East, that is life.

Talking about having the EU spend a bit longer discussing how to sort itself out and then not quite offer Central Europe any access to this particular marketplace on a necessary scale simply consigns Central and Eastern Europe into a sort of difficult position of not being able to stabilize their own internal structures, to have full access to marketplaces.

That is, we would rather abandon aggressive liberalism because we want to protect our own internal structures. The truth is that the EU must not use this as some sort of an excuse to hang onto absurd bureaucracies and policies, which are projectionist, but rather as an excuse to break them down and return to that free-trading model that was the essence of the beginning. We cannot just offer Central and Eastern Europe some sort of comprehensive supranational structure to discuss matters with Russia. The system must be firmly based on trade, or there is no reason at all for having it. To conclude that Russia is relevant is not to conclude that we acquiesce in all Russian preferences.

We certainly want to go slowly in the expansion of the EU. But one can make the case that such an opportunity occurred three years ago. If we drag this process out, we could find ourselves facing a much more costly decision, from which we might recoil. The sooner we take this action, the better: enlarge NATO and, in the immediate aftermath of that, enlarge the EU. If we allow a gap to develop between the members of the principal security organization and the principal economic organization, we are asking for trouble; the two must move in tandem.

13

Extending Free Trade

Discussion

BRIAN HINDLEY (United Kingdom): The members of the Trade and Economics Committee meeting in Karlovy Vary in November all agreed on three points. First of all, the European Union should remove all obstacles to accession of all countries of Central Europe at the earliest possible date. Second, the enlarged EU and members of NAFTA should prepare a joint initiative for further liberalization of the World Trade Organization. Third, in the event that the initiative is rejected by other members of the WTO, then the EU and NAFTA should proceed with the liberalization of transatlantic trade and investment.

Clearly, there is substantial resistance in the European Union, couched in terms of the practicalities of the Central European states joining the European Union, if not in terms of the principle. In the past week, a report of the European Parliament suggested that the accession of the Eastern European states be delayed because of practical difficulties. The difficulties identified in the report concern the impact on the EU budget of any attempt to extend the Common Agricultural Policy (CAP), as it now exists, to the Central European states and the impact on regional funding and regional policies and the political problems this expansion creates for beneficiaries of the CAP.

KAREL KANSKY (Czech Republic): I see a certain ambiguity in the term *Central Europe*. What states are we talking about? People use this term in many different ways. We should be more specific, by identifying the outreach or size of Central Europe, if it exists. I am an economist, not an authority on geographical definition. The states I was concerned with were Poland, the Czech Republic, and Hungary, and possibly Romania and Bulgaria, the Baltics, and states further east. But certainly those core states—Poland, the Czech Republic, and Hungary—are included.

MICHAEL SPICER (United Kingdom): There can be no doubt at all that the CAP is the big obstacle to enlargement to the East, however one defines that. And that is bad. CAP provides a wonderful excuse for the European Union to be an extremely protectionist organization. The British government also thinks that is bad. But what do we do about it? The only sensible solution in the end would seem to be some kind of breakup of the CAP. This would mean a return to some kind of national-based deficiency payment system focused on the particular problems of particular countries: there is little doubt that the big payers in the CAP at the moment—Germany and Britain—would not be able to sustain the massive increased expenditures that would be required if they were to support the farming industries of the east. And this situation has been used as an excuse for delaying matters. The CAP has to be radically redone if this issue of trade is to be addressed properly.

MR. HINDLEY: A fairly radical reform of the CAP has been suggested: that the CAP should not be extended to the Central European states. We argue that the CAP should be reformed in the sense of being detached from current production, so that farmers in existing member-states who have been receiving support will continue to receive it. But because support would not be dependent on production, there would be a free market in agricultural products within the EU. Between the EU and the rest of the world, support would be by means of direct income support, which would not necessarily go to farmers in Central Europe.

ROBERT D. HORMATS (United States): First, one of the major problems is that political support for free trade has encountered a great, and indeed growing, resistance in virtually all of our countries. The primary objective must be to reestablish in the minds of our electorates and in the minds of our legislatures the importance of resuming a process of reducing trade barriers around the world, particularly among the major trading countries. Finding an initiative that generates political support is therefore extremely important in the current environment, so that countries that are tending to turn inward will once again see the advantages of global engagement. That is particularly important in the United States. Second, the so-called central negotiations will not work well.

EDWIN J. FEULNER, JR. (United States): For those of us on the Right who believe in free trade in the United States, the pace of activities at the Uruguay Round of the GATT and at the WTO is always the pace of the slowest ship in the convoy. Little progress is made, and we must look for other ways to liberalize trade. We also must contend with other realities, most importantly the fact that the EU, instead of removing internal walls and external walls, as we had hoped, is increasing them.

As a consequence, there is an inbalance in U.S. policy as we look for opportunities either in our own hemisphere or across the Pacific. It is unfortunate; it is something that we should all decry. But, at the same time, as Milton Friedman said about tax cuts, I will take these opportunities whenever and wherever I can find them. Most of my colleagues in the United States would say that we are in favor of expanding trade, of opening markets, and of moving in the right direction wherever and whenever we can and at as fast a pace as we can—keeping the momentum in the right direction and trying to resist some of our own internal political pressures.

REGINALD DALE (United States): In the United States, there will not be backing for a transatlantic free-trade area that does not include agriculture. Without agriculture, there is a question of how much would be achieved in other areas, given that tariffs are already so low. And without agriculture, it would be hard to prove good intentions to the new and much tougher WTO. In the European Union, it would be hard to get a mandate for a transatlantic free-trade area *with* agriculture, largely because of the French position. France, acting through the European Union, has already killed any specific reference to a transatlantic free-trade area. Negotiations have started between the United States and the European Union on the basis of a transatlantic agenda that does foresee exploratory contacts between the two to determine whether trade could be encouraged, whether tariffs could be reduced or even eliminated.

But referring to a transatlantic free-trade area runs into all sorts of ideological problems. The European Union's approach at the moment is to try to get as far as it can through the back door, through these negotiations, and hope that, in the end, there might be something like a TAFTA, although it would not be called that. But, at the same time, the European Union and Britain are calling for a new round of global trade, multilateral negotiations, and other Uruguay Round–type negotiations. Various other straws in the wind seem to indicate that as a possible way to go. And it would be the best way to go.

By the end of the century, under the terms of the Uruguay Round, there will be new negotiations on agriculture and services; many other negotiations are proceeding at the moment. These may all come together at the end of the century, into something that looks like a new multilateral round. At the same time, the Asia-Pacific Economic Cooperation (APEC) is saying to the European Union, "Why don't you match step by step all the liberalization moves that we implement?" Now, if APEC were to implement those moves, and the European Union were to match them and accept also the deadline of 2010 for free trade, there would be a global negotiation. The whole of APEC, NAFTA, and the European Union must account for 90 percent of world trade. The omens now are quite favorable toward a new global initiative, although the ground has not been prepared politically yet. But that is the direction we should push at the moment.

At present, negotiations based on the Madrid declarations are not proceeding rapidly. There are problems in the tariff field between the United States and the European Union. Because of the Uruguay Round, countries feel that they need not pursue changes that were not accepted in the Uruguay Round. In specific areas where U.S. tariffs are high and in others where European tariffs are high, bargaining is difficult. We cannot rely on such talks as a driving force to liberalize trade.

QUESTION: Given the liberalization and free-trade movements going on in South America, given the new governments coming forward in Spain, the new attitudes in Portugal, and the links that exist between those countries and South America, is there a case for extending the concept of the Atlantic further south than has been traditional?

MR. HINDLEY: There is no reason in principle why discussions should not be extended to South Atlantic relations.

If you were looking around the world for sensible customs unions or free-trade areas, the North Atlantic is not, from an economic point of view, particularly sensible. There are no potentially huge gains, except in the sensitive areas such as agriculture, where gain would come from disassembling the CAP.

If the project is cast in political terms, a fear in the United States and in Europe is that the United States is moving in isolationist directions. From a European point of view, in terms of a need to link the United States to the rest of the world, and to Europe in particular, the proposal makes more sense.

COMMENT: The argument for extending the concept is twofold. One, the more all-embracing the concept of free trade, the better. But there is a more specific point: both sides of the North Atlantic share certain Western values and, therefore, there is some substance on which to base both free-trade arrangements and perhaps some kind of political arrangements.

Those arguments until recently would have been restricted to the North Atlantic, but deep-rooted Western values are emerging fast in South America, in terms of democracy and of jurisdictions and in terms of the whole attitude toward running an economy. South America has much more in common with Europe than twenty to thirty years ago, when some of these ideas about North Atlantic cooperation first arose.

QUESTION: Would it be fair to state the position of the committee as follows: The development of the North Atlantic industrial policy called TAFTA is not a good idea, either to strengthen U.S.-European cooperation or to promote the liberal idea of free trade? Would it be fair to say that perhaps the committee was of the opinion that a TAFTA project did not serve or could not serve either of those two purposes and was a bad rather than a good idea?

MR. DALE: On the point about the South Atlantic, the EU is already negotiating with MERCOSUR—a situation that the United States slightly resents. The action rather breaches the Monroe Doctrine. The United States will sooner or later be extending NAFTA. It would be hard to isolate a TAFTA from the rest of the Atlantic, because these moves are happening at the same time.

It has been noticeable in Europe that the United States has committed itself to deadlines for free trade with the whole of the Pacific and the whole of Latin America but not with Europe. Although there may be practical reasons, there is a symbolic message, which people in Europe do not always appreciate, coming as it has with statements from some members of the Clinton administration that Europe is no longer the center of the world. This further signals a shift in U.S. attention.

There is an argument in the United States, particularly from the labor unions, that a country should have free trade with countries that are more like oneself, not with the developing countries and low-wage countries: the United States should have free trade with Europe because Europeans are easier to compete with and have high costs.

Another political argument on the other side, from a more liberal point of view, is that an Atlantic free-trade agreement could be seen as ganging up on the developing world. That is an extraordinary argument. APEC includes half the world's economy, and the competitive countries now are the developing countries. But with all these networks of agreements reaching out in one direction or another, they will have to be pulled together, and the more arrangements that can be globalized, the better.

MR. HORMATS: The argument that the United States is becoming isolationist is a bit overdone. The United States is turning its interests and its energies regarding trade away from Europe and toward Asia and toward the Western Hemisphere. This is not isolationism, but it is a sign that there is more growth in those markets and that the United States needs to spend more of its political energy and its negotiation energy to find ways of opening them up for American goods and services.

There does seem to be a feeling in the United States, and perhaps in Europe as well, that it is more comfortable and fairer to have trade with countries that have relatively the same wages and relatively the same working standards and relatively the same social standards as the United States. This is the kind of argument one might associate with Patrick Buchanan: that somehow trade with countries with lower wages is unfair, and either the United States should not trade with them or it should impose a tariff—what he called a social tariff—to make up for this differential. But productivity levels are different. Whatever we do, we ought not to sell it on the basis that it is somehow easier to deal with countries of like economic structures as opposed to those with differences.

Any effort to spread trade among the Atlantic countries should be seen as part of a broader effort to expand global trade. That reinforces the case for expansion in the context of the World Trade Organization. Thus we deal with both the Latin American issue and the Asian issue. But there is no reason why the United States and Europe could not lead the way in the World Trade Organization. The United States and Europe ought to take the initiative, perhaps with the involvement of APEC countries—which would be beneficial—to create new momentum to expand trade in the WTO. This should be done at the head-of-state level. Margaret Thatcher made this point about a head-of-state summit.

KEVIN MURPHY (United States): There is a temptation to limit trade to the areas where it is not painful, but the gains to trade occur in the cases that are painful and cause changes. Trade without changes in prices would not have any impact. Without tough decisions such as opening trade in agriculture with Europe, one is paying only lip service to the ideals of free trade. Free trade is embraced with the difficult cases: the less developed countries. That reasoning implies free trade in agriculture. Someone must take the initiative and have the perseverance to push through on the difficult choices. If we ignore the most difficult cases, we are not really talking about free trade. The same argument pertains to trade with Eastern Europe.

DOUG SEAY (United States): Bringing the South Atlantic in on this would be an excellent idea because of its beneficial effects on motivation. One can talk about why free trade is good in general, but the political aspect of providing a sufficient motivation has nothing to do with rationality. The problem is not the Latin Americans, because virtually all of them have signed on to free trade with the United States. We in the United States are dragging our heels. The other countries would love to be brought in, almost overnight. The rate of NAFTA's expansion is unknown. We cannot bring in even Chile or El Salvador at this point, and tackling Argentina or Brazil is not in the picture in the immediate future. But the interests of the Latin Americans in expanding trade with Europe and the somewhat cynical desire of the EU to have a separate trade agreement with the Latin Americans would pressure those in the United States who have to make the argument for free trade. Like most countries and most people, the United States does not value something until there is a threat to take it away. Latin America is simply looked on as our backyard, and we can do with it as we wish in terms of trade. Those countries will knock at the door and wait until we are ready. But if the perception is that these two rival areas are about to get together and exclude the United States—even better would be a Japanese–Latin American free-trade area—that would mean headlines, and people would rush to bring the Latin Americans in to preserve what is ours.

The same applies to Canada. For a long time, Canadians have wanted to have a special economic relationship with Europe, precisely because they wanted to have some political leverage to use against the United States. The Europeans have always turned them down, because they fear that Canada is a stalking-horse for the United States—a matter of reverse logic. The issue of any baneful economic effect at all is irrelevant. Such an arrangement would push the United States toward a more urgent look at this whole process.

The other aspect of this problem is that we talk about Europe and the EU in economic terms here as almost synonymous. Some areas in Europe are not likely to be part of the EU in the near future. Now the EU exerts a domineering role. It tells these applicant countries that they may or may not do this, even though they are not members or are going to become members. I have long advocated that the United States look at trying to make special trade arrangements, even a free-trade area, with East Europeans or with any country—Norway, Switzerland, Russia, etc.—for the same reason: that arrangement would upset the EU. It would get the EU not to look more favorably on the United States but more favorably on the idea of economic expansion to the east, precisely to block the United States—again not for economic reasons but for narrow political ones. That aspect—forcing these countries against their political desire into these agreements—must be part of the strategy, not just outlining why it would be a good thing.

Mr. Hindley: The thrust of this New Atlantic Initiative is to make the strongest possible case for a new link between the United States and the European Union. Clearly, to rush straight to a TAFTA, leaving aside the questions of political feasibility, would raise all kinds of questions about the WTO. I would not wish to see the WTO damaged. The initiative is about the future of trade relations between the European Union and North America.

COMMENT: It has been stated that agricultural policy is expensive and probably fundamental to the problems that have to be addressed if the economic union is to be expanded to the east. I think that the problem caused by agricultural policy in Europe must be solved and is fundamental to anything else in terms of either European trade or North Atlantic trade.

MR. HINDLEY: How could the CAP be reformed in such a way that it was not a barrier to desirable initiatives elsewhere? If the political power of farmers in Europe is a political fact of life, it is still possible to make transfer payments to them without creating a structure that blocks desirable relations with the rest of the world. This can be done by detaching subsidies from production.

It is not a minor issue at all. It is truly an extremely major issue. Reform of the CAP and these initiatives to include Eastern Europe do not in any logical sense threaten the support that is paid to farmers in Western Europe. They do threaten the way that it is done but not the fact of doing it.

MR. SPICER: Should the subsidies be given on a country-by-country basis? Or will there be some EU pool for this?

MR. HINDLEY: The EU could make the payments or fund them or administer the funds.

MR. SPICER: On an EU basis, from the point of view of the feasibility of reforming the CAP in such a way that the trade barrier point is addressed, it does not make much difference whether reform comes through prices or whether through deficiency payments. The interesting change would be on a country-by-country basis to overcome this fundamental excuse on the part of some countries that pay into the pot at the moment when they say that they simply cannot afford to anymore. The crucial point is whether it is to be done on a European basis or a country-by-country basis.

MR. HINDLEY: Deficiency payments have not been proposed as the alternative. What is proposed is that any payment should be detached completely from current production. Farmers who have received so much support in the past ten years should be given a commitment based on production in the past ten years, not in any way affected by current production. That proposal does not arise from a passion to reform the CAP in that direction. My own preferred reform of the CAP would simply be to do away with it totally. It is a proposal made in recognition of the fact that farmers do seem to have substantial political power in the European Union—and that the present arrangements are making it extremely difficult to expand to the east. Farmers would make it extremely difficult to form a customs union across the Atlantic. Therefore, it is necessary to think of some politically feasible way of reforming the CAP that does not stand in the ways of these initiatives. There may be all kinds of ways of doing it, but a deficiency payment scheme was not proposed here.

MR. SPICER: It is still money coming out of the rich countries' pockets to put into the poor countries' pockets. The question is whether the rich countries will accept that politically. If they will not, this situation will continue to be a barrier to trade. One must go to a country-by-country basis of support to overcome this barrier to trade.

MR. HINDLEY: What is important here is that the payments to farmers detached from production could be zero in principle. That is not the core of the issue. If payments to farmers are detached from current production, then the CAP is no longer a barrier to initiatives of the kind we are talking about here.

JAN KRZYSZTOF BIELECKI (Poland): When obstacles to entry are identified, the issue of the burden for the existing member countries is raised. There is, however, a kind of deception that is often used by fans of deepening against the goal of enlargement. But the argument about the extent of the burden is often wrong—possibly because of depreciation factors and economic growth. All the calculations submitted to the European Parliament several months ago were simply not correct, because the figures have changed and economic relationships have changed.

Second, it is not a one-way equation, because there are also benefits from enlargement, not only costs. When raising the issue of a heavy burden caused by enlargement, we put ourselves into a trap, which works against enlargement. Finally, the most important problem facing any further enlargement is the monetary union. If the monetary union and the single currency are introduced on time, then in 1999 we have a redivided Europe instead of an integrated Europe.

And we have a situation in which there is a Europe of two or three speeds and two or three circles.

If we really want to touch on the dilemma facing the EU, the main problem is not the CAP. The dilemma is whether to go with monetary union on time and launch it for the hard-core six or seven countries and to provide for the others a transition period until 2001 or 2003. The Intergovernmental Conference has been inaugurated, maybe with trumpets, and is now doing its work in conspiracy. Something, however, should emerge quickly, and then with great speed in Europe and redivided Europe. The question of transatlantic partnership in securities, trade, or economic organizations is important, but I am trying to indicate some sense of priorities.

COMMENT: If the objective is to create freer transatlantic trade and, if possible, even wider than that, there are two main obstacles at the present time in Europe. Obstacle one is the plan for monetary union. Monetary union is the end to the single market in Europe. It is another tool in this managed-trade industrial policy device.

And problem two is indeed keeping agricultural policy on the European level. The only way that might be politically feasible and economically sensible—to make sure that agricultural policy is no longer the major obstacle to free trade—is to transfer it back to the national level. As long as the current projects for monetary union stay in the works, and as long as the renationalization of agricultural policy is not seriously considered, TAFTA will be only another tool in the global industrial policy scheme.

Following the reference to the Buchanan rhetoric, I understand public reaction to it when all they hear is that "we want these free-trade areas in order to increase competitiveness because it is a battle-field out there, and only the best can win." Nobody talks about the mutual benefits of free trade anymore. All we hear is the need to increase competitiveness. Now, are we then surprised that the average citizen has some questions about that approach? So the free-trade rhetoric needs careful examination. Certainly, we should stop using the free-trade argument in the sense of planned competitiveness, and we should start using the free-trade argument again in the sense of mutual benefits.

MR. HORMATS: On the question of the issue of free-trade rhetoric, we must generate political support for expanding trade, and the competitiveness point is only one of many. What troubles me in some of our debates in the United States is the notion that people identify a particular trade deal with a particular number of jobs. Such claims as NAFTA will create one hundred thousand or a million jobs are common. The impact on numbers is hard to determine, and in a way those claims are bogus. When there is a setback, like a recession in a country such as Mexico or a collapse of the currency, people say, "It failed, it failed because it really didn't create those jobs, and it turned our trade surplus into a trade deficit that also cost jobs." How we present the point is important.

The job argument is attractive politically, but it knifes you in the back if you are not careful. Another argument is inadequately reflected in the debate: locking countries into free-trade agreements is important because it strengthens the hands of the reformers. Mexico is a good example of this. There are limits to what governments can do to intervene in the economy if things turn downward. Mexico, for instance, did not impose, during this crisis as it did last time in the early 1980s, trade barriers against the United States or revert to more protectionist types of domestic policies, because NAFTA had locked in the reform.

The other element is that increasingly investment must be part of this. It may well be that in NAFTA we need to improve, clarify, and expand the rules for investment.

We have to find a more imaginative and more accurate way of explaining the benefits of free-trade agreements but, more important, this expanded idea of free trade. The direction most of us hope we can go is to emphasize expanding trade in the context of the WTO as the primary and the most substantial way of achieving benefits across the Atlantic and across the Pacific, including Latin America.

14

Trade, Security, and
Social Conscience

Discussion

BRIAN HINDLEY (United Kingdom): Is a transatlantic free-trade agreement (TAFTA) an attractive project? Maybe it is, maybe it is not. There is a way of going at it that makes it attractive; there is a way of going at it that makes it unattractive. And what has been proposed is that the attractive route is an effort to construct a TAFTA only after further liberalization has failed in the World Trade Organization. It is much more desirable to have free trade at large than free trade simply across the Atlantic.

FRANCIS BLANCHARD (France): Should a so-called social clause be introduced through the World Trade Organization or outside that organization? This is not a theoretical question, nor is it indeed a new question. Indeed, when the International Labor Organization, for which I was responsible, was created in 1919, it had two objectives: social justice and fair competition.

As long as the industrialized countries were in control of the world economy, the problem of the so-called social clause did not come up. Globalization of the world economy increased, alongside the fierce competition among all countries of the world, increasing fears among the trade unions, especially in the West, that the workers of the world were suffering and would suffer from low wages and bad working conditions.

As a result, a strong demand was made by those trade unions

in the West for the inclusion in the GATT agreement of a social clause, that is, a provision to link trade to human rights and workers' rights. But the reaction on the part of developing countries has been negative. At times, they have been passionate in their opposition, and it remains passionate; we should have evidence of that at the WTO assembly in Singapore in December. That is one of the issues that is bound to come up.

The developing countries have argued that a social clause is a disguised attempt to introduce protectionist measures. In the West, the trade unions have argued that conditions in developing countries are the consequence of the malfunction and dislocation of industry. In other words, there is a deadlock on the subject; there is no chance of a social clause being introduced through the WTO. Can nothing be done to see that the process of trade liberalization will parallel the improvement of labor conditions in the world at large? There seems to be more readiness on the part of both sides, developing countries and industrialized countries—including trade unions in the latter—to take a more dispassionate view of the situation and to explore the possibilities of meeting this kind of problem.

We could make progress on the basis of common-sense notions and principles. The first principle, one that has not been recognized in the heated discussion on the subject, is to accept that each country must determine the level and content of its social policy in accordance with its economic possibilities, choices, and preferences, provided that it is understood that such a principle does not allow the search for a comparative advantage resulting from abnormally low levels of social protection. The second principle is that there should be general acceptance—regardless of the level of economic development—of a number of fundamental workers' rights that must be recognized, regardless of the level of economic development. The number of those workers' rights, or conventions, is small, but their importance is great. If there were a general agreement to have strong action on the following issues, we would make substantial progress.

Issue one concerns interdiction of forced labor; forced labor is still a fact in the world today. Issue two asserts the freedom of association and collective bargaining. Issue three concerns the equality of treatment and the fight against any form of discrimination. And issue four is about the fight against child labor. On those four headings—forced labor, freedom of association and collective bargaining, equal treatment, child labor—there should be general agreement

135

regardless of the level of economic development.

The third common-sense principle concerns the growing need to recognize that the interdependence resulting from the globalization of the world economy carries with it obligations for each country—not only the ILO because the ILO over the years has become the good conscience of the world. By the way, the ILO headquarters is less than one mile from the headquarters of the WTO. I wish I could say that there is close collaboration between the two, but this is not the case. We are on polite terms and are friendly to each other, but there is no exchange of views or experience between the two. This must change. I would say the same about the World Bank and the International Monetary Fund.

At this juncture, in relation to this difficult problem of the social cause, the ILO is not equipped to deal with the increasingly complicated problems related to the globalization of the economy. The ILO is in the process of trying to equip itself for that objective.

JAN KRZYSZTOF BIELECKI (Poland): I would like to emphasize two points. First, we need the United States in Europe, and, second, it is not an easy task. For the United States and for some other Europeans, it is not obvious that America should be present in Europe forever, even if the prosperity, peace, and stability of Europe in the past forty years are thanks to the U.S. presence and the NATO umbrella that it provided.

The task is to convince the Americans why they are important, why we need them. From my Polish perspective, it is particularly important that we answer these questions not merely from the perspective of investments, trade, or technology transfer, all of which are immensely important in achieving progress in Central Europe, but also from the perspective of ideas and values. Among these I would include the ideas of free enterprise, limited government, and free trade. I would also include Anglo-Saxon systems of accounting, Anglo-Saxon systems of financial standards, and Anglo-Saxon standards of transparency, which we in Poland introduced on a large scale. If we look at these matters even from a Western European perspective, we can see that their introduction is in the interests of Europe as a whole. But the more I travel to the United States, the more I am conscious that we cannot take a strong U.S. presence for granted. We must demand it; we must show interest in it; and we must explain why we need it.

Look at the changing structure of Polish trade, which was in the postwar period almost welded to the Soviet bloc via Comecon. It has been reorientated, and today 70 percent or so of trade is with the European Union. For the sake of the economy, we need more diversification. We need not only an access to European markets, we need better access to the U.S. market. Some diversification of the economic orientation of our countries is conducive to growth; the list of reasons why we need a U.S. presence is long indeed.

ROBERT D. HORMATS (United States): First, it is clear that support for free trade in the United States and elsewhere has encountered growing political resistance, largely because of concerns about jobs, about global competition, and about the impact on wage differentials. We must realistically understand that there is not the level of support for free trade that there was several years ago. Making further progress is going to be difficult and will require more effort from the point of view of structuring a negotiation that carries strong political support.

Second, we need to recognize that the attention of the United States with respect to trade has shifted away from Europe, away from the Western Hemisphere, to Asia. Much of the energy in the United States today, much of the attention of the American trade negotiators, much of the political emphasis, much of the discussion of trade in the Western Hemisphere is certainly on an open Asia and the Asia Pacific Economic Cooperation.

Third, it is hard to make a success of sectional negotiations. Reciprocity is much more difficult within a single sector, whereas in a broader negotiation there is intersectoral reciprocity. When sectors are crossed, there is a better chance of a negotiated deal than in a specific sector because of the greater scope for a trade-off. We ought to bear that in mind and seek a broader base for negotiation than the sectional negotiations that have been mandated by the Uruguay Round.

The fourth requirement is to reject the notion that somehow it is fair to have trade between countries that have the same, or roughly the same, wage levels or roughly the same workplace standards and that it is somehow unfair to have trade negotiations or free trade with countries that have different wage levels and different workplace standards. According to that view, negotiating a free trade agreement between the United States and Europe rests on the grounds that it is comfortable because these countries are relatively the same.

137

But this can only come at the expense of trade expansion with other countries with different levels of wages and workplace standards. Unfortunately, the idea that somehow trade with developing countries is unfair and we should not negotiate any more trade agreements with them has gained ground because of the campaigns of certain presidential candidates.

It is important to realize that the United States cannot, and will not, negotiate exclusively with Europe on trade. An American-European trade deal is simply not an acceptable proposition for the United States to the exclusion of trade negotiations in the Western Hemisphere or trade negotiations in Asia through APEC. There is a lot more activity there than there is with Europe in terms of American discussions at the moment.

The way to integrate the process of negotiating between the United States and Europe, between the United States and Asia, and between Asia and Europe (which is becoming a more important nexus) and Europe and Latin America (which is also growing in importance) is to have a broader negotiation within the World Trade Organization. If we are looking for an area in which the United States and Europe can lead, it is in that context. The United States and Europe together, using the Madrid agenda as a starting point but working beyond that, can identify a number of priorities on which the WTO should focus, above and beyond what it is already committed to do, and try to regenerate support for trade in the WTO.

That will not be easy because there is not much support for that, but that is the best way of acknowledging the United States will not deal exclusively with Europe; it also must negotiate with Asia and with Latin America.

If there is momentum in the WTO for a new round of negotiations, then the next-best solution—not the optimum but the next best—is to have parallel negotiations that integrate those going on between the United States and the East Asian countries, between the North American countries and the Asian countries in APEC, between the United States and North America and the EU, and also those negotiations that will probably be taking place with the Western Hemisphere.

But it is important to develop a major effort with strong political support to liberalize trade beyond the Uruguay Round. It is important to do it within the WTO. To the extent that it is not possible in the WTO, then negotiations with Latin America, Europe, Asia, and

North America must be integrated or dovetailed in some way. We do need, however, to establish a new momentum, and we do need to develop some more ambitious idea and then develop strong political support. Free trade is best for consumers and best for producers and does increase the general wealth. It is up to political leaders to explain that to people, rather than to retreat in the face of neoprotectionist, Buchanan-style measures.

LANE KIRKLAND (United States): Francis Blanchard gave a precise definition of the social clause, and the social clause has been so defined by the international trade union organizations involved in its advocacy. As he said, it means freedom of association, the right to collective bargaining, opposition to slave labor, to child labor, and to discrimination. That is the social clause. It has nothing whatever to do with and does not propose a minimum wage or elimination of wage differentials between countries—something that is widely misunderstood. These are not only trade issues; they are deep-seated moral issues. Any pattern of trade that is based on the denial of those propositions is not free trade. To call it free trade is a fraud. It is the worst form of protectionism, the worst form of turning trade to one's advantage at the expense of human beings, who, after all, are the ultimate objects of good economic policy.

If the idea that I put forward, of extending the European common market across the Atlantic, is somewhat antithetical to the terms of the WTO, then you are surpassing my understanding. If that is the case, then why is the European single market not antithetical to the WTO? Why is NAFTA not antithetical to the WTO? If a transatlantic free trade agreement is antithetical to the WTO, so much the worse for the WTO. The organization I represented never felt any stake in the WTO, and we were never able to get action on the creation of a study group to contemplate the consideration of a social clause.

Trade exists for a purpose, and I assume that purpose is to elevate the conditions of human beings, not to satisfy the abstract thinking of negotiators, who engage people in that process.

IRWIN M. STELZER (United States): The concerns of Mr. Kirkland are concerns with the costs imposed on consuming and importing countries, not solely with the costs imposed on producing countries that tolerate these conditions. In other words, the political problems arise because the importation of these goods should create costs on the consuming and importing nations, but we have a long tradition in America and in other nations of reflecting in the prices of goods— through legislation if necessary—the social costs imposed by consumers of those goods, whether they are environmental costs or others.

I am having trouble holding onto my free-trade theology concerning the question of whether to impose the social costs of imported goods on the consumers of those imported goods. Second, can we discuss the movement of goods and so on without talking about the free movement of resources? Free trade holds good if both goods and resources, which means people, move freely. Can we be for free trade and against open immigration policies?

COMMENT: In two successive sessions, I have heard protectionism defended under the guise of culture. It is said that we cannot import films because they will degrade our culture. Then I hear protectionism advocated under other guises—in terms of social and other agendas. Protectionism is rarely explicit and is usually promoted under some other guise.

Second, over the past decade and a half, the evidence is that expanding trade and expanding wage differentials in the United States are not as closely related as the popular press and other people might lead us to believe. It would be useful if we could get that message out. A social cost is unlikely. Europe and the United States are net exporters of high-skilled products; net importers of low-skilled products would certainly benefit as a whole the United States and other countries.

Third, the countries of Europe and the United States are huge producers of human capital. There is a huge gain now in the return from investment in skill and human capital. In the United States, this is higher than it has ever been and presents a huge opportunity for us, which many of the young today are starting to take advantage of. I would hate to see us try to undermine that return at this point by somehow subsidizing ourselves away from human capital investment. That would be counterproductive, counter to economic growth.

ROBERT L. POLLOCK (United States): I take issue with Mr. Kirkland and Mr. Blanchard, particularly in regard to the idea that the social clause should be a serious obstacle to liberalizing world trade. In history, rarely if ever have the actions of government, free-trade agreements, or anything else been the force behind improving labor standards. It has been economic growth. Rich countries do not have forced labor; in rich countries you have freedom of association. Rich countries have a good record of equal treatment. Rich countries do not have child labor because they can afford to not have children working. We are not doing the workers of poor countries a favor by keeping them out of free-trade agreements on the grounds of labor conditions. The economic benefits of free trade are great and important, but there is a reason for trade liberalization that has nothing to do with reducing tariffs and reducing other barriers. It is a moral issue, it is a political issue: free trade is the foundation of a liberal world order.

MR. HINDLEY: There is absolutely nothing antithetical about a free-trade area between the United States and the EU and the WTO. There would be a problem, however, if the customs union did not substantially cover all trade. Not including the sensitive areas—audiovisual, agriculture, steel, chemicals, for example—would be antithetical to the WTO. In other words, an incomplete free-trade area would be antithetical to the WTO, as well as bad for both the United States and Europe. There is no obvious willingness to negotiate about those sensitive areas in the United States or in the EU. Do we want to go with an incomplete free-trade area? We should not: it would be too damaging. There is a great deal one can say about the minimum standards for labor. From the point of view of someone concerned with free trade, the problem stems from the fact that regulations designed to protect labor in certain ways can be distorted to serve other purposes. It would be extraordinarily difficult for anyone to argue against the provisions dealing with slave labor or traded goods produced by slave labor. But it is always difficult to write an agreement that cannot be distorted so that it covers things that were not the original target of the wording.

Finally, a transatlantic free-trade area would represent an economic gain, provided that it was inclusive in kind. There is an attempt to solve a political problem with an economic solution. A TAFTA would not involve heavy economic losses if it could be constructed in such a way as not to damage the WTO. My first preference would be to try to seek trade liberalism through the WTO and only seek to create a TAFTA in the event that we fail.

I would not argue that there are no losers as a result of free trade. There are winners, and there are losers. I have always felt un-

141

comfortable with people who say that NAFTA will lead to an increase of 100,000 or 200,000 jobs. The numbers bandied around are bogus numbers. While a liberal system results in an improvement in the general welfare and many other benefits, for a certain group of people there is pain. This is a consequence of the adjustments to a more open, more competitive global order. And if we are to move even more dramatically toward open trade, we must figure out within our own societies how we are going to address that. We have not done it all that well. Unless we can demonstrate the economic benefits of more open trade and deal with the pain of adjustment and the loss of jobs in some quarters, then rekindling support will be hard. Free trade is a broad winner, but there are real pains, real adjustment costs, and some unemployment connected with the transition to more competition that have to be dealt with economically and certainly politically to generate the support we need.

15

Meeting the Challenges to Political Cooperation

Discussion

CHRISTOPH BERTRAM (Germany): In many ways, political cooperation is the most important part of any new Atlantic initiative. And it is, of course, difficult to get a discussion going on it. The problem seems to me not just the fault of our limited minds, but the contradiction between, on one hand, a desire to hold onto NATO, and, on the other, a sense that perhaps NATO alone is not good enough.

We have to be much more ruthless. The New Atlantic Initiative is necessary because NATO no longer provides the backbone for the Atlantic relationship. And if we want to retain the military and security aspects of that, we need to put it on a firmer and wider base. Otherwise, the security relationship will wither, simply because there are very few threats that still unite us. And so I suggest we must be more imaginative than talking about an Atlantic free-trade area or summits chaired by the American president. We have to understand that the future relationship across the Atlantic will have to include other well-defined activities and institutional arrangements different from the one that we have at the moment. And perhaps we even have to "de-NATO-ize" to make that arrangement more cohesive.

GYÖRGY GRANASZTÓI (Hungary): It was easy to enlarge NATO from twelve to fifteen or sixteen member countries and the European Union from twelve to fifteen. But now, with the Central and Eastern European countries, we have a completely different situation, with coun-

143

tries at different levels of development and facing different problems. Now, we need a more strategic and conceptual view. The stability of the Central European region and the rapid integration of
these countries into international security and political organizations
are vitally important. This point needs to be declared because public
opinion in this part of Europe is not fully persuaded. In fact, public
opinion polls now show that public interest in this goal is declining.
This is the moment when a new, true Atlantic initiative has an opportunity to deliver a clear message to this part of Europe.

IRWIN M. STELZER (United States): My comment concerns the case for a
new organization along the lines of the OECD. I question the need for a
new organization, and I wonder about using the OECD as an example.
While the OECD has been successful in rapidly revising its last fore-
cast, beyond that, I have some difficulty in deciding what it does. Second, I have some difficulty understanding the need for meetings between the U.S. president and the president of the European Union. That
is a lot different from Lady Thatcher's suggestion of meetings between
the U.S. president and the European heads of state. Meetings with the
president of the EU would encourage the illusion in America that there
is something called Europe, to which it can make one phone call and
then deal. That notion might indeed be very dangerous. I wonder if in
the future such meetings might be counterproductive to a new Atlantic
initiative, which, in the end, will have to be between nation-states and
not between the United States and the European Union.

I sympathize with the point put forth by György Granasztói
about the attitude of countries in Eastern and Central Europe. But I
believe we must look at dynamic politics as they evolve at the moment. Although the domestic political pressures that push the European Union toward insularity and protectionism and away from
enlargement are strong, we believe that the long-term interest of EU
members will be best served by resisting those pressures.

Within the EU, some countries are determined to create a federal system, and a limited number of countries that would be highly
protectionist, preferring in security matters some separation from
the United States. Other members of the European Union, such as
the United Kingdom, oppose all of those goals and would regard
enlargement of the EU and the improvement of relations with the
United States as far more important than any development of integration within the present EU. These are political facts at the mo-

ment, and we cannot understand our subject if we pass over them.

CHARLES POWELL (United Kingdom): I agree with Irwin Stelzer's point that you cannot "stitch up" Europe with a single telephone call, although there are, of course, areas where that is actually the case. Trade policy is an example, where the European Commission, sometimes accompanied by the presidency, does speak for Europe.

The three points I wanted to make are these. First, the main issue is how to keep alive the habit of consultation across the Atlantic. The problem, it seems to me, is that the European Union has become so obsessed with reaching common positions that by the time it reaches a common position it is so exhausted by the effort that there is no question of its ever changing that position. It is therefore pointless to talk to the European Commission because all you get is a gramophone record that plays the same tune. I see a danger, now that the security threats in Europe look less formidable, that the United States will be less inclined to take account of the views of others in formulating American policies than in the past. It is hard to overcome that problem, but perhaps that is something we should bear in mind.

Second, I have sympathy with what Christoph Bertram said. The United States and Europe could meet in any number of institutions: the G-7 summit, the OECD, the GATT, and innumerable bilaterals. I do not think that political consultation in NATO was ever a huge success. Although it was valuable, I do not recall that it was ever regarded as the main forum for political cooperation. We do need to look for new institutions. Lady Thatcher's suggestion of a summit is a new one, although I think that the value of summits is generally overplayed. We have too many of them, and they often lack clear objectives. Possibly we need to be very inventive, to think of something entirely new—an Atlantic Security Council, for example, that would comprise the United States and two or three of the larger European countries and a revolving membership of two or three of the smaller ones.

Frankly, the voices of those countries that count the most, those with the most influence, are the ones that provide the bulk of the military strength of Europe. I think three countries provide 70 percent of that military strength. Inevitably, it is their voices that are heard loudest. It is never popular to propose institutions in which not all countries are full members, but I am afraid that life is like that.

Third, I would like to underline the importance of Asia. I spend a lot of time these days in the Far East and am struck by the degree to which multinational institutions there are developing, particularly institutions that are especially concerned with security and political issues in the broadest sense. The Association of Southeast Asian Nations and APEC come to mind, and, of course, those institutions draw in the United States. Moreover, the economic balance of the world is shifting rapidly in that direction. If, in twenty years' time, you wanted to construct a G-7 summit from the biggest economies of the world, several would be in Asia: China, India, Korea, and Indonesia. We then get a very different picture from the one we are comfortably used to in which European countries sit by right in the G-7.

If we are not to lose the interest of the United States in Europe and see it overwhelmingly attracted by the economic possibilities of Asia—and, indeed, the growing security problems of Asia, with a more assertive China wanting to display military power and influence in the area—then we in Europe have to strengthen transatlantic cooperation. Otherwise, if Europe spends its time simply trying to formulate its own common foreign security policy and becomes unable to deal with the outside once it has reached a common position, the United States will become bored with Europe, quite understandably so. It will come to find Asia-Pacific area more attractive. In that case, we should have done ourselves a great disservice.

To come back to my starting point, I endorse the vital importance of keeping alive the habit of transatlantic discussion before policies are finally settled and resolved.

GÉZA JESZENSZKY (Hungary): We do not intend to create the impression that there is a Hungarian relay team here, but I wish to continue where Mr. Granasztói left off by stressing the importance of the inclusion of Central Europe in a European security and political system at this moment. Indeed it is a rare moment when history is open and its course may be altered. By profession, I am a historian. It has been my conviction that there are relatively short periods when there is a chance to take a new course. We are at such a stage now, but it is coming to an end very soon. That is why we should make hay while the sun shines.

Why include Eastern Europe? I will refer to one of the strongest advocates of including Eastern Europe, the late Hungarian prime minister Antall. He surprised many Americans when in 1990, before he became prime minister, he expressed a strong commitment to the Atlantic idea when even in Western Europe that idea was weakening, rather than strengthening. His argument, though not unique, was that the United States had been involved in two world wars in Europe, and its contribution was essential. But the two world wars were followed by less successful peace settlements. That is the key issue.

Why were the two world wars concluded in a way that disappointed the hopes raised? I think that the issue of Central Europe was not sufficiently dealt with in those settlements. This failure was due in part to a political philosophy—as exemplified by Walter Lippmann and others who influenced President Roosevelt—that the new Atlantic world should include only the two sides of the Atlantic, while Central Europeans should be left to their own devices and seek a relationship with the Soviet Union. Later on it was said that there should be an organic relationship worked out by these countries among themselves, without any outside help.

We are now in a new situation, when Central Europe and perhaps eventually the other countries, can really be part of this Atlantic world. There could be many arguments in favor, but I propose just one. All those with doubts about Central Europe's having a place in the new Atlantic community should first visit Russia, Ukraine, and Romania and then go to Warsaw, Budapest, and Prague. Then, I think they will require no further argument that these countries are really part of Europe and part of the Atlantic world.

ALAN LEE WILLIAMS (United Kingdom): I would like to make two points. First, it would be a mistake to launch a new Atlantic initiative by making it sound like an attack on the European Union. It is a mistake I think that we will avoid, but it is important to make that simple point just in case there are any lingering doubts about the objective.

Second, I offer a comment on the role of the voluntary sector. Sitting next to the secretary general of the North Atlantic Assembly as I do, I raise the point with trepidation. I think I can say, however, as a former member of that body, that the assembly should be the center of some of the activities that we have in mind, because it bridges the all-important gap between the two sides of the Atlantic and, of course, has an amazingly educative effect on parliamentarians. One of the sad facts at this present moment is that a number of members of the U.S. Congress and Senate are no longer as active in promoting the cause of Atlanticism as they used to be. I find that a very depressing situation about which I hope something can be done.

Much the same is true of the Atlantic Treaty Association. I was asked by that association to head a committee exploring ways to make it more effective; there are some difficulties, though, trying to do that. And so I see the need for something new.

I would like to pursue whether there is a case for launching something more effective than the Atlantic Treaty Association without, of course, damaging that association. The task has to be done with some care.

SERGEI A. KARAGANOV (Russia): Let me be as frank as possible, all the more since Russia was not included in the possible scheme of Atlantic political cooperation, and that gives me certain freedoms. There is an error, if not an error then an unreality, about the whole idea of political cooperation that does not involve one of the most powerful countries on the continent. Without that cooperation, how would you deal with regional problems? How would you deal with problems like the former Yugoslavia? What would happen in the end? We would return to great power diplomacy with everything being decided among Washington, Moscow, London, and Paris. Budapest, which is obviously a more European city than Moscow, would be left out. If we really want to build up something like a transatlantic political initiative, we have to involve all countries that are influential in the area. That means Bulgaria, for example, as well as some of the countries of the former Yugoslavia.

VIKTOR ORBÁN (Hungary): I would like to offer a response to our friend from Russia. In my essay, I tried to define the nature of Atlanticism, saying that some common characteristics, shared values, and historical experiences belong to the Atlantic area or ethos. This observation does not apply to Russia in present circumstances.

We on the European Integration Committee tried to be as imaginative and inventive as possible, but we were not successful in finding new institutions to assist the cooperation among the countries that consider themselves part of the Atlantic area. The reason for the inadequate cooperation between the countries is a lack of political will, not an absence of certain institutions.

The major task is not to find new institutions but to convince the decision makers to reach certain conclusions and to make decisions accordingly. For that reason, we are cautious about advocating new institutions, because we—the majority of the members of the European Integration Committee—do not believe that new institutions themselves are a substitute for political will.

FRANS A. M. ALTING VON GEUSAU (Netherlands): I remember that during the first years after the fall of the Berlin Wall we spoke of a once-in-a-lifetime opportunity to make Europe whole again. Today I think we must realize that in many respects our governments, our countries, and our institutions have failed to stand up to that challenge. On the basis of that observation, I have a few remarks.

First, we should not look at Atlanticism as a way to do some Europe bashing. It is no use saying that the European Union is all about protectionism; it is even worse to think that protectionism and federalism go together, but that is the British view. The European Union in many respects is a successful enterprise, which like NATO should be enlarged to include Central and Eastern Europe. Let us not forget that Franco-German reconciliation could not have taken place without it.

Principle number one, then, is that if we talk about enlargement and political cooperation, we must talk about enlarging the EU and NATO. Point number two concerns the failure of the past year, which is that while we have been speaking about adaptation, all we have done is increase the number of summits, free-for-all consultation, and arrangements without commitment. Our ministers have been flying around the world, discussing the same things many times without reaching conclusions. And the EU is unfortunately no exception to that rule. Another thing that we should clearly establish is that whatever new institutions or arrangements we propose must be institutions that clearly commit the member states and enforce the requirements of entry.

The great danger we are running, and I take the Council of Europe as an example, is that we say countries that respect human rights can be admitted and then we decide to admit countries where that situation has not yet been achieved. We must have clear commitments, and we must impress on everyone that those commitments have to be observed. Rather than creating new institutions, let us look at those institutions where commitments can be realized.

The third aspect concerns political reality. Political reality tells me that none of our objectives can be achieved without a strong partnership between the United States and Germany. The United States and Germany are the central forces in the Atlantic world today, and any initiative must be built on such a partnership. Because I am from the Netherlands, you may be surprised to hear this from me, but that is why I am saying it, rather than leaving it to others.

Last, if there have been some moderate successes in rebuilding Europe, they have primarily been through the voluntary civil society. And what we have left out—but what should be included in any declaration we make—is the importance of civil society. We need to return to a system of law as one of our principal tasks in making Europe whole again. Ties between universities, law firms, civil institutions, and the like make the Atlantic world strong. If we want to open up Europe to the east, we must make this one of our basic purposes.

ALUN CHALFONT (United Kingdom): I would like to comment on Islamic fundamentalism. We should be careful about using the phrase *Islamic fundamentalism*, as some have done, in a crude way. Islamic fundamentalism is not a political movement of any kind and in itself does not pose a threat to stability. It has become a phrase in use; perhaps this has something to do with Samuel Huntington's famous essay on the clash of cultures. Using this phrase as though Islam were a threat to the West causes great resentment and great bitterness, and I hope we will be more careful.

DANIEL PIPES (United States): I take issue with Lord Chalfont's comment that fundamentalist Islam is not necessarily anti-Western and is not necessarily a political movement. One must distinguish between Islam, the religion of a billion people, and fundamentalist Islam, which is a twentieth-century radical Utopian movement. That movement is political, is necessarily anti-Western, and therefore deserves to be regarded as a current and potential opponent of the West.

MR. CHALFONT: Although I do not want to get into a confrontation with Daniel Pipes about Islam, I would like to explain what I was hoping to say in my earlier remarks. I think we have got two problems here. The main one is possibly a problem of semantics. To many Muslims, fundamentalism is simply a fundamental belief in the tradition of Islam, the Sharia, and the whole Islamic religion. And they resent disparaging references to fundamentalism and feel bitter about them. I think perhaps that we could avoid this problem if we called it *Islamic extremism*, because there are extremists in Islam, and fundamentalists get caught up in extremist movements when they are exploited by people with political, usually national, motives, not religious ones. I want to avoid an argument about this. If we include a reference to Islam as a threat in any of our discussions, we should not just throw it away in half a sentence; we ought to explain what we are talking about.

16

The Form of Political Cooperation
in the Context of Atlanticism

Discussion

PETER W. RODMAN (United States): I would like to address two points. The first concerns suggestions to change the alliance, and the second regards our relations with Russia. I disagree with the notion that the alliance should change its nature and become more of a political rather than a military institution. NATO has always been a political as well as a military alliance; clearly the commitments to mutual security reflect a political consensus. To dilute the security dimension of NATO in the process of strengthening its political dimension is dangerous. The function of NATO is still to maintain security. The mutual exchange of guarantees maintains the balance of power in Europe. One reason the political committee found it difficult to develop a new institutional framework is that NATO's role in maintaining security is taken for granted. Proposals that would diminish NATO's military strength are dangerous precisely because both Soviet and Russian policy long aimed to dilute the degree of security consensus within NATO. The Russians continue to suggest that NATO reform is a possible quid pro quo for enlarging NATO. They say that only if it is restructured would they tolerate it. I think their statements are dangerous and mischievous; they would like to neuter NATO.

An additional danger is that the Clinton administration is flirting with the idea of changing the alliance. A recently reputed telephone conversation between Presidents Yeltsin and Clinton and their press conference April 21, 1996, provided evidence of the administration's position. It is essential to maintain NATO as the defensive alliance it always has been. Giving the Russians assurances that that aspect of NATO will change is dangerous.

My second general point addresses how to deal with the Russians when we talk about enlarging NATO. We need to talk to the Russians. The continent is not secure and stable if they continue to declare war on the enlargement of NATO. I am not inclined to make major concessions, certainly not for free. The point I would make is that NATO is a *defensive* alignment. Two-thirds of American troops have already left Europe, so there is no conceivable threat to Russia from enlarging the alliance. That ought to be the premise of the whole discussion.

I am willing to talk to the Russians about the military dispositions in Europe, about nuclear weapons, or whatever, because I do not want to see the remilitarization of Central Europe. I am willing to discuss other things with them, provided that they accept the enlargement of NATO. Russians have many desires. They want membership in the G-7, and they would like the contact group in Bosnia to be continued as a kind of political directorate. I have mixed feelings about some of those proposals. But we should not even discuss them until we settle the question of NATO enlargement. We owe the Russians no reassurances of any kind if they continue to make threats, including threats against the Balkans or Ukraine of the "shooting the hostages" variety. The Russians have threatened to retaliate if we bring Central Europe into the alliance; they have used the Balkans and the Ukrainians as hostages. If they behave in that manner, we owe them no reassurances at all about what kind of weapons we deploy in Central Europe. If they call off their campaign against NATO enlargement, we can have productive discussions with them, for example, about military restraint on a reciprocal basis—but only on the condition that they "call off the dogs" on NATO enlargement.

I am appalled that some European governments are making free concessions to the Russians. We should withhold discussing concessions of these goodies until we see how the Russians behave on the most central security question right now—enlarging NATO. The long-term relationship with Russia can be stable. If Russia accepts the new status quo that emerged from 1989, there is no basis for conflict. I interpret NATO enlargement not as a new act, but as the consolidation of the new status quo. If the Russians accept that view, they have no objective basis for a power conflict. I can see a long-term relationship with Russia that is cooperative, transparent, and benign. A sensible relationship with Russia is possible, but we cannot purchase it at the expense of sacrificing our interests, particularly our interests in consolidating the security of Central Europe.

CHARLES POWELL (United Kingdom): One of the main tasks here is to sell Atlanticism. Political cooperation is a rather narrow technical term—an exercise in producing statements that reflect the lowest common denominator among fifteen or sixteen different opinions—and is of no use for transatlantic purposes. For our purposes, we must base political cooperation on a much broader concept, embracing the totality of transatlantic relations: politics, trade, and defense. The essence of political cooperation has to be the entrenched habit of consultation in the *formative stage* of policy making.

At the moment, those on the European side of the Atlantic tend to exhaust themselves in titanic struggles to agree on a position and then are totally unable, thereafter, to change it. On the American side the problem is slightly different; leaders make decisions and only then remember that they have allies, whom they should have consulted and who are mortally offended that they did not do so. Lady Thatcher made an important point when she said that we should rely on powerful alliances, not on international institutions, to ensure our security in the world.

In the forums of international institutions one can pass endless resolutions that mean nothing. In an alliance one has to be serious, and the transatlantic relationship is a serious matter. Clearly we must maintain the concept of an alliance, widen it, and underpin it with a trade relationship and political consultation. With respect to trade, while many of us support the idea of a transatlantic free-trade area, the notion is not so widely supported by senior government officials in the United States. Indeed, we should not get the idea that Europe opposes and the United States favors a transatlantic free-trade area.

Political consolidation is absolutely vital to Europe: Europe has global interests, but it does not have all the means to pursue them. Europe has great influence in the trade field and considerable influence when it comes to dispensing aid. Europe has negligible influence worldwide on security and defense issues. If Europeans want to have a role in seeing that their interests are protected, transatlantic political cooperation is vital.

Protectionism is not confined to trade. It also applies to politics.

153

Europe has a degree of political protectionism—an obsession with internal discussions that lead to reaching unalterable positions rather than focusing on the broader issues. Is NATO the best forum for such political cooperation? I am certainly not in favor of creating new institutions if they are just going to become fresh obstacles to action. NATO has not been very effective in the political field, even it has been extremely successful on the defense issues. The NATO institutions do have to be revitalized and revivified; they can be made better.

One possibility is to create an Atlantic security council, consisting of the United States, three or four of the larger members of NATO, and perhaps two or three of the smaller ones on a revolving basis, rather like the UN Security Council. Another is a permanent coalition of the willing. If that is anathema to some countries, then we can just have a coalition of the willing within NATO—those who are prepared to sign on and act in the real world, not just in Europe. Finally, we have all agreed that the Central European countries should enter NATO. The Russians are not the problem, as Peter Rodman made absolutely clear. The Russians have no conceivable leg to stand on; NATO presents no threat to them. If there ever was a threat, it certainly does not exist now. The problem is with our own governments. We must find a way to convince them to move decisively.

PAVEL BRATINKA (Czech Republic): I subscribe to the provisions of the committee's report, which addresses the need to enlarge NATO and the European Union. That will take some time, and in the meantime those of us who are not members of NATO and the European Union would appreciate being involved in a deeper discussion.

As far as the noises coming out of the Russian Federation, we should make no compromises. Any compromise with them only enhances their respectability domestically, because they can show that they can deliver and they want to assuage inherent Russian pride. Today, their goods have a large market, so we should not compromise.

To achieve cooperation in a world full of diverse changes, the European side of the Atlantic requires an institution with a political will and the capability to implement the will. One does not need to be a historian to know that a large group of people can act as a coherent whole only when it has established a set of rules defining the ways of decision making under all possible contingencies.

Unfortunately, so far Europe has almost no such rules. Speaking about enhancing governmental cooperation will not outweigh that hard fact. Such a strategy might have worked during the cold war, when the powerful Soviet threat focused minds and brought about exceptional unity of purpose and wills. But there is no certainty that future challenges will have the same disciplining effect on all the governments concerned.

On the American side of the Atlantic, we do not deal with a single government. We deal with the United States and Canada. Nevertheless, failure to reach a government consensus between the United States and Canada on a joint response issue does not lead to paralysis. Thus, the ball is on the European side of the court.

I am aware of the difficulties involved in trying to get the second stage of the Maastricht Treaty to work. The only way to do so is to establish rules and procedures in institutions, so that one can secure guarantees that the things that need to be done are done.

Finally, I disagree with Lady Thatcher's contention that if Europe creates a kind of quasi-federal state, that state would be bound to become in the long run hostile to the United States, or it would become a historical anomaly. To the contrary, American states united themselves into a federation and they developed their own army and interests, but they never were a threat to Europe. Instead, the United States came three times this century to save Europe from the worst sides of its own history.

JAN NOWAK (United States): I agree with the suggestion that Russia should be offered participation in the security architecture of Europe, and I agree that the expansion of NATO should not create the perception that the rest is up for grabs. I do not agree that those problems should prevent or delay enlargement or expansion of NATO. I am very concerned, however, by the suggestion of a return to four or five European powers making decisions about the security of Europe. That would be a return to the idea that larger countries should decide the fate and security of smaller countries. We have the very sad precedent of Potsdam and Yalta. I believe that the European and Central European countries would never accept such an idea.

JAN FIGEL (Slovakia): I have two points. First, there is a good source for spreading Atlanticism that has not been mentioned. Hundreds of thousands of people fled from Central Europe before, after, or during communism, because of economic or political oppression. Those now living in the United States or Canada could serve as good personal ties for Atlanticism and for keeping the United States engaged in Europe.

Second, I represent the Slovakian parliament and am a member of the Christian Democratic Party, which is the opposition party. During the security debate, Slovakia was not among the many other countries that were mentioned—the Baltics, Ukraine, Moldova, and of course Russia. There is neither a panelist nor a speaker from my country. Slovakia appears to be somewhere between the first and second leagues or last. Slovakia understands that it needs to settle its domestic troubles and orientation and democratic principles and human rights at home. Our neighbors are bigger, and by itself Slovakia is vulnerable and cannot feel secure. I want to express gratitude for support from the EU and U.S. diplomatic services.

ARRIGO LEVI (Italy): Lady Thatcher spoke of the wider world and of how the New Atlantic Initiative must take into account the wider world and the very unstable balance of powers in the twenty-first century. She was talking about the enlargement of what is, after all, old Atlanticism. To arouse public opinion to the real dangers of the coming century, we need a new Atlantic initiative, not an old one.

MAX BELOFF (United Kingdom): Although from the European side of the Atlantic one could say that the United States was a threat to no one when it was created, an American Indian would not have said that. Furthermore, and even more important, the creation of that federation led to the first major bloody war in the history of the Western world. People who talk about federalism should start by studying American history. One of the great weaknesses on the continent of Europe and to some extent even in Britain is the neglect of studying American history, which has major lessons for us all. Remedying that weakness should be one of the aims of a new Atlantic initiative.

COMMENT: One lesson from the proceedings is that one definition of NATO is now no longer valid. When asked to describe the purpose of NATO, General Ismay, an early secretary-general of NATO, replied, "To keep the Americans in, the Russians out, and the Germans down." That was a fairly simplistic view, and one we can all now agree is no longer valid. Today's issues are far more complicated.

PART FOUR

Imperatives for the Atlantic Community

17

The Czech Republic and the Great Historic Challenge

Václav Havel

Thanks to our geographical location, the Czech lands have been a crossroads for the spiritual currents of Europe as well as of a variety of geopolitical interests. Here, many times in history wars have started or ended. As a result, we have traditionally had a heightened sensitivity toward possible threats or approaching dangers.

We can give ample evidence of that awareness. We have traditionally thought about the broader context of the European order, about the global issues of our civilization; we have regarded them as matters vital to ourselves. We know that the Czech problem cannot be resolved in isolation, that it will always be related to the solution of global problems. King George of Podìbrady, Jan Amos Comenius, Palacky, Masaryk, and even as far back as Patoèka, each of them in one way or another manifested the better part of the Czech tradition and related Czech matters to the broader context.

Of course, there has also been another side to the Czech tradition, that is, provincialism. But I believe that the Czech Republic of our times and its political representatives have learned a lesson from our past, and they link this to the better tradition: the tradition of thinking beyond ourselves and our own affairs. We pay close attention to what is happening beyond our country and beyond our own backyard.

We have often heard the voices of warning coming from the Czech environment. For example, Franz Kafka, whose work anticipates so many of the disasters that were to come, lived and worked here. Let us remember that in September 1938, the League of Czech Writers appealed to the conscience of the world, warning against appeasement and against concessions to Hitler. The voice of Czech writers found tremendous response among their colleagues abroad. Regrettably, that warning failed to find the same kind of response from the representatives of the Western democracies. The Munich Accords were concluded, and those who believed that by making concessions they would save peace later had to pay a heavy price for the defeat of the aggressor.

But even later in the 1970s and 1980s, in the times of the Charter 77 movement, we heard from here voices that were not quite usual. I remember, for example, the Prague Appeal, a Charter 77 document, which even then at the time of the bipolar division of Europe called for dialogue, for a quest for a new European order, for tearing down the iron curtain. That appeal of Prague, in fact, mentioned Germany's unification as a prerequisite for European unification. It was not usual to talk like that then, and many of our German friends were surprised that we presented this view.

The old, unnatural order has now collapsed. The bipolar division of the world has fallen apart, and Europe is no longer divided by the iron curtain. We live in a period marked by a great historic challenge to find a new order for Europe and for the world too, an order that will meet the challenges of our time.

Perhaps we are entering an era of Baltic cultural and multipolar civilization. In this era, the global order will be built, or should be built, on the principles of cooperation, coexistence among various, larger regional groupings; such entities range between the nation-state and the whole world. We can see the emergence of such regional entities on different continents.

The key to future global cooperation seems not to lie in one entity forcibly exporting its own values or its own ideas about what the system should be like. I believe we should go another way, to search out the common roots of all cultures. The cultures are more closely related to each other than we realize. While some cultures may emphasize their differences rather than their affinities, in reality, the roots of those cultures, though differing in outward appearance, are in fact quite closely related. To foster truly meaningful cooperation, we must look for these common roots, for the elements that unite our different worlds and from which the principles of cooperation are derived and on which our shared values rest.

It is no disgrace to be a part of any one of the world's regions or any one of these cultural spheres. None of them is a priori better than the others. They are equal, but so that they can enter into good cooperation, they must first define themselves. Only those entities that are clearly defined can work together in a creative fashion. The worst alternative of all would be not knowing where one ends and another begins, to have undefined areas, areas of vacuum. The existence of such undefined areas would encourage certain forces to look anew for opportunities to penetrate these "no man's lands." That is why I find it tremendously important that the European Union and the North Atlantic Alliance be expanded by admitting the countries of Central Europe and possibly Eastern Europe.

We live in a time when Europe has a chance it has never had throughout its previous history—namely, a chance to order itself on the principles of equality of rights and peaceful cooperation. Up until now, the European order has always been based on a dictate of the stronger and more powerful nations, which the less powerful ones just had to accept. Now, for the first time we have a chance to build a fair arrangement, a fair order. But because Europe in essence is one political entity, though intricately structured and multifaceted, the fates of its peoples are interconnected, and there can be no lasting peace in Europe without lasting peace in every part of Europe.

It would be hardly thinkable that one half of Europe should flourish, be able to defend itself against various dangers, and work together on the basis of democratic principles while the other half of Europe is left permanently in an undefined vacuum. That is not thinkable as a long-term prospect, just as it would not be thinkable for one half a room to be warm and the other half cold. Time is growing ripe for this new European order and eventually a global order as well to be built with a renewed energy and renewed vigor.

Although six years have passed since the fall of the iron curtain, little has happened during those six years, and time is working against the democrats and against those who want peace and peaceful cooperation. Unless democrats proceed with greater vigor to build the European order, others will start to do so, and we know who the "others" are.

The story of the former Yugoslavia should be a clear warning for Europe and for the whole world about what can happen if there is too much hesitation, if democrats fail to show enough energy and enough courage for broad-minded solutions. We need the same kind of courage that the postwar politicians, such as Adenauer, Churchill, or de Gaulle, had when they proceeded to unify Western Europe. It was not easy to achieve reconciliation between France and Germany. It sometimes required going against the prevailing opinion of their own citizens. Nevertheless, these politicians achieved that unity, and I believe that the present time needs the same kind of bold and broad-minded politicians capable of building this new order. This new order, of course, includes an Atlantic link between the North American world and Europe. Although these two continents are distant from each other geographically, they share profound bonds of civilization, and it is therefore entirely logical that they belong together and that they should be joined together within this global arrangement that is being born. The North Atlantic Alliance is one of the instruments of this connection.

I believe that NATO should give thought to its position in this new era. It should rededicate itself to the principles of the Washington Treaty, where its origins lie. And it should understand its new objectives: it will no longer be just a defense alliance against a common enemy; it will also be called on to deal with regional conflicts, as it has done for the first time in Bosnia and Herzegovina. And it will be called on to tackle other than military threats such as organized crime, terrorism, and the like. Furthermore, it is tremendously important that NATO should gradually start to embrace the sphere of civilization that it is called on to defend, an imperative that includes enlarging by admitting those countries that have belonged to the European-American tradition through their entire history. The countries of Central Europe should be admitted since not only do they belong to the same civilization, but they have in fact for centuries taken part in shaping that civilization.

Questions remain about Russia. Russia is a huge Euro-Asian power, with which all spheres of the world and all regions have to have good relations. We could hardly imagine peace in the world without having good relations with the Russian Federation or with the Commonwealth of Independent States. NATO too should build a genuine partnership with the Russian Federation. NATO's enlargement should take place against the background of such a partnership. I believe, however, that such a partnership can be built only if both entities are clearly defined. And the North Atlantic Alliance must not permit an outside entity to decide which countries should be allowed to join the alliance and which should not.

In conclusion, the appeal of this congress to the conscience of the politicians of the world has touched my heart. Let this message not suffer the same fate as the manifesto of the Czech writers of 1938, which was heeded only by those who had no actual influence on political affairs.

18

The Atlantic Idea in Modern Politics

Discussion

PAUL JOHNSON (United Kingdom): Mr. Martino, you have just come back from a hard-fought election campaign. Could you tell us how international issues are seen from the grass roots of the European electorate?

ANTONIO MARTINO (Italy): This question can be answered on several levels. First, international issues do not have much appeal in Italy. Even though I had been foreign minister and presumably, had I won the election, would have been foreign minister again, I never talked about international issues in the campaign. In this campaign, voters were interested in unemployment, welfare reform, taxation, and federalism.

And yet, there was a hint of internationalism in the debate, because the Left made a big point of saying that international markets favored a victory of the Left. As an unrepentant free marketeer, who has always believed in the market and has consequently been in a position of almost complete isolation, I found it quite satisfying to observe those who have opposed free markets for decades claim that they had the support of markets. Usually people are more interested in things they want changed. That is why they were more concerned about domestic issues, because there they wanted change: welfare reform, fiscal reform, and federalism. They did not want the international position of the country changed. Italy has always been very pro-Western, very pro-European. In fact, after the elections, a distinguished (or I should say *notorious*) commentator, a former Italian ambassador, claimed that the Right lost because the Left was perceived as the party in favor of European unification and the Right was perceived as the party opposing European unification. On this hypothesis, I should be held responsible for the defeat of my party, being perceived as anti-European.

MR. JOHNSON: Did the enlargement of NATO come up at all in your campaign, or is there any Italian feeling one way or the other about that?

MR. MARTINO: It was not discussed much by the electorate. In general, the majority of Italians probably would favor the enlargement of NATO. Another interesting aspect of the election was that the Left, which in the past sought accreditation by going to Moscow, now sought accreditation by going to the city of London and by going to Wall Street.

MR. JOHNSON: That is something we have noticed in London, too, actually. David McCurdy, could you comment on the enlargement of NATO? America is the centerpiece of NATO; without the United States, NATO would never have been constructed in the first place nor would it exist today. How do ordinary Americans feel about NATO now? Does it come into their consciousness at all, and if it does, how do they feel about the idea of enlarging it?

DAVID MCCURDY (United States): It is a good question, and I would add one point to what Antonio Martino said because the similarity between the politics of Italy and those of the United States is close. We Americans do not change governments quite as rapidly as the Italians, but we have had some recent experience of change. Interest in foreign policy among the American public and in the elections is probably at an all time low, maybe its lowest point in a century. Because there is little interest there, specific issues such as NATO do not come up in the campaigns. Paradoxically, if interest in foreign policy is low, the incumbent president often has unusual power to influence the outcome of debates such as those on NATO or other foreign policy issues or crises.

The 1992 election, in my opinion, represented a rejection of the status quo; and George Bush and the Republican administration were

165

the embodiment of the status quo. When, however, the Republicans swept Congress and the Democrats were dealt a severe blow in 1994, that, in my opinion, was a rejection of the elites, the elites being seen as the congressional party, the party in power.

As for NATO, Americans have a long tradition of support for that organization. In our conversation here, we have been speaking about common culture and values. In America, the foundations of support for NATO are there, along with support for an enlargement of NATO.

Unfortunately, in the United States people have actually conducted opinion polls on the issue. (I wish they would throw the things out of politics, but we have to live with them.) The poll findings are surprising, showing something of a split, depending on how the question is asked. On one hand, if you ask whether there is support for expanding NATO, most Americans, the majority, would say yes. If you explain, "If you expand NATO, there would be a requirement to protect Poland from attack," the majority would say no. So they are for expansion but do not want to defend the new members. That is part of the dilemma.

An interesting point, though, would arise if the administration and the foreign policy elite in America supported the expansion of NATO. The question is whether the U.S. Senate, if controlled by the opposition party, would ratify or agree. As you know, two-thirds of the U.S. Senate would have to ratify or confirm. That would be a very close fight. It would take sixty-seven votes. The Republicans would have to count on a number of Democrats.

On a related topic, a number of commentators have described the rise of isolationism in America. In addition to one group of opponents to expansion, the Pat Buchanans and the like, there are a surprising number of supposed internationalists—including many liberal Democrats—that would oppose expanding NATO for fear of alienating Moscow or because of other concerns, such as arms control. So NATO expansion would be a challenge. But, again, I believe that the president, if he put the whole weight of his office behind it, could have the support of Congress.

MR. JOHNSON: Isolationism can take more than one form. Margaret Thatcher, for example, has criticized the notion of deepening Europe rather than enlarging it. She voiced fears that Europe might be in danger of becoming a self-contained fortress and could possibly face reactions from other parts of the world. Mr. Martino, do you think there is danger of a fortress Europe emerging, with the consequent threats of world trade wars? Is that a serious possibility, or is it just a debating point?

MR. MARTINO: Today we face two equally plausible scenarios following the development of regional arrangements like NAFTA and the European Union. On the one hand, they can be perceived as first steps toward a freer, more multilateral world order. On the other, they could be stumbling blocks; they could result in a fortress Europe and the like.

The contradiction arises because these customs unions and regional arrangements have two quite different effects: they create trade within their borders by reducing tariff barriers, and at the same time they divert trade because of direct external barriers.

Now this second scenario would be really frightening. There are the possible consequences for peace—trade wars have often preceded real wars—and trade wars among big blocs would be dangerous. Even barring the possibility of trade wars, that scenario would be negative because it would hurt poor countries. Poor countries are almost all excluded from these arrangements. And the protectionist attitude of the big blocs would hurt the poor countries the most.

In reference to your question about a fortress Europe, I have no empirical evidence to offer. The picture is mixed; though on balance the effect has been favorable. The European Union has created more trade than it has diverted. I am convinced that if we left trade policy in the hands of sovereign national governments, we would have had protectionist warfare among European governments. The American Founding Fathers understood this tendency very well when they introduced the commerce clause in the American Constitution.

But the question is, What next? One of the key issues of this congress is to devise some kind of mechanism whereby we ensure that the pessimistic scenario does not prevail, that is, that Europe opens its borders. At the present moment, the European Union is exporting unemployment and instability among its neighbors, especially along its southern shore. When the people in that area are not allowed to sell what they produce, they will no longer produce it, and therefore mass unemployment and instability will result. We should form a more open policy toward the southern shore of the Mediterranean. But I still believe that a more optimistic scenario can prevail.

MR. JOHNSON: One way in which we could avoid the possibility that a fortress Europe will emerge, followed by fortress Far East or fortress America and so forth, is by merging groups. Margaret Thatcher has suggested that Europe and the North American free-trade area should come together into an enlarged free-trade area. How would that idea go down among the American people?

MR. McCURDY: It is probably more than they could swallow at one time, or even understand. Unfortunately, we would have to bifurcate the question to distinguish between policy makers and the American public as a whole. We would also need to consider how the policy makers would sell such an approach. In *The Federalist Papers*, the Founding Fathers declared that "promptitude of decision" is more often "an evil than a benefit." Unfortunately, it appears that the European Union likes to take that maxim to the extreme and that its members will delay and debate. The layers of bureaucracy and the layers of committees and resolutions are such that it seems very difficult to come to a final conclusion. I believe that finding a mechanism to impose an enlarged free-trade area would be very difficult.

The United States had a unique position following World War II. It had the dominant economy and military force, and it had a choice to make. Either it could support open trade, or it could be a fortress unto itself as an independent economy. It chose the former. It became an open trading system and supported multilateral agreements and shallow integration within the economies. We are now integrating more deeply. With that deeper integration, it becomes far more difficult to get agreement on complex trade issues.

MR. JOHNSON: You have rightly stressed the technical and constitutional difficulties of getting that kind of thing through, but leaving those problems aside for the moment, do you feel that it would be in America's long-term interests to have such an arrangement? Obviously, if we had one, the notion itself would underpin NATO, which I think is what Margaret Thatcher had in mind. It would be a very convenient solution to the geopolitical problem if we could get an enlarged free-trade area.

MR. McCURDY: From a trading standpoint, I support the General Agreement on Tariffs and Trade and the World Trade Organization, with some reservations at times. Most arguments in the United States are based on sovereignty; and every country, when it debates trade, always has sovereignty issues. Any time a country enters into such agreements, it gives up a bit of its sovereignty. I support that concept, but I also support, where possible, establishing trading relationships, not necessarily blocs, but organizations and zones. We have seen it in NAFTA, where the next step is to include Chile and other countries. We see it in APEC as well. I support any mechanism that would reduce trade barriers, internally and externally. And if there is a way to increase the relationship between the two regions, then I would support that.

MR. JOHNSON: Mr. Martino, would you, speaking as an Italian and as a European, welcome, both for its own sake and as a means of underpinning NATO, some kind of agreement between NAFTA and the European Union?

MR. MARTINO: Definitely. While I am in favor of using the multilateral way to increase free trade, that may be slower at times than regional arrangements. I believe in unlimited free trade; I favor any decision that increases trade and oppose any decision that limits trade. And I think that an agreement between NATO and the European Union would be an intermediate step toward free trade for the world and would certainly reduce commercial difficulties between these two regional arrangements.

Saying that I am in favor, however, does not mean that it will be easy to accomplish. It is a simple answer but difficult in practice. But we have to try. Someone once said that reasonable men adapt themselves to the world they live in; unreasonable men stubbornly insist on trying to adapt the world to themselves; therefore, all the progress depends on unreasonable men.

MR. JOHNSON: Can I press you a bit on that? David McCurdy has outlined some of the technical and constitutional difficulties of getting that kind of agreement through Congress.

In your view, would there be comparable or possibly even greater difficulties in getting it through the European Union? How do you think the French and the Germans would react to such an idea?

MR. MARTINO: First, an optimistic answer to the question. I think it was much harder to get an agreement on NAFTA than it would be to get one between Europe and America, because the issues are closer to home and they are felt more deeply. Next, the pessimistic answer. It is true, as Adam Smith told us some years ago, that the monopolizing spirit and mean rapacity of merchants and manufacturers will always exert pressures on governments to prevent the removal of trade barriers.

Why should that be more difficult on the regional level than on the national level? It is much easier for producers to put pressure on national governments than it is to influence international arrangements. And one of the reasons I favor such international agreements, as Mr. McCurdy indicated, is that they reduce national sovereignty. I think national sovereignty in the past has been responsible for a great many crimes, and anything that constrains national sovereignty is welcome.

MR. JOHNSON: Let us turn to security questions. Underlying much of the conversation and many of the statements at this conference has been the thought that the West, to use the term in a loose sense, needs some sort of antimissile system that would be collectively available to all of us. Mr. McCurdy, how would the American public receive the notion of America as the centerpiece of a working antimissile system to protect the entire West?

MR. MCCURDY: This is not a new question. During my fourteen years on the Armed Services Committee and as chairman of the Intelligence Committee, my subcommittee dealt with the research and development budget for the Department of Defense. Following the 1983 speech by Ronald Reagan that launched the Strategic Defense Initiative, there was a fierce debate on the type and amount of spending for ballistic missile defense. And it went through certain phases. The initial phase envisaged a global, space-based system, and the initial program was focused in that direction. Consequently, there was a great deal of technology developed that will be of use in the future.

Following the experience in the Persian Gulf with SCUD missile attacks, the emphasis shifted to theater missile defense. A bipartisan consensus, essential to support large systems, emerged in favor of these; and that support went beyond the Patriot missile system, which presented something of a psychological problem for the Iraqis but did not really amount to much as a tactical defensive system. Patriot missiles were not particularly successful.

Today we have considerable funding, in excess of $3 billion a year, for ballistic missile defense. John Kyl, the senator from Arizona, has been a major proponent of that system. After development, then comes deployment. I think technologies will develop for the eventual deployment of a broader-based system, but clearly the United States is now moving toward deployment, or eventual deployment, of a tactical theater missile defense. And the question is, Where are those theaters?

We also have a debate in the United States about whether to defend just the continental United States. My friends in Hawaii and Alaska ask themselves, and each other, whether they would be included in that defense. Even that debate has not been resolved.

As technology continues, I think there will be growing support for some ground-based systems with space-based detectors, a technology that is not very far off. Tactical high-energy lasers are being developed, and I think there will be tests in conjunction with certain countries, such as Israel, of tactical systems in which ground-based laser systems could defend against incoming missiles such as those that have recently been launched from Lebanon. Those sorts of systems are not far into the future. If they are seen to be successful and an international regime is established, then perhaps a type of regional defense could evolve.

MR. JOHNSON: If Hawaii and Alaska are not sure whether they are under the umbrella, the same applies to Europe. We would like to be under the umbrella, too, and, of course, we would be prepared to contribute in all kinds of ways, I think and hope.

MR. McCURDY: You would need to see the price tag before you made that statement, because beyond the political questions lie those of cost. Most countries around the world are decreasing their defense budgets. The U.S. defense budget, for instance, has declined steadily over the past six or seven years.

I do not say this as a point of pride or ego, but it is clear that little is done militarily around the world without U.S. leadership. Americans are therefore asking, What is the cost of this? There is a great deal of pressure in the United States to reassess our commitments. And that debate is still to be resolved. We have cut our military personnel by nearly 40 percent, and the procurement budget has been cut by half. These cuts are starting to have an impact, and I think people are rightly questioning our priorities. Ballistic missiles will be a part of our defense, but they will not be the leader for some time.

MR. JOHNSON: Mr. Martino, how anxious, in your view, is Europe to get under an antimissile umbrella and to share in the cost and construction of that umbrella? Would we be prepared to pay the price, and are we keen to have it in the first place?

MR. MARTINO: The collapse of the Evil Empire has contributed to making European governments, even more than in the past, a bunch of free riders. They would be very happy to take part in the initiative, provided that American taxpayers foot the bill. We have been cutting military expenses in my country, and military expenses are being cut elsewhere. Maybe the case for this kind of protection is so strong, however, that politicians will see the light and feel the heat. If the threat from local, small nuclear powers is seen as real, then politicians may come around. I am afraid that this change may come too late to avoid some accident, though.

MR. JOHNSON: Where do Europeans now see the danger? While the Soviet Empire is finished, Russia is still a great power in many respects, and there is also the emerging power of China, so that is one possibility, one type of threat. Do we see the main threat as Russia or China, or do we see a much more likely possibility of some rogue power, possibly from the third world, getting hold of nuclear weapons and delivery systems and therefore constituting a threat to us? How seriously are we taking this threat?

MR. MARTINO: The second is more likely. The prevailing opinion in many European countries, including mine, is that instability at the local level—a country's getting hold of nuclear weapons by accident—is perceived as more of a threat than that coming from China or Russia. But it worries me that they do not attach enough importance, in my view, to this threat. That is why they would not be prepared to foot their part of the bill in the event of an initiative from the United States on an international level.

MR. JOHNSON: Mr. McCurdy, you have heard that European opinion on the problem of freeloading and unwillingness to foot the bill. But of course, a rogue nuclear power could be as much a threat to European nations as to the United States. How far do you think America, in its endless generosity, would be prepared to come to our assistance if we faced that kind of threat? What is the mood of the American public on this question?

MR. McCURDY: There are two levels. The American public has developed an interesting view toward the defense posture. On one hand, they are willing to support a very strong U.S. military. But on the other hand, as indicated in the previous polling on NATO enlargement, they are very hesitant to engage that force. And some of the most reticent of the opinion leaders wear a uniform and stars on their shoulders. The U.S. military is usually the most reluctant to engage force, and it is the State Department that is usually trying to push the military into doing so.

The United States has national interests around the globe, and there are threats to our interests. In a ranking of those threats, it is clear that the threat from the Soviet Union and the Warsaw Pact has expired. We still believe, however, that there are some threats to our interests in the Middle East and in southwest Asia. We also have concerns about northeast Asia. We have close to 35,000 troops on the Korean Peninsula. Even though the American public in a recent poll indicated they were not sure they would support the defense of South Korea, I think that is nonsense. I think we would, and we are there and are prepared to do it.

As for great power threats, China is at a crossroads. The Chinese have a choice to make. They can either enter the community of nations and be a responsible player or continue in a more isolated direction and become a threat to the region. Japan has a choice to make, as well.

If you ask policy makers what the top question is, I would think proliferation of weapons of mass destruction continues to head the list. And it is clear that nonproliferation itself is a very difficult task, and you probably do not succeed 100 percent—hence the call for some sort of limited missile defense.

MR. JOHNSON: Would you regard it as more likely that the American public would be prepared to accept European powers under the umbrella of missile defense in these contingencies if, in fact, we had a formal enlargement of NATO and a refurbishment of NATO so that American treaty obligations were specific?

MR. McCURDY: Because of the unique relationship of Americans with NATO, I think that NATO could be extended and would survive. I believe, however, that the general perception that there is not a direct threat, which also exists in Italy and other European countries, will continue to undermine that relationship.

We in the United States have certain advantages, however, that Europeans and others should consider. That is, we are the only country that has the airlift capability, and we are the only nation with advanced observation capabilities. We have command of space; and in fact, we have tools that can be used in a cooperative way. I think that if Europeans really want to avail themselves of those advantages, then they ought to start to engage at that level as opposed to just expecting to see U.S. troops deployed around the world and expecting the United States will unilaterally pay for some system that will protect free nations against missile attack. It is not going to happen that way.

MR. JOHNSON: The Czech prime minister has said that when he was asked to make a statement about "the crisis," he was inclined to ask, What crisis? He felt that talk about a crisis was a little exaggerated. Do either of you have a feeling of crisis in the world today, or are you fairly happy about the way the world is getting on?

MR. MARTINO: I think that my nationality gives me a comparative advantage in talking about "crises." Shortly before the elections as I was coming out of Parliament, I saw a BBC TV crew. I was asked, "How long is the Italian crisis going to last?" And I said, "That all depends on how you define *crisis*. We have been having one for twenty-five centuries."

My view is that "crisis" is a description of any moment in time. There are no moments in time without a crisis. The concept of crisis points to the fact that we have problems, and we shall always have problems. In times like these it is good to remember that the perfect society in which freedom is secure and protected shall never be. Freedom has always had challenges, and each century has its own. If we look back, however, I tend to agree with Václav Klaus. The twentieth century has been a terrible century. In the encyclopedia entry "Fascism," signed by Benito Mussolini—but not written by him—he says that the nineteenth century was the century of the individual and of liberalism but that the twentieth century will be the century of the state, a fascist century.

There is no doubt that history is proving him right. The twentieth century has been the century of big government. If it has been a century of big dictators—Stalin, Hitler, Mussolini, Idi Amin, and Pol Pot—it has also been a century of big government. We have seen the exponential growth of the welfare state and the exponential growth of taxation, of regulation, and of government intervention of all kinds. We have a reason for being optimistic, however. All the various statist recipes have been tried, and they have uniformly produced disasters. No one, in any country, has the courage to advocate socialism on a global level any more. No one wants wholesale socialism. It is true that at some level socialist solutions are still advocated, but no one still believes in a socialist society. So as this century comes to an end, I think we can be optimistic. We shall have other crises, but they will be different from those we have had in this century.

MR. JOHNSON: I agree with your optimism. Mr. McCurdy, are we in a crisis?

MR. MCCURDY: I agree with Mr. Martino that we cannot use the term *crisis* in the traditional sense. If we have learned anything, however, we should have learned over the centuries that if we are not prepared, problems become crises. And my concern goes beyond the immediacy of issues such as those we have been discussing. Having served nearly fifteen years in elected office, I have deep concern about the state of politics—globally and in America specifically—and about how we make decisions. I am deeply concerned that we live in an age when modern politics are defined as the "CNN age," an era of "sound bites," of short reports, and investigative reporting. The national sport in the United States is no longer baseball: the national sport is destroying heroes.

I said that the 1994 election signified the rejection of the elite. What that means is that the American public's attention span has grown even shorter; it wants immediate answers, immediate solutions. Instead of dealing with long-term problems, the public is focused on the short term.

175

We hear a lot about expanding "rights" around the world; and Mr. Martino is correct that governments tend to foster that trend and give in to demands for more "rights." But few talk about the commensurate responsibilities. To me, that is deeply troubling. I think our political system in the United States is in trouble. I grew up in rural western Oklahoma where my parents were factory workers. If it had not been for public school and the existence of a recognized elite I could look up to and aspire to join, I would have lacked the spur to public service, and I would have lacked a role model. I would have had no incentive to use my mind and talents to help others and to help my country. Without such role models and such incentives, we undermine the stability of countries.

Thus conferences such as this are important, although they are not the solution or panacea. I think we must ask ourselves whether politics is still a noble calling. Each of us falls into the habit of decrying politicians, but I believe that when we do so we take a little bit of our own liberty away. And I think that erosion is heading toward a crisis.

When I was here in Prague six years ago, just after the change of government, it was a very exciting time; there was an electricity in the air. When I met with the new leader of the Czech Parliament, who was so excited, so new, so fresh, he wanted to show me the chamber where the Parliament was to meet. It was the middle of the afternoon, and he took me into this spectacular building. But he could not find the light switch. No one could. There was not a person in the entire building who knew how to turn the lights on because there had been such a revolutionary change. I hope that we can capture some of that electricity and excitement in reinvigorating our political parties.

The political parties in the United States are threatened, rejected by most Americans. Maybe it is time for us to rise above partisanship and rise above the political parties, to rise above nationalism and start to address these bigger and more fundamental issues. If we can do that, then I think I, too, will be the eternal optimist.

19

Atlantic Economics

Leszek Balcerowicz

When the Berlin Wall collapsed in 1989, many people were caught by surprise. Most of us—and I do not mean only the former rulers of Communist Eastern Europe—believed that the division of Europe was eternal and that we in the center of Europe were condemned to communism. For those were the views of many decision makers and academics in the West. We now know how wrong they were.

We can enjoy our liberty today because of those brave individuals, like Václav Havel, who decided to live in peace and, by their actions, showed that as long as the human spirit exists, liberty will prevail. Liberty prevails, but only if we fight on its behalf at every step. The recent history of Central Europe shows us that, despite all our security and prosperity, we must never let down our guard or disregard the need for leadership in times of difficulty. I say that not without reason. The same leadership for an Atlantic community has to be demonstrated throughout our regions and also to be displayed on a broader, interregional basis if we are to achieve global liberty and prosperity.

We cannot, however, separate a regional issue of liberty and prosperity from its global context. Just as freedom within our region is a condition of global freedom, so only by securing global freedom and prosperity can we make the freedom for which we have all fought permanent. I will focus my attention on the relationship between regional and global freedom and prosperity.

The truths of economics are often provable when they are violated. In the past, ideologues have believed that economic laws can be broken. The consequences of such arrogance come to be felt only later. That is the story of socialism and the source of the economic failures of much of the third world. Those of us gathered at the Congress of Prague know that the experience of the past few decades shows that Adam Smith was right. Economic freedom is the key to economic prosperity, and suppressing economic freedom is sufficient to condemn society to economic stagnation.

The history of the past two decades is the history of the victory of Atlantic economics over what some call *socialism*. The past two decades are a great testament to visionary leaders who understood these principles and fought to implement them.

In the European economies Great Britain was the first, under Lady Thatcher in the 1980s, to achieve the highest growth combined with the lowest inflation, leading to significant job creation. In the United States, it was the principle of supply-side economics—and not a demand stimulation—in the 1980s that laid the foundation not only for continued prosperity but also for an intellectual climate that bore fruit in the remarkable Republican Party victories two years ago.

In the 1990s it was the turn of reformers, or should I say revolutionaries, in Central Europe to grapple with the dinosaurs of state socialism and introduce economic policies that have produced gross rates that are now the envy of many Western European countries. And now those experiences are spreading worldwide. A circle of those countries feeding off the success of others is now developing.

We have similarly seen a victory of the principles of free trade in recent years. The postwar period has been one in which, step by step, the principles of free trade have been extended on a global scale, culminating in the completion of the Uruguay Round and the creation of the World Trade Organization. The establishment of the North American Free Trade Agreement was also a milestone. There must be a further step, however, to ensure that the benefits of free trade are spread further afield.

The dramatic economic developments of recent years have gone hand in hand with the development and strengthening of democracy. Historically, democracy usually followed the development of capitalism. In the case of Central Europe, however, it was the rejection of Communist autocracy that allowed economic reformers to come to power.

Uniquely, we have been asked to grapple with the problem of introducing capitalism after the birth of democracy. But it is the introduction of free-market capitalism that provides the greatest security for democracy in the long run, by providing the opportunity for obtaining worth for those who aspire to it and by acting to create the liberal middle classes, on whose support democracy rests. I am also convinced that the reforms of Lady Thatcher and the American Right are profoundly democratic, in that they seek to remove the shackles of collectivism from the lives of ordinary men and women. Socialists speak of freedom but rely on centralized power.

Margaret Thatcher showed that she was the real liberator by giving people power over their own lives and private property, by right of which they would realize their independence and their ambitions. No less important was the intellectual effect of the New Right of the 1980s, in creating a new consensus on the permanence of capitalism and the flawed nature of socialism, which men even on the Left have come to accept. We in Central Europe salute Lady Thatcher's achievements, her legacy, and the encouragement of our efforts, which her successes provide.

I noted earlier that, to preserve liberty, we must never rest in our readiness to confront challenges and threats to our achievements. Among our great successes there indeed have been, and will continue to be, pitfalls and failures. The cause of liberty is never won forever. In my own region the forces of the past have returned to power in most countries. In many cases the policies they are pursuing—slowdowns in privatization, growth in state spending, and increased protection—are threatening to undermine the prospect for creating the only true model of wealth creation. That model is the economic system based on economic freedom, on private property, and on sound money. In Western Europe, many economists, some albeit grudgingly, are facing up to the fact that they can no longer cope with the burdens of state spending for interventionist policies. No longer are there sick men in Europe—there seems to be a Europe of sick men.

Just as we need more reform in Central Europe, so most European Union countries also need to make painful but necessary decisions. These decisions are also very important for reformers in other parts of Europe by providing a good example; conversely, the failure to carry out these reforms provides a bad example and is negatively influencing the balance of forces in Western Europe. We have needed to be aware of the threats to free trade. There are significant economic and social groups in Central Europe that are the creations of state socialism, which fear the rigors of competition. But the protectionist impulse is not the remedy for Central Europe.

Our special interest groups have learned important lessons from special interest groups not far away from Central Europe. The West is missing a window of opportunity to help reform in Central Europe by not opening its market more quickly to our products and by delaying decisions on widening of the European Union. The solution is for democratic leadership to face up to the challenges on a local and global scale and to build up a new coalition of popular support for the changes and reforms that must come if economic reform growth is to be set in motion or sustained. In Western Europe there has been an intense debate on the future of the European Union and its relation to Central Europe. The history of the past few years has shown large constituencies in Western Europe unconvinced of the benefits of further integration at the political level. More has to be done to address these concerns. The alternative, again, is the growth of resentment and alienation and the search for political alternatives that may well challenge the established system.

Nevertheless, the extent to which the European Union recognizes the importance of assisting European reforms through a greater opening in trade will largely determine the success of a historical transformation in Central Europe itself. Closing the European Union to Central Europe only encourages those political forces in Central Europe who feed on anti-Western sentiments. And that would be bad for Europe, bad for reform, and bad for democracy itself.

For the Atlantic community, the years to come will provide two key challenges that prompt reflection on the relationship between democracy and prosperity. The first challenge is that of Asia. Some might view such a challenge as a threat, but I view it as an opportunity—as long as the right decisions are made and the correct lessons learned.

We rightly admire the growth rate of the "tigers," but we also reflect that economic reform there has been achieved without democracy. In Central Europe, the 1989 revolutions were carried out to restore democratic freedoms—disproving the claims of those who said that capitalism can be introduced only against the will of the people. So the Asian road to reform was not an option. And we must remember that democracy is crucial in safeguarding the dignity of man in his relation to the state and in removing fear from the public life.

Truly, important noneconomic dimensions of the quality of life arise from democracy. Reforms can be made only through democratic persuasion, and this is an additional reason for an emergence of a strong, united, democratic leadership committed to the reforms in Central and Eastern Europe.

At the same time, Asia provides us with optimistic conclusions about the democracy-capitalism relationship. Democracy has come to Asia as a result of capitalism and the development of middle-class aspirations that come with it. So in looking to Asia, we can gain hope for the victory of democracy in Central Europe, as long as the free-market reforms continue.

Capitalism is necessary not only for economic prosperity but also for preserving democracy. There is not a single example of a lasting coexistence of democracy and socialism. To be an "anticapitalist democrat" is a contradiction in terms. And by defending and strengthening the free-market economy, we are defending democracy. Those who block privatization and other free-market reforms endanger democracy. And the civil society described by Mr. Lubbers in this volume cannot exist without the free-market economy. Without free markets, civil society degenerates into interest groups that endanger economic growth and poison public life. So there is a synergy between free markets and civil society of the right shape.

Another challenge posed by Asia is the challenge of trade. If you are to embrace the principle of free trade, then we must also accept that our own markets must be opened to those economies that produce goods our consumers want to buy at prices they find competitive. In practice this must mean a strengthening of the WTO. The interest-group global growth cannot be served by the creation of two warring blocs. We must not replace one global political division with a global economic division.

We must also not fall into the trap of thinking that economic division can be prevented from spilling over into political discord. One of the great achievements of postwar leadership was the establishment of friendly relations with Asian countries, and that achievement must be preserved.

Asia presents one key challenge. The second, more dramatic challenge for the years to come is that of Russia. Some say that the Russian experience shows that there is no relationship between capitalism and democracy. My view is different. This issue is not that in Russia there is no link between the two, but that in the Russian case neither democracy nor reform has ever been implemented with the necessary rigor and conviction. The courageous reforms of Yegor

Gaidar, for example, were not continued with sufficient dynamism. The reformers in Russia have a much more difficult job than in some other post-Socialist economies. Reformers in post-Socialist countries are like runners who have to overcome the same distance but with different burdens on their backs. To compare outcomes without considering those different burdens is a spectacular fallacy.

I am skeptical as to what can be done from the outside, as far as Russia is concerned—especially in terms of direct aid to assist in a task that, at the end of the day, remains for the Russians themselves to implement. But unless we in the West—and I use that term in relation to us Central Europeans deliberately—recognize that we have a role to play, then we will soon be facing a second challenge. Some in the West believe that the appropriate policy toward Russia is to act in the same way the West acted sometimes toward the Soviet Union: "Let us offer Russia unlimited funds in order to keep her inefficient economy afloat, and let us turn a blind eye to abuses of human rights and great power ambitions. Then perhaps the Russian authorities will start to like us and not be horrible any more." I have a word for that; it is called *appeasement*.

Russia needs help, but not in a fashion that acts against our own interests and endangers European stability. The phrase *partnership for peace* is well known. Why not a partnership for democracy to assist reform in Russia? Such a partnership would involve Central Europeans, West Europeans, and the Americans. Our role in Central Europe would be to ensure the success of economic and political reform in our own countries. I believe that the failed reforms in Central Europe will encourage resistance to reform in Russia; conversely, successful democratic and free-market reforms in our region will be a beacon for reformers in Russia and evidence to the Russian people that reforms bring prosperity. That is the best help we in Central and Eastern Europe can give to Russian reformers.

Western Europe, for its part, can act to support reform through greater openness to trade with Russia. Closer trade links between the European Union and other Western countries and Russia are an important condition of reforms.

Speaking about Russia, one should not forget another crucially important country, which is Ukraine. A strong and prosperous Ukraine is the key condition for the preservation of the present political order in Europe. And, consequently, to support the Ukrainians' economic reforms, so bravely launched in 1994 under President

Kuchma, is of utmost strategic importance.

I would like to underline the central importance of the relationship between democracy, prosperity, and leadership. The key that will bring all of these elements together is free trade. And let me end with a note on free trade.

In entrenching capitalism, free trade is an instrument for encouraging internal reform. Free trade undermines vested domestic interest groups and assists in developing regional cooperation. Free trade carries with it the spirit of capitalism to further reaches of the globe. Finally, because it creates mutual economic benefits and dense social contacts, it builds the human infrastructure for peace. And this is being discovered every working day by millions of Poles, Germans, and Russians who trade with one other. This is a great contribution to mutual understanding.

Leadership also implies responsibility to the values that our civilization represents. Those values are represented in the European ideals and in the Atlantic community. We must make those values secure for future generations in an increasingly global environment, where there are as many challenges as there are opportunities.

20

The Importance of Civil Society

R. F. M. Lubbers

I have been reflecting on the things basic to our societies: the roots of our civilization and our common heritage.

When I grew up after the Second World War, we lived more than four decades with the concept of three worlds. One used to speak about the first world, that is, the free world; the second world, the Communist world; and the third world, the nonaligned countries, marked by traces of colonialism. The nonaligned countries could make the choice between the first world and the second.

And now, after the end of communism, we see, almost everywhere, the choice being made for our kind of democracy and in favor of market economics. We achieved our triumph over communism, thanks to the resistance in Central and Eastern European countries, and that is a source of enormous joy. That triumph was brought about by their courage. Of course, it was also thanks to NATO and our common stance. To a certain extent, the victory also had something to do with European integration and the European Union, which presented an alternative model for Central and Eastern Europe.

But now, we have to take stock. I stressed from the outset the importance of democracy and of the market. The market is not only a technical device but the foundation of choice. I would like to take the liberty of adding my observations on civil society.

What is civil society? Civil society concerns the basic need to live in truth and dignity. It provides means to restore and protect the moral integrity of the person, and it can serve a strategy of resistance against tyranny, as it did in Central Europe. This faith in civil society was essential to resist communism, but our dependence upon it has not diminished. After the thorough mental cleansing of Communist dictatorship, we once again need civil society. To repeat, civil society offers the means for lives lived in truth and dignity. In Central and Eastern Europe, people were courageous; they threw off the shackles of communism by affirming exactly those values we associate with civil society.

That is now the situation that exists in the liberated countries, but democracy will last and economic transformation will be successful only if the values of truth and dignity pervade the deepest layers of society. Indeed, we are right to be proud of being so successful in establishing democracy and the basis for a free market economy. Those were needed, but they are not enough. People in these countries need a vision of hope for the future. That vision has to be a part of a new Atlantic initiative, because this initiative is about the individual's right to express his or her human dignity through shared responsibility and to experience the truth in doing so. That is what is needed in the post-Communist era.

But let us be honest. A new Atlantic initiative must also be about reanimating civil society in the established democracies to avoid a form of the unreserved application of the capitalist model, which would have an adverse effect on the quality of life. Market democracy will not suffice; it never did. There was always a need for a civil society. Citizens fought for liberty and for their rights, and they did so rightly. And the market concept proved to be an enormous success. At the same time, our citizens have to live—want to live—in truth and dignity. That goal can be achieved only when we have the opportunity to give shape and substance to a civil society based on values that we cherish, on individual initiative, and on the free association of citizens who care.

A few years ago, Francis Fukuyama explained to us that we are at the end of history. Only a few years later, he had to write a new book, a book about trust. Without trust, he explained, the market could not function. He was right.

Moreover, society cannot function if it is based only on a formal democracy. Society needs responsible citizens, citizens empowering each other and taking responsibility. We talk about a new Atlantic initiative and our roots, but if we have to convince other civilizations, other traditions, about our values, we tend to say that it is about

185

democracy and free markets. But beyond that, we also need to explain how civil society can enhance the quality of life. Only in that way can we be credible to other continents, other civilizations. Democracy, the market economy, civil society: these are the foundations of a society in which freedom is prized and our values cherished.

What sort of values? First, we must recognize the importance of each single human being and of life itself. Second, we must prevent violence and push it back when it occurs. This task requires external security and internal security. The third value is respect for and care of the environment. Nature in America and Europe is really too beautiful to be spoiled. Next is the need for equity. Equity is not something that can be arranged by government; equity can be achieved only by society itself through the initiatives of citizens.

My list of values characterizing our civilization would be incomplete without a reference to the need to honor the generations of the past and take some responsibility for the generations to come. As Burke wrote, society is a bond between those who are dead, those who are living, and those who are not yet born.

Let the world say important things about the market economy. But the market economy cannot look after all aspects of life. Neither should politics and government be seen as the ultimate arbiter of values. No, that role is for society itself. The New Atlantic Initiative is concerned with the transformation of societies in Central and Eastern Europe. But we must recognize that the need for a civil society based on values is not less in the established democracies. There, individual human beings can achieve great things. There is the essential strength of our society. And there we see the continuity with the roots of our civilization.

21

The Golden Age of the Twenty-first Century

Jon L. Kyl

In no other period of history has one country occupied a position of economic and military strength and general influence throughout the world as great as that of the United States now, in the aftermath of the Soviet Union's disintegration. And I believe this is a good thing, for no great state in history has ever before combined such a position of power with so benign an outlook toward other nations as America does today. The United States has no ambition for empire and no impulse to take the property of others or to interfere with their freedom.

In my view, the United States should not and usually does not think of its actions in world affairs as a matter of narrow national interests. When we act on the world stage, we do so conscious of our membership in a community of allies. If I had to sum up in one sentence the U.S. national interest in the world, I would say that it is promoting the security, well-being, and expansion of the community of nations that respect the democratic rights of their people.

With this in mind, though much in today's world is disturbing and ominous, I believe we have grounds for hoping that if we think wisely and act courageously and morally, we can achieve a degree of prosperity, international peace and security, and human freedom that will qualify as a new era—a golden age in world affairs.

Defining the Alliance

It cannot be overemphasized that the essence of our ties to other democratic states—and in particular to our European allies—is not just the practical benefit of the relationships, though that is great. The essence, rather, is philosophical and humane. What unites us grows out of a moral conception of the human being: that each individual has inherent worth and individual rights. The power of government should be limited by respect for those rights. Our concepts of the democratic election of officials, due process of law, private property, freedom of conscience and speech—all arise from moral ideas with profound religious and philosophical roots. This is the bedrock of our alliance with our European friends and other democratic partners around the world.

We should not hesitate to discuss this idea in terms of civilization. The *civilized world*—I use the term to refer to those countries that genuinely respect human rights—is of course broader than the West, including as it does people from many cultures. It is the world's misfortune that not every state behaves in a civilized fashion, neither to its people nor to its neighbors.

The Case against Isolationism

Europeans are concerned about isolationism in the United States. And it is true that even Americans who supported an interventionist U.S. national security policy to oppose communism during the cold war are now asking whether a similarly internationalist U.S. policy is justified today. I believe it is sensible, when U.S. resources are at issue, for Americans to ask, "What is the interest of the U.S. taxpayer in international affairs and in the ability of the United States to influence them?"

But while the question is legitimate, at the end of the day, isolationism does not serve as an answer. This is true for both philosophical and practical reasons. First, the philosophical. The cold war was won by an idea—freedom—and our determination to defend it. Communism failed because it was built on a wrong idea: an unnatural conception of man. Ideas—no less than guns and money—have powerful consequences in world affairs; and truly strategic thinkers never fail to grasp the importance of philosophy. Truly strategic thinkers appreciate that what sustains the Western Alliance is not mere *realpolitik,* but the common attachment of our people to moral and political convictions that we harbor in our heart of hearts.

Lady Thatcher demonstrated the point when she spoke on the fiftieth anniversary of Sir Winston Churchill's famous iron curtain speech:

> The West is not just some cold war construct, devoid of significance in today's freer, more fluid world. It rests upon distinctive values and virtues, ideas and ideals, and above all upon a common experience of liberty.

To preserve these values, she concluded, we need the Atlantic Alliance.

The essence of community is a sense of mutual responsibility. This is true of domestic communities, and it is true of our international community of democratic states. President Havel, in his address to the U.S. Congress just weeks after his arrest, release, and ascendancy to the leadership of his people, warned that we can avert "a general breakdown of civilization" only if we "put morality ahead of politics." He observed: "The only genuine backbone of all our actions, if they are to be moral, is responsibility." Leaders of the Atlantic Alliance should cultivate among their citizens an appreciation of the alliance's moral foundation as well as the practical benefits it yields, so that the sense of mutual responsibility is kept vivid. This is insurance against isolationism.

America's membership in the alliance and its active role in world affairs in general have practical benefits. Many are obvious. For example, it is not necessary to expound on the economic interest we have in imports and exports. And it should go without saying that our interests in national military security are best protected not at the water's edge but through "forward defense" and that promoting democracy can reduce our military burdens because democratic states tend to be nonaggressive. It is well to highlight, however, some of the less obvious ways in which international affairs affect the personal interests of average Americans.

As democracy expands around the world, the freedom of Americans expands, for there are more places where we can trade, tour, and study—where we can feel secure, where the governments honor our individual rights, where the courts are available to protect us, where there is less danger of war. The expansion of democracy boosts our standard of living.

And consider this matter from the opposite end: if the democratic community is deteriorating, if our allies find themselves challenged by antidemocratic adversaries and if they are undermined or overcome—this weakness not only harms our interests in U.S. activities abroad but tends to endanger our democratic values at home. The domestic freedoms that Americans enjoy and boast of come under strain when the world at large becomes dangerous and threatening.

It is good for Americans to be reminded of the link between our civil liberties and our nation's sense of security. The anarchist scare at the beginning of this century and the Communist threat in midcentury both affected the civil liberties of Americans at home. The point is made clear by an exaggerated proposition: if the United States were the only democracy left in the world, would we be able to maintain our democratic freedom?

In sum, our lives are influenced by world events whether we want to engage in the world or not. We can work to help shape world affairs or abdicate leadership, but we cannot prevent international affairs—and in particular the fate of our fellow democratic states—from profoundly affecting our people's lives.

Defending the Alliance

We have thus identified ourselves in national security affairs not as a solo performer but as a member of the community of democratic states, and we have noted that the United States in fact has no realistic isolationist option. What will this, then, mean as a practical matter—especially with respect to military challenges to the community?

First, we should appreciate that the West's victory over the Soviet bloc has greatly enhanced our security in important respects. Liberal democracy now has no serious philosophical challenger with universal pretensions. Neither fascism, Nazism, nor communism can compete with democracy as a system for organizing society. We can approach our defense responsibilities with powerful moral confidence.

Why, then, do we still have defense responsibilities? Much commentary about national security policy nowadays reflects the view that defense is an outdated concern—a vestige of the cold war. If the Soviet Union is no more, then why do we need to spend billions more on defense—for example, on weapons research, long-range bombers, or missile defense?

As great as our cold war victory was, it eliminated only our major ideological foe. It did not eliminate evil from the world. It did not eliminate aggression or all aggressive regimes, whether motivated by ideology or not. And it most assuredly did not eliminate the ability of such regimes to do great harm to us and to others. What type of harm can outlaw states wreak?

The principal threat is weapons of mass destruction—nuclear, biological, and chemical—and missiles that can deliver them over long distances. Recall that Lady Thatcher has characterized this as "quite simply the most dangerous threat of our times." And that is true for two major reasons. First, the weapons themselves, obviously, can cause an enormous amount of death and destruction. And second, they can be useful politically, even for countries that could not actually defeat us or our allies militarily.

We should be clear on this important point. The danger of nuclear weapons in the hands of Iran, for example, is not that Iran would use them to invade the United States or Europe or even to triumph over American or allied forces on the battlefield (though this is a scenario worth some worry). The main danger is that an Iran armed with such weapons, and with missiles, may succeed in deterring us from challenging aggression directed at others.

It bears recalling that the U.S. Congress came very close to voting against the use of force against Iraq after the rape of Kuwait. If we had believed that Iraq had nuclear-armed missiles, Congress might not have supported U.S. military action to protect our interests in that region. For that matter, would our European partners have participated in a grand coalition if they were vulnerable to missile threats?

The true measure of our strength is not simply whether we can be defended but whether we can be deterred or intimidated. This is a critical reason why we must concern ourselves with dangerous weapons in the hands of states that are weaker than we are.

The Options

Short of engaging such nations preemptively through offensive military action, there are three alternatives available for addressing the threat. The first and, I submit, least effective is arms control. Unfortunately, bilateral or multilateral arms control agreements have not historically prevented states determined to acquire or develop weapons from doing so.

For example, Iraq, Iran, North Korea, and other troublesome regimes have all made strides toward nuclear capabilities despite their treaty obligations, despite international inspections, and despite the widespread knowledge that they are pursuing such capabilities. And it seems reasonable to expect that the same will be true of chemical weapons proliferation despite the Chemical Weapons Convention. We simply cannot rely on treaties to constrain regimes that do not respect their own domestic laws, let alone that weaker species known as international law.

Second, export controls: these can be highly valuable—though they cannot entirely solve the problem. Cooperative international arrangements (like COCOM, the Missile Technology Control Regime, and others) have been useful in driving up the financial costs of dangerous programs, delaying such programs, or imposing serious political penalties on the relevant regimes. To the degree that these arrangements are rigorously enforced, export controls can be of real value. And that brings us then to the question of how to defend ourselves if a bad regime realizes its ambition for the capacity to deliver weapons of mass destruction over long distances.

The Need for Missile Defenses

My principal point is that we should move rapidly and wholeheartedly to create defenses for ourselves against these missiles. Our publics, by and large, do not realize that if Syria, North Korea, or Russia launched a missile at one of our cities, we could not stop it. Opinion research shows that Americans believe we have in place systems to intercept missiles launched against us. They are often outraged to learn that we do not—particularly when they discover the principal reason is that political leaders, relying on theories of arms control, assert that we can have greater security if we remain vulnerable to missile attack. The public's outrage is well grounded.

Is there any weapon other than missiles to which we believe we are better off being vulnerable? No one suggests that we would be more secure by renouncing defenses against strategic bombers or warships. It makes no more sense to conclude that we should remain without a defense against missiles.

The theory of mutual assured destruction (MAD) does not provide the answer. First, it is morally repugnant. Second, while the theory may have had a role in preventing two responsible superpowers from attacking one another, it would not necessarily prevent a rogue nation from attacking us. Indeed, it could prove extremely risky to rely on MAD doctrine when dealing with a number of autocratic regimes operated by individuals of dubious stability and judgment. Finally, mutual assured destruction lacks credibility. Would a U.S. president use nuclear weapons against the civilian population of a rogue state whose leaders employed chemical or biological weapons? or if a nuclear weapon were used against an ally?

In short, the problem cannot be handled entirely by deterrence policies because the stakes are too high if deterrence fails and because we cannot effectively deter a regime that believes it can deter us from entering into a fight with it. If the community of democratic states is to protect itself and preserve its ability to safeguard law and stability in the broader international arena, we must maximize our deterrence capabilities, not only by maintaining general military strength but also by deploying sensible, multitiered global missile defenses. This goal should be among our alliance's chief priorities. It is clearly within our means—technological and financial—but it requires effort. It requires intellectual and political leadership. It requires a commitment of resources—a substantial amount, but small in comparison with the value of preventing a Libyan missile from hitting Rome, a Chinese missile from hitting Los Angeles, or an Iranian missile from hitting London (not to speak of Russian missiles, which can already hit anywhere in the world).

As the Security Policy Committee's report concludes, the required effort to deploy missile defenses will be optimized if it is concerted among the leaders of the alliance. The project is worthy. It is moral, valuable, practicable, and affordable. It should be embraced as an alliance mission. And if it is, it will serve as a powerful answer to anyone who questions why we still need an alliance in the post–cold war period.

Expanding the Alliance

I return to my one-sentence summation of the U.S. national interest in the world—that is, promoting the security, well-being, and expansion of the community of nations that respect the democratic rights of their people. Our security and well-being improve when this community is expanding. The foundation for our security and material prosperity is a well-ordered state system in which more and more countries operate with respect for fundamental principles of international law.

This goal cannot be achieved by giving respectability to disreputable actors or by entering into arms control or peace treaties with terrorists and war criminals and pretending they are good-faith parties. This goal cannot be achieved by pretending that law will constrain lawless regimes. No one thinks that domestic crime can be eliminated by having the police and criminals enter into agreements, and no one should think that international "crime" can be controlled by having outlaw regimes sign agreements with their intended victims. The key to peace lies elsewhere.

The key has several parts: first, keeping democratic states and responsible members of the international community strong; second, preventing dangerous regimes from obtaining especially dangerous weapons; and third, doing what we can to have outlaw regimes—those that threaten other states, employ terrorism, or deal in illegal drugs, for example—replaced by relatively responsible governments.

This is not a call for rampant interventionism or for the complete abandonment of long-standing concepts of sovereignty. It is crucial, however, that we recognize that peace and security will not be available to us if outlaw regimes have the means and the will to violate the rights of others. And we should have no illusions about our ability to constrain such regimes by means of talk and paper—by means other than military and economic pressure.

To bring the point home, I would observe that the recent, enormous increase in the security of Europe was not due to arms control agreements with the dishonest Communist regimes of the Soviet Union and Eastern Europe. It was due to the replacement of those regimes by governments headed by individuals like President Havel. The point here is that if we can facilitate the end of bad regimes—replacing them with democratic governments—it will enhance security far more than attempts to work out arrangements with such regimes would.

Our alliance should move decisively to lock in the benefits of those changes. We should be working to bring the new democracies of Europe into the alliance. Cautionary voices warn us not to expand our military commitments beyond our capability to fulfill them, and those cautionary voices make a wise point. But what this means is not that we should drop plans to expand NATO, but rather that we should commit ourselves to maintaining the capabilities necessary to support the kind of NATO expansion that will serve our interests in preventing Europe from slipping backward.

Conclusion

Political leaders have a tendency to announce the dawning of new eras. But such announcements often have more to do with the dawning in the speaker's mind of the importance of world affairs than with the arrival of a genuinely distinctive period in human history.

Having issued that warning to myself, I nevertheless want to highlight the unusual nature of the current moment in world history. The cold war's end puts us in one of those rare postwar periods that can be likened in recent centuries only to the era following the Napoleonic Wars and those following World Wars I and II. We have a rare opportunity to reshape the world.

It is, therefore, more important than usual that we think about national security strategically, philosophically, systematically. We can do so if we are clear about the moral foundations of our community, if we cultivate popular appreciation of the practical benefits we each derive from that community, if we are willing to protect ourselves against missiles and other military threats, and if we work diligently to constrain and oppose aggressive, tyrannical, outlaw regimes and help more and more countries join the community of democratic states.

We in the Atlantic Alliance have the economic and military power to facilitate great improvements in the world. We also need the wisdom and the resolve. We must aspire to have historians of the future look back on us and say, "Those were the leaders who ushered in the golden age of the twenty-first century."

22

Conclusion

William E. Odom

The Congress of Prague was a response, as Gerald Frost rightly observed in the introduction to this book, to a mood of "introspection, drift, and the thoughtless subordination of fundamental and long-term interests to parochial and short-term ones" besetting the Atlantic Alliance. It is a dangerous mood if allowed to persist, but its emergence should occasion little surprise. It is the predictable reaction to the intellectually paralyzing events of the early 1990s. Consider only two of several reasons why they were likely to have this effect.

First, in the course of about two years Europe experienced the largest strategic realignment in modern history—far greater than the one occurring in the wake of Napoleon's collapsing empire after his retreat from Russia. Germany was reunited, the Warsaw Pact collapsed, Soviet forces were withdrawn, and the Soviet Union dissolved into fifteen independent states. The breathtaking magnitude of these events simply deprived our minds of the oxygen necessary to think seriously about the fundamental questions posed by such fundamental change.

Second, this dramatic breakup of the Soviet Empire occurred without war. Previous upheavals in Europe's interstate system have been accompanied by large wars. War tends to focus leaders' minds on basic questions and long-term interests, albeit not always successfully. On this occasion, the absence of war has contributed to the sedative mood. In some circles on both sides of the Atlantic, the illusion suddenly took hold that the very nature of politics had been transformed to exclude war as one of its instruments. Had not

Gorbachev lectured his generals that Clausewitz was no longer relevant, ordering them to put his book back in the library for good and to forget war as a means of pursuing foreign or managing international relations? Perhaps this view did not apply to the rest of the world, but it seemed to many that it did in Europe. Through some magic, Europe had been transformed into a permanent zone of peace. By 1993, however, the civil war in Bosnia was making this illusion difficult to maintain, although some politicians and pundits continued to try. The mood of introspection and drift, therefore, was understandably strong but no less dangerous for its naturalness.

Thus the Congress of Prague sounded the tocsin. It dispatched a number of warning messages, as this book makes clear, but some stand out above the others. The first and most important is that strategic realignment is incomplete. Germany's reunification within NATO so far exceeded anyone's expectations about what could be achieved as Gorbachev wound down the cold war that we have lost sight of the strategic limbo created in Central and Eastern Europe. The longer the Atlantic Alliance waits to fill this vacuum, the more difficult it will be. And whether, by whom, and how it is filled will make a huge difference for Europe's stability. Lady Thatcher and Senator Kyl eloquently made the strategic case for NATO's expansion, while other featured contributors added their own variants to these compelling calls to face up to the new security challenges.

Although most of the discussion of European security was at a level above the detail of NATO's military organizational adaptation and force structure requirements, one such issue—the need for ballistic missile defense—was raised repeatedly. Not all agreed that the need is so urgent, but the emphasis it received seems to portend a central place for missile defense in future alliance military requirements analogous to the one occupied by nuclear weapons during the cold war. Considerations of missile defense embrace arcane technical issues with enormous significance for strategy, diplomacy, international alliance cooperation, and military planning.

A second message was sounded most clearly by President Havel but also by others—the moral, cultural, and political reasons that the Atlantic Alliance cannot stand by, leaving Central Europe formally disconnected from Western Europe. The pretense that nothing really needs to be done to achieve the reintegration of Central Europe is not only unconvincing but also morally and politically irresponsible. The mood of "introspection and drift" has dulled sensitivities to this reality in the very circles that were most attuned to it during the cold war. One cannot read the words of Havel, Thatcher, and others without wondering if we have lost our moral compass. The opportunity of hearing them in Prague was even more compelling.

A third message was meant mainly for the United States—the "we won" and therefore "we can go home and celebrate" attitude is dangerous. It is dangerous for the alliance even if Washington rephrases it as "we can stay in Europe and celebrate" because it reflects an unwillingness to take the lead in the alliance at the very time when strategic vision and determined leadership are most needed. The Partnership for Peace and numerous economic and technical assistance programs are not enough. A stronger sense of new purpose is needed. Hence the name, the *New Atlantic Initiative*, and there cannot be an adequate initiative without committed American involvement.

A fourth message concerned Russia. Here participants showed divisions, a few expressing grave concern about offending the noisier anti-NATO expansion factions in the Russian leadership. The prevailing opinion, however, shared by at least one of the Russian participants, was that NATO's expansion is objectively in the interest of a Russia on the road to a liberal political system with a market economy. Putting a NATO umbrella over much of Central Europe to facilitate successful political and economic transitions there can only benefit, not threaten, Russia. The danger to both Western Europe and Russia is a repetition of the political and economic meltdown that occurred in Central Europe in the interwar period when all states of the region began with democracies but by the mid-1930s all but one had become dictatorships. Furthermore, these circumstances encouraged diplomatic competition among the Soviet Union, Britain, Germany, and France for influence in the region, facilitating the outbreak of war in the 1930s. Although speakers did not draw this analogy so explicitly, the awareness of it was palpable in some of the discussions.

These messages, of course, concern what Gerald Frost calls the "fundamental and long-term interests" of the Atlantic Alliance. As the panel discussions and extensive corridor debate quickly revealed, however, consensus on how to secure them will not emerge easily. A lot is going on in Europe, and not just in Western Europe. Moreover, some of it does not always fit comfortably in an Atlantic Alliance framework. Other regional organizations have their own rationales, constraints, and interests.

The European Union, the most conspicuous example, has its internal problems concerning next steps in economic integration. Carrying them through and also maintaining well-established European Union transfer payments policies do not mesh well with the economic needs of the former Warsaw Pact states. That was apparent, implicitly if not always explicitly, from the statements and speeches by participants from these states. The "widening" versus "deepening" debate in the European Union had its echo at the Congress of Prague.

The European Union's aspiration to a common foreign and defense policy is also at issue as NATO expansion goes forward. Moreover, it raises the question of the Western European Union's security role in Europe and its relation to NATO. Since the Congress of Prague, the United States has conceded to the idea of a purely European entity within NATO. Precisely what that "entity" entails and how it will operate have yet to be defined. How all these things can be effectively melded within an expanded NATO could not be addressed in depth at the Congress of Prague, but the inherent problems were much on the minds of many of the participants. More important, they reflected differences among some Europeans about what kind of U. S. security role is most appropriate in Europe.

Central and Eastern European participants raised their own issues with no less force and clarity. Several of them spoke equally if not more emphatically for the idea of a "new Atlantic initiative." The potentially most divisive issue among them, of course, is which states are to be offered NATO membership. The queue of aspirant members is long. What will happen to those who are not initially included in this exclusive club? And for those that do not realistically expect to be included, or have not yet expressed an official desire for admittance, will a limited NATO expansion increase or diminish their security?

Economic issues also loomed large in the commentaries by these participants. Sharing their own countries' experiences with market transition policies and explaining their needs, they tied their short-term economic interests to the larger and longer-term interests of the alliance. And at the same time, they could not avoid an implicit clash with some of the short-term economic interests of the European Union.

Although cultural issues did not rival security and economic issues for intensity of attention, they were not neglected. Notwith-

199

standing the long division of Europe during the cold war, the cultural foundations of Central Europe make it an integral part of Europe. The Atlantic Alliance, as it now stands, draws an artificial boundary down the middle of cultural Europe, and that is not healthy for the future of the new Europe.

These summary observations are meant not only to draw out key themes of the book but also to provide some sense of the rich informal discussions in Prague. Their complexity and breadth are far beyond what a single meeting could explore in depth, and that was not its purpose. Rather, it was to provide a wake-up call by demonstrating just how much the Atlantic Alliance has to do, much of it urgently. The unprecedented strategic realignment produced by the ending of the cold war was no small achievement, especially because it was peaceful. But the process is far from complete, and war has already raised its head in the former Yugoslavia as an ill omen if it is not completed. During the last decades of the cold war, the central issues for the alliance were few, clearly framed, and focused by years of transatlantic dialogue and cooperation. In the changed strategic environment, they are many, amorphous, and diffuse, crying out for transatlantic attention. The overarching impression they convey is that a "new Atlantic initiative" is imperative if they are to be brought into sharper focus, given coherent form, and subjected to policy action. Because all this cannot be done by Europe alone, the emphasis is on *Atlantic*.

Finally, NATO enlargement is the single most important "initiative" that can revitalize the alliance, give it a new sense of purpose, and make it aware that it faces not a period of respite but one of huge challenges. Merely the consideration of admitting new members forces the accumulating neglected issues onto the alliance's official agenda. That is why the Congress of Prague and this book endorse that action so strongly.

I fully share my coeditor's judgment that this book provides a "unique guide to the issues that will determine the profiles and fault lines of a fluid and uncertain international order." And I would add that it also makes abundantly clear why a new Atlantic initiative is necessary, one inspired by no less vision and inspiring no less hope than the one in 1949.

AGENDA FOR THE CONGRESS OF PRAGUE

May 10-12, 1996

Friday, May 10

POLICY COMMITTEE OPENING MEETINGS

Security Policy
Cultural Policy
Trade and Economic Policy
Political Cooperation

OPENING CEREMONY

Welcome,
Karel Schwarzenberg

Introduction,
Edward Streator

The Czech Republic and the Great Historic Challenge,
Václav Havel

Saturday, May 11

Introduction,
Christopher C. DeMuth

The Common Crisis: Is There Any?
Václav Klaus

Are There Common Answers?

Chairman: Irwin M. Stelzer
Panelists: Paul Fabra, Tomás Halík, Eberhard von Koerber,
and Wilfried Prewo

What Role for International Institutions?

Chairman: Géza Jeszenszky
Panelists: Max M. Kampelman, Adrian Karatnycky, and Lane Kirkland

Introduction,
William C. Steere Jr.

The Common Crisis: Atlantic Solutions,
Margaret Thatcher

Solutions: Four Policy Perspectives

"Security Policy"

Chairman: Richard N. Perle
Panelists: Christoph Bertram, Michal Lobkowicz, William E. Odom,
and Hanna Suchocka

"Cultural Policy"

Chairman: William H. Luers
Presenter: Anthony Hartley
Panelists: Alicia Borinsky, Nikolaus Lobkowicz, Georges
Liébert, and Zdenek Mádl

"Trade and Economic Policy"

Chairman: Pete du Pont
Presenter: Brian Hindley
Panelists: Jan Krzysztof Bielecki, Francis Blanchard,
and Robert D. Hormats

"Political Cooperation"

Chairman: Alun Chalfont
Presenter: Viktor Orbán
Panelists: Peter Rodman, Charles Powell, Peter Corterier,
and Pavel Bratinka

"Response"

Moderator: Paul Johnson
Antonio Martino and David McCurdy

Sunday, May 12

The Importance of Civil Society,
R. F. M. Lubbers

Atlantic Economics,
Leszek Balcerowicz

The Golden Age of the Twenty-first Century,
Jon L. Kyl

Closing Remarks,
Edward Streator and John O'Sullivan

Ceremonial Signing,
The Declaration of Atlantic Principles

ATTENDEES

D. Thomas Abbott
Mees Pierson Holdings Inc.

Martin Adam
Nadace Jiriho z Podebrad pro Evropskou

Frans A. M. Alting von Geusau
Leiden University

Digby Anderson
Social Affairs Unit

György Antall
Hungarian National Committee

Anne Applebaum
Evening Standard

Alex Bachmann
Pfizer Inc.

Whitney Backlar
The Advertising Council

Leszek Balcerowicz
Unia Wolnosci

Monica Baldi
European Parliament

Christopher P. Ball
Hungarian Atlantic Council

James Balog
The William H. Donner Foundation, Inc.

Brian Beedham
The Economist

Paul Belien
Centre for the New Europe

Max Beloff
House of Lords, United Kingdom

Václav Belohradsky
Lidove Noviny

Marek Benda
Parliament, Czech Republic

Václav Benda
Ministry of Interior, Czech Republic

Christoph Bertram
Die Zeit

Alain Besancon

Czeslaw Bielecki
100 Movement

Jan Krzysztof Bielecki
European Bank for Reconstruction and Development

Vladislav Bizek
Ministry of the Environment, Czech Republic

Conrad Black
The Daily Telegraph

Francis Blanchard
International Labor Office (retired)

Eva Blechova
Ministry of Foreign Affairs, Czech Republic

Gary Bogard
Encounter Foundation

John Bolton
National Policy Forum

Eduard Bomhoff
Nijenrode University

Jan Bondy
Czech Centers

Alicia Borinsky
Boston University

Pavel Bratinka
Ministry of Foreign Affairs, Czech Republic

Peter Brimelow
Forbes Magazine

George Brock
The Times

Petr Brodsky
Parliament, Czech Republic

David Brooks
The Weekly Standard

Viliam Buchert
Mlada Fronta Dnes

Zora Bútorová
FOCUS Center for Social and Market Analysis

Joseph A. Cannon
Geneva Steel Company

Geoffrey Carlson
The Windsor Foundation

Alun Chalfont
House of Lords, United Kingdom

Viacheslav Chornovil
People's Movement of Ukraine

Marek Cieslak
Institute for Eastern Studies

Robert Conquest
Hoover Institution, Stanford University

Peter Corterier
North Atlantic Assembly

S. W. Couwenberg
Erasmus University

Frans Crols
Trends Magazine

Victoria Curzon-Price
University of Geneva

Ryszard Czarnecki
Christian National Union

Gert Dahlmanns
Frankfurter Institut

Gonzales d'Alcantara
Antwerp University

Reginald Dale
International Herald Tribune

James DeCandole
Klub Mediator

Midge Decter
The Heritage Foundation

Christopher C. DeMuth
American Enterprise Institute

Paula J. Dobriansky
Hunton & Williams

Jan Dohnal
IBM Czech Republic, s.r.o.

Robert W. Doubek
American Friends of the Czech Republic

Iain Duncan-Smith
House of Commons, United Kingdom

Pete du Pont
Richards, Layton & Finger

Karel Dyba
Ministry of Economy, Czech Republic

Douglas Eden
Middlesex University

Paul Fabra
Centre for the New Europe

Hynek Fajmon
Ministry of Foreign Affairs, Czech Republic

Luigi Vittorio Ferraris
Società Italiana Organizzazioni Internazionali

Joachim Fest
Frankfurter Allgemeine Zeitung

Edwin J. Feulner Jr.
The Heritage Foundation

Jan Figel
NRSR Christian Democratic Movement,
Slovak Republic

Daniel Finkelstein
Conservative Party Research Department

Jens Fischer
Fischer & Limberger GmbH

Joseph Fitchett Jr.
International Herald Tribune

Lluís Foix
La Vanguardia

John Fonte
American Enterprise Institute

Kelly Forsberg
The National Review Institute

Andreas Freytag
Institut fur Wirtschaftspolitik

Bruce W. Friedman
Department of State, United States

Gerald Frost
New Atlantic Initiative

John Fund
Wall Street Journal

Robert Gabor
Interco Press

Frank J. Gaffney, Jr.
Center for Security Policy

Yegor T. Gaidar
Institute for the Economy in Transition

Charles Gati
Interinvest

Jeffrey Gedmin
American Enterprise Institute

Leonhard Gleske
Directorate Deutsche Bundesbank

Dean Godson
The Daily Telegraph

György Granasztói
Institute for Central European Studies

Hanna Gronkiewicz-Waltz
National Bank of Poland

Miriam Gross
The Sunday Telegraph

Eniko Gyori

Kurt Hans Hahn
Pfizer Inc.

Tomáš Halík
Ceska Krestanska Akademie

Stefan Halper
Brown Communications Inc.

Owen Harries
The National Interest

Robin Harris
Margaret Thatcher Foundation

Anthony Hartley
Independent Writer on International Affairs

Václav Havel
President, Czech Republic

Andrew Heath
Pfizer Inc.

Craig R. Helsing
BMW (US) Holding Corp.

Derrick Hill
The Daily Express

Brian Hindley
London School of Economics

Robert D. Hormats
Goldman Sachs International

Marta Hubova
Parliament, Czech Republic

Peter Huncík
Marai Sandor Foundation

Rod Hunter
Centre for the New Europe

Jirí Hybner
Czech Atlantic Commission

ATTENDEES

Jaroslav Janda
Institute of International Relations

Géza Jeszenszky
Hungarian Atlantic Council

Tomás Jezek
Parliament, Czech Republic

Roman Joch
Civic Democratic Alliance

Paul Johnson
Historian

Eugen Jurzyca
Center for Economic Development

Vladimir Kabes
Bohemiæ Foundation

Max M. Kampelman
Fried, Frank, Harris, Shriver & Jacobson

Karel Kansky
CERGE

Sergei A. Karaganov
Institute of Europe

Adrian Karatnycky
Freedom House

Jan Kasal
Parliament, Czech Republic

Fernand Keuleneer
Centre for the New Europe

Ihor Kharchenko
Ministry for Foreign Affairs, Ukraine

Conrad Kiechel
Reader's Digest

Andras Kiraly
Hungarian National Committee

Lane Kirkland
AFL-CIO

Václav Klaus
Prime Minister, Czech Republic

Stephen Klimczuk
A. T. Kearney

Mary Kohler
National Review Institute

Terry Kohler
Windway Capital Corporation

Petr Kolar
Ministry of Foreign Affairs, Czech Republic

Judit Körmendy-Ékes
Hungarian National Committee

Jan Koukal
Mayor of Prague

Dusan Kovác
Slovak Academy of Science

Bruce Kovner
Caxton Corporation

Maciej Kozlowski
Ministry of Foreign Affairs, Polamd

Piotr Krzywicki
Institute for Eastern Studies

James Kurth
Swarthmore College

Oldrich Kuzilek
Parliament, Czech Republic

Jon L. Kyl
United States Senate

William P. Laughlin
National Review Institute

Philippe Lefournier
Groupe Expansion

Arrigo Levi
Corriere Della Sera

Georges Liébert
Robert Laffont Publishers

Brooks Lobkowicz
American Friends for the Preservation of Czech Culture

Michal Lobkowicz
Ministry of Foreign Affairs, Czech Republic

Nikolaus Lobkowicz
Katholischen Universitat Eichstätt

Veronika Lombardini
Office of the President, Slovak Republic

R. F. M. Lubbers
Former Prime Minister, The Netherlands

Jaroslav Ludva
Ministry of Foreign Affairs, Czech Republic

William H. Luers
Metropolitan Museum of Art

William Luti
*Office of Representative Newt Gingrich,
United States*

Ferenc Mádl
University of Budapest

Zdenek Malek
Czech-Moravian Chamber of Trade Unions

Robert H. Malott
FMC Corporation

Peter Mandelson
The House of Commons, United Kingdom

Budzisz Marek
Polish Television

Václav Marhoul
AB Barrandov Holding

William Marsteller
The WEFA Group

Antonio Martino
University of Rome

Janos Martonyi
Hungarian National Committee

Ivan Masek
Parliament, Czech Republic

Marek Matraszek
The Windsor Group

Dorothy McCartney
National Review

David McCurdy
McCurdy Group L.L.C.

Gary L. McDowell
University of London

Anne McElvoy
The Spectator

Robert McGeehan
University of London

Andrew McHallam
*Institute for European Defense and Strategic
Studies*

Ivan Medek
Office of the President, Czech Republic

Paul Mentre
Crédit National

Jim Michaels
The Budapest Sun

Ivan Miklos
Democratic Party, Slovak Republic

Kenneth Minogue
The London School of Economics

Michael Mosbacher
New Atlantic Initiative

Ladislav Mravec
*Ministry of Foreign Affairs,
Czech Republic*

Joshua Muravchik
American Enterprise Institute

Kevin Murphy
University of Chicago

László Nagy

Piotr Naimski
Movement for the Reconstruction of Poland

Petr Necas
Ministry of Defense, Czech Republic

Milan Nic
Radio Free Europe

Grover Norquist
Americans for Tax Reform

Jiri Novak
Ministry of Justice, Czech Republic

Jan Nowak
Polish American Congress

Jerzy Marek Nowakowski
The Windsor Group

William E. Odom
Hudson Institute

Daniel Oliver
Preferred Health Systems, LLC

Louise V. Oliver
The William H. Donner Foundation

Viktor Orbán
FIDESZ

John O'Sullivan
National Review

Jan Parys
Atlantic Club in Warsaw

Peter Passell
New York Times

Tomas Pav
Parliament, Czech Republic

Jiri Payne
Parliament, Czech Republic

Marguerite Peeters
Center for the New Europe

Jiri Pehe
Open Media Research Institute

Victor Perez-Diaz
University Computense of Madrid

Richard N. Perle
American Enterprise Institute

Karel Pezl
Office of the President, Czech Republic

Jean Paul Pigasse

Lucie Pilipová
Bohemiæ Foundation

Daniel Pipes
Middle East Forum

Andrej Pniejnia-Olszynski
Christian National Union, Poland

Norman Podhoretz
Hudson Institute

Stephen Pollard
Social Market Foundation

Robert L. Pollock
Wall Street Journal Europe

Charles Powell
Jardine Matheson

Clyde Prestowitz
Economic Strategy Institute

Wilfried Prewo
Hannover Chamber of Industry & Commerce

Gergely Pröhle
Friedrich Naumann Foundation

Jeremy A. Rabkin
Cornell University

Therese Raphael
Wall Street Journal Europe

Alfred A. Reisch
Hungarian Atlantic Council

Vladimir Reisky
Czech Foundation for International Studies

Tatiana Repková
Narodna Obroda

Peter Robinson
Atlantic Council of the United Kingdom

Roger Robinson
Center for Security Policy

Peter W. Rodman
Nixon Center for Peace and Freedom

Jan Maria Rokita
Parliament, Poland

Sebastian Rybarczyk
Institute for Eastern Studies

Giuseppe Sacco
University of Rome

Felipe Sahagún
El Mundo

Antxón Sarasqueta
Multimedia Capital

John P. Schmitz
Mayer, Brown & Platt

Karel Schwarzenberg
Bohemiæ Foundation

Roger Scruton
Writer and Philosopher

Michael Scully
Pfizer Inc.

Doug Seay
The Heritage Foundation

John Seidler
Pfizer s.r.o.

Pavel Seifter
Office of the President, Czech Republic

Gustavo Selva
Chamber of Deputies, Italy

Michal Semin
Civic Institute

Miroslav Sevcik
Liberal Institute

Jochen Siemens
Frankfurter Rundschau

Radek Sikorski
National Review

Rudolf Slansky
Ministry of Foreign Affairs, Czech Republic

Vaclav Slavicek
Ministry of Agriculture, Czech Republic

Eva Slivkova
Christian Democratic Youth of Slovakia

Veronika Smigolová
Ministry of Foreign Affairs, Czech Republic

David J. Smith
Global Horizons, Inc.

Vitezslav Socher
Parliament, Czech Republic

Henry Sokolski
Nonproliferation Policy Education Ctr.

Miroslav Somol
Ministry of Trade and Industry, Czech Republic

Reka Somssich

Michael Spicer
House of Commons, United Kingdom

William C. Steere Jr.
Pfizer Inc.

Natalia Stelmashchuk
Ukraine-Europe Fund

Irwin M. Stelzer
American Enterprise Institute

Jiri Stepanovsky
Czech Atlantic Commission

Edward Streator
New Atlantic Initiative

Andrew Stuttaford
National Review Institute

Hanna Suchocka
Parliament, Poland

Pavol Sud'a
Trend, spol. s.r.o.

Vladimir Suman
Parliament, Czech Republic

Johnathan Sunley
The Windsor Group

Tomás Svoboda
Parliament, Czech Republic

Martin Syka
Parliament, Czech Republic

Zsolt Szekeres
Hungarian American Coalition

Boris Tarasyuk
Embassy of Ukraine

Pavel Telicka
Ministry of Foreign Affairs, Czech Republic

Margaret Thatcher
Former Prime Minister, United Kingdom

Pavel Tigrid
Ministry of Culture, Czech Republic

R. Emmett Tyrrell Jr.
American Spectator

Isabel Anne Upham

James Upham

Nancy Upham

Darió Valcarcel
Estudios de Politica Exterior

Magdalena Vásáryová
Slovak Foreign Policy Association

Bulcsu Veress
Hungarian American Coalition

Daniel Vesely
Office of the President, Czech Republic

Barbara von der Heydt
The Acton Institute

Alexandr Vondra
Ministry of Foreign Affairs,Czech Republic

Eberhard von Koerber
ABB Europe Ltd.

Otakar Vychodil
Parliament, Czech Republic

Jenonne R. Walker
Embassy of the United States of America

W. Allen Wallis
American Enterprise Institute

W. Bruce Weinrod
Allen & Harold, PLC

Richard A. Wilde
New Encounter

Alan Lee Williams
Atlantic Council of the United Kingdom

Catherine Windels
Pfizer Inc.

Jan Winiecki
Viadrina-European University

Jan Zahradil
*Office of the Government,
Czech Republic*

Tomás Zálesák
Democratic Party, Slovak Republic

Krzysztof Zanussi
The Windsor Group

Joseph Zieleniec
*Ministry of Foreign Affairs,
Czech Republic*

Anton Zijderveld
Erasmus University

Jan Zizka
Hospodarske Noviny

Editors and Contributors

GERALD FROST, coeditor of this volume, is the research director of the New Atlantic Initiative. An author and journalist, he has written extensively on political issues in the United States and Britain. He was director of the Centre for Policy Studies in London and founder-director of the Institute for European Defence and Strategic Studies, where he now remains a consultant director.

LT. GENERAL WILLIAM E. ODOM, USA (RET.), coeditor of this volume, is director of National Security Studies for the Hudson Institute and an adjunct professor at Yale University. He was director of the National Security Agency from 1985 to 1988 and military assistant to the president's assistant for national security affairs, Zbigniew Brzezinski. His military service includes duty in Germany, the United States, and Vietnam.

LESZEK BALCEROWICZ is a Polish historian and economist and the president of Unia Wolnosci. He was the deputy chairman of the Council of Ministers and the minister of finance from 1989 to 1991. Mr. Balcerowicz was a member of the Council of Economic Advisers to President Walesa, chairman of the Centre for Social and Economic Research, and head of comparative international studies at the Warsaw School of Economics.

CHRISTOPH BERTRAM is the diplomatic correspondent of the leading German weekly, *Die Zeit*. He joined the International Institute for

Strategic Studies in 1967 and was director from 1974 to 1982. The institute is an internationally renowned research center focusing on foreign and security policy. Mr. Bertram has published on international affairs, in particular on European politics and international security. His most recent publication is *Europe in the Balance—Securing the Peace Won in the Cold War*.

JAN KRZYSZTOF BIELECKI is an economist and former prime minister of Poland. In the 1980s he was active in the Solidarity Trade Union and in 1989 became a deputy to the Polish Parliament. In 1992 he was appointed minister for European integration.

FRANCIS BLANCHARD joined the International Labor Office in Geneva in 1951 and retired as the director general in 1989. Mr. Blanchard was a member of the French Economic and Social Council from 1989 to 1994. He is an officer of the French Foreign Legion.

ALICIA BORINSKY is a novelist, poet, and scholar. She is professor of Latin American and comparative literature at Boston University. She is the author of, among other works, *Theoretical Fable: The Pedagogical Dream in Contemporary Latin American Fiction*.

PAVEL BRATINKA is the deputy minister of foreign affairs of the Czech Republic. Previously, he was the deputy minister for international relations for the Czech Republic. Mr. Bratinka was elected to the Federal Assembly of the Czech and Slovak Federal Republic in 1990 and served as the vice chairman of the Foreign Affairs Committee. He is a founder of the Civic Democratic Alliance, a member organization of the Civic Forum, a broad coalition of anti-Communist forces.

ALUN CHALFONT is president of the All-Party Defence Group in the British House of Lords. He was a minister of state in the Foreign Office from 1964 to 1970. His published works include *Star Wars: Suicide or Survival?* (1985) and *Defence of the Realm* (1987). He is vice president of the European Atlantic Group and a fellow of the Atlantic Council.

PETER CORTERIER is the secretary-general for the North Atlantic Assembly, the interparliamentary organization of the sixteen countries of NATO and sixteen associate member countries from the former

Warsaw Pact. For sixteen years, Mr. Corterier was a member of the German Bundestag from Karlsruhe, and he was the minister of state for foreign affairs from 1981 to 1982.

CHRISTOPHER C. DeMUTH has been president of the American Enterprise Institute since 1986. He was previously the managing director of Lexecon, an economics consulting firm; administrator for regulatory affairs at the U.S. Office of Management and Budget and executive director of the Task Force on Regulatory Relief in the Reagan administration; lecturer and director of regulatory studies at Harvard's Kennedy School of Government; and an attorney with the Consolidated Rail Corporation and the law firm of Sidley & Austin. His articles on government regulation and other subjects have appeared in *The Public Interest*, the *Harvard Law Review*, the *Yale Journal on Regulation*, the *Wall Street Journal*, and elsewhere.

PETE DU PONT is the chairman of the National Review Institute. He is a director in the law firm of Richard, Layton & Finger, P.A., in Wilmington, Delaware. He was a member of the U.S. House of Representatives from 1971 to 1977 and governor of the state of Delaware from 1977 to 1985. Mr. du Pont is policy chairman of the National Center for Policy Analysis, a nonprofit, nonpartisan public policy institute.

PAUL FABRA is the director general of the Centre for the New Europe and a columnist for *Les Echos*, the leading French economic weekly newspaper. He was a columnist for *Le Monde*.

TOMÁŠ HALÍK is an associate professor of philosophy of religion at Charles University in Prague. He is also president of the Czech Christian Academy and rector of the University Church. He was general secretary of the Czech Bishop Conference and was the consultor of the Pontifical Council for Dialogue with Nonbelievers. Mr. Halík was secretly ordained a priest in 1978.

ANTHONY HARTLEY is a journalist specializing in European affairs and a contributing editor to *The National Interest*. He is a former editor of *Encounter*.

VÁCLAV HAVEL is president of the Czech Republic, and before that he was president of Czechoslovakia. He is the chairman of the Prague Heritage Fund and a member of the jury awarding the International Prize for Human Rights. Mr. Havel is a writer and playwright; he has written more than thirty plays, books, and essays. He was imprisoned for more than five years for incitement and obstruction, sedition, and subversive and antistate activities.

BRIAN HINDLEY is reader in trade policy at the London School of Economics. He is a consultant on trade policy issues to a number of international organizations and is codirector of the Trade Policy Unit of the London-based Centre for Policy Studies.

ROBERT D. HORMATS is the vice chairman of Goldman Sachs (International). He received the French Legion of Honor in 1987 and the Arthur Fleming Award in 1974. Mr. Hormats was senior staff member for international economic affairs on the National Security Council from 1974 to 1977 and was a senior economic adviser to Henry Kissinger, General Brent Scowcroft, and Zbigniew Brzezinski. He is a board member of the Council on Foreign Relations and of the Columbia University School of International Affairs.

GÉZA JESZENSZKY is a professor at the University of Michigan. He is a historian with a Ph.D. from Eötvös University, Budapest, which has been attached to the Budapest University of Economics since 1976. He was a founder of one of the first major political movements challenging communism in Hungary. Mr. Jeszenszky served as minister for foreign affairs from 1990 to 1994. He is the president of the Hungarian Atlantic Council.

PAUL JOHNSON is a historian and journalist. He was the editor of the *New Statesman* from 1965 to 1970. Mr. Johnson contributes to magazines and newspapers worldwide. He is the author of many books, including *A History of Christianity*, *A History of the Jews*, *Modern Times*, *Intellectuals*, and *The Birth of the Modern*. His most recent book is *A Quest for God* (1996).

MAX M. KAMPELMAN is an attorney with the law firm of Fried, Frank, Harris, Shriver & Jacobson in Washington, D.C. He was a counselor for the U.S. Department of State and the ambassador and head of the U.S. delegation to the Negotiations with the Soviet Union on Nuclear and Space Arms in Geneva. Mr. Kampelman is now the chairman of the American Academy of Diplomacy, chairman of Georgetown University's Institute for the Study of Diplomacy, and, by presidential appointment, vice chairman of the U.S. Institute of Peace.

ADRIAN KARATNYCKY is president of Freedom House, a nonprofit organization that promotes democracy, the civil society, and the rule of law and monitors human rights, political rights, and civil liberties around the world. He was assistant to the president of the AFL-CIO, director of research in the AFL-CIO Department of International Affairs, and editor of the Interco Press Service, the AFL-CIO's international editorial features service. Mr. Karatnycky has written scores of articles on East European and post-Soviet issues, and his most recent book is *New Nations Rising: The Fall of the Soviets and the Challenge of Independence.*

LANE KIRKLAND was president emeritus of the AFL-CIO from 1979 to 1995, where he previously served as secretary-treasurer and executive assistant to the president. Mr. Kirkland was director of research and education at the International Union of Operating Engineers. A licensed master mariner, he is a member of the International Organization of Masters, Mates, and Pilots.

VÁCLAV KLAUS is prime minister of the Czech Republic. He was minister of finance from 1989 to 1992; since 1991, he has been chairman of the Civic Democratic Party. Mr. Klaus won the Schumpeter Prize for Economics, the Freedom Award, and the Konrad Adenauer Prize. He has written several books and numerous articles on economic theory and economic reform.

JON L. KYL is a U.S. senator from Arizona and serves on the Judiciary Committee, the Energy and Natural Resources Committee, and the Intelligence Committee. Previously, he served four terms in the U.S. House of Representatives. Mr. Kyl practiced law at the firm of Jennings, Strouss & Salmon in Phoenix, Arizona, and served as the chairman of the Phoenix Metropolitan Chamber of Commerce from 1984 to 1985.

GEORGES LIÉBERT is the editor of *Pluriel,* a paperback series of essays and social science studies. He is also professor of political science at the Institute of Paris and in charge of a seminar on French cultural policy and practices. Mr. Liébert is the producer of a classical music radio program on the state radio station. He is the author of numerous books and articles on music, most recently, *Nietzsche and Music* (1995).

MICHAL LOBKOWICZ is a member of Parliament and a member of the Foreign Affairs Committee in the Czech Republic. He had been the *chef de cabinet* to the minister of foreign affairs. In 1993, Mr. Lobkowicz was elected to the board of directors of the Christian Democratic Party, which later merged with the Civic Democratic Party.

NIKOLAUS LOBKOWICZ is the founder and director of the Institute of Central and East European Studies at Eichstätt, Germany. He previously taught philosophy at the University of Notre Dame, the University of Munich, and the Catholic University of Eichstätt.

R. F. M. LUBBERS was the prime minister of the Netherlands from 1982 to 1994. He is a member of the Second Chamber of States-General in Parliament. Mr. Lubbers has been the minister of economic affairs. He is a member of the board of the Netherlands Christian Employers' Federation and of the Federation of Mechanical and Electrical Engineering Industries and is a member of the Programs Advisory Council of the Catholic Broadcasting Association.

WILLIAM H. LUERS is president of the Metropolitan Museum of Art in New York City. In the Foreign Service from 1957 to 1986, he served as ambassador to Czechoslovakia from 1983 to 1986 and as ambassador to Venezuela from 1978 to 1982. Mr. Luers was a visiting lecturer at the Woodrow Wilson School at Princeton University, the Johns Hopkins University School of Advanced International Studies, and George Washington University. Mr. Luers has written extensively on the arts, the Soviet Union and Eastern Europe, Atlantic relations, and Latin America. He is a member of the Council on Foreign Relations and a fellow of the American Academy of Arts and Sciences.

DAVID MCCURDY is chairman of the McCurdy Group L.L.C. He is also a partner and a member of the board of directors of the American Medical Group, Inc., and a senior adviser at the Center for Strategic and International Studies. He is a member of the board of advisers for the Asia-Pacific Policy Center, the Aspen Institute, the Progressive Policy Institute, and the Committee for the Common Defense. Mr. McCurdy served fourteen years in the U.S. House of Representatives from the fourth district of Oklahoma (1980–1994) and attained numerous leadership positions, including chairmanship of subcommittees, full committees, and the national Democratic Leadership Council.

FERENC MÁDL is professor of international economic law at the University of Budapest. He is a member of the Hungarian Academy of Sciences and of the European Academy of Sciences. Mr. Mádl was the minister of privatization from 1990 to 1992 and was the minister of education and culture from 1993 to 1994.

ANTONIO MARTINO was the minister of foreign affairs in Italy from 1994 to 1995 and now is a parliamentary deputy. He was a lecturer on monetary history and politics, the chairman of the Political Science Department, and a member of the board of directors of Libera Università Internazionale degli Studi Sociali in Rome.

VIKTOR ORBÁN is the editor of the political and cultural periodical, Századvég. A 1987 graduate of the Faculty of Law at Lóránd Eötvös University, he is a founder of the István Bibó College of Law and Social Sciences.

JOHN O'SULLIVAN has been the editor of National Review since 1988. He had been a special adviser to Margaret Thatcher, an associate editor of the Times in London, an assistant editor of the Daily Telegraph in London, and editor of Policy Review. Mr. O'Sullivan was the director of studies at the Heritage Foundation and a fellow at the Institute of Politics at Harvard University. He was made a Commander of the British Empire in 1991.

RICHARD N. PERLE is a resident fellow at the American Enterprise Institute. He was the assistant secretary of defense for international security policy and the chairman of the North Atlantic Treaty Organization High Level Defense Group from 1981 to 1987. From 1969 to 1980 he served in the office of Senator Henry M. "Scoop" Jackson and worked on the Senate Committee on Government Operations and the Committee on Armed Services. Mr. Perle is a contributing

219

editor of *U.S. News & World Report*, a consultant to the secretary of defense, and a member of the Defense Policy Board. He is the author of *Hard Line*, a political novel.

CHARLES POWELL was private secretary to Prime Ministers Margaret Thatcher and John Major, in which position he was responsible for foreign affairs and defense. A former member of the British Diplomatic Service, he is now a member of the board of directors of Jardine Matheson, National Westminster Bank, and several other international companies.

WILFRIED PREWO is chief executive officer of the Hannover Chamber of Industry and Commerce in Hannover, Germany, and a fellow of the Centre for the New Europe. He has held positions at the Institute of World Economics in Kiel, Germany, and at the University of Texas. An extensive writer on economic and social policy, he is active in the Christian Democratic Union.

PETER W. RODMAN is the director of National Security Programs at the Nixon Center for Peace and Freedom in Washington, D.C., and a senior editor of *National Review*. Previously, he served as deputy assistant to the president for national security affairs and as director of the State Department's policy planning staff. In the 1970s Mr. Rodman was a special assistant to Henry Kissinger. He is the author of *More Precious than Peace: The Cold War and the Struggle for the Third World* (1994) and *America Adrift: A Strategic Assessment* (1996).

KAREL SCHWARZENBERG is a founder and member of the board of directors of the Bohemiæ Foundation. He was chancellor to President Václav Havel from 1990 to 1992. Mr. Schwarzenberg was the chairman of the Helsinki Conference for Human Rights from 1985 to 1990, and he actively supported Czech political exiles.

WILLIAM C. STEERE, JR., is the chairman of the board and chief executive officer of Pfizer Inc. Joining Pfizer in 1959, he has been president of Pfizer Pharmaceuticals Group and president of Pfizer Inc. Mr. Steere is a member of the board of directors of the Pharmaceutical Research and Manufacturers of America.

IRWIN M. STELZER is the director of regulatory policy studies at the

American Enterprise Institute. He is a U.S. economic and political columnist for the *Sunday Times* (London) and the *Courier Mail* (Australia), a member of the publication committee of *The Public Interest*, and an honorary fellow of the Centre for Socio-Legal Studies, Wolfson College, Oxford. Mr. Stelzer is the author of *Selected Antitrust Cases: Landmark Decisions* and coauthor of *The Antitrust Laws: A Primer*. He founded the National Economic Research Associates in 1961 and served as its president until a few years after its sale in 1983 to Marsh & McLennan.

EDWARD STREATOR is a member of the executive committee of the International Institute for Strategic Studies and a director of the South Bank in London. He was the governor of the Royal United Services Institute for Defense Studies. Mr. Streator held positions in the U.S. government as the State Department's director of NATO affairs, the deputy permanent representative to NATO, the minister at the U.S. embassy in London, and the ambassador and permanent representative to the OECD.

HANNA SUCHOCKA is a member of the Polish Parliament and serves on the European Treaty and Foreign Affairs Committees. From 1992 to 1993, she was the prime minister of Poland and served as vice chairman of the Parliamentary Assembly of the Council of Europe and chairman of the Polish delegation to the council. Ms. Suchocka is the author of numerous academic publications on constitutional law and human rights.

MARGARET THATCHER was prime minister of the United Kingdom from 1979 to 1990. She was a Conservative member of Parliament, representing Finchley, from 1959 to 1992, and was Opposition leader from 1975 to 1979. Lady Thatcher was awarded the Order of Merit in 1990. She is the author of two volumes of memoirs: *The Downing Street Years* (1993) and *The Path to Power* (1995).

EBERHARD VON KOERBER is executive vice president and member of the group executive committee of ABB Asea Brown Boveri Ltd., Zurich. From 1988 to 1994, he was chairman of the managing board of Asea Brown Boveri AG in Mannheim, Germany. Before that, Mr. von Koerber was executive vice president and member of the group executive committee of BBC Brown Boveri & Company Ltd. in Baden,

Switzerland. He held several executive positions at BMW AG in Munich between 1972 and 1986. Mr. von Koerber was an attorney in international law and was the assistant to the chairman of the managing board of Glanzstoff AG (later Enka AG).

Acknowledgments

A number of people deserve thanks for making the Congress of Prague possible. Many worked hard to make this conference successful, and I apologize to those whom I will unintentionally, but inevitably, neglect to mention.

First, I would like to thank the Bohemiæ Foundation, whose young people worked with such efficiency and ability: if I were President Havel or Prime Minister Klaus, I would be absolutely confident about the future of the Czech Republic. I want to thank in particular David Bednar, Johanna Dvoraková, Jenna Whitman, Martina Parchanská, and all the rest of their staff. I am especially grateful, too, to the foundation's director, Lucie Pilipová, who worked with such dedication on this conference and whose contribution was indispensable to our endeavors.

Second, the American Enterprise Institute has been a tower of strength in getting the New Atlantic Initiative off the ground. Its president, Christopher DeMuth, and its scholars Richard Perle, Jeffrey Gedmin, and Irwin Stelzer have done much to give our preparations real intellectual muscle. And the practical arrangements were handled with great dispatch on short notice by Isabel Ferguson, Elizabeth Drembus, and their colleagues. Without them, this congress might not have taken place and none of us would have been here.

In Europe, I want to thank the Institute for European Defense and Strategic Studies, which was our first organizing home and which did so much to get us started, and in particular its director, Andrew McHallam.

A special thanks must go out to all our sponsors, whose generous support made this endeavor possible, particularly the William H. Donner Foundation, the Margaret Thatcher Foundation, the John M. Olin Foundation, the German Marshall Fund of the United States, the National Review Institute, Hollinger International, Pfizer International Inc., Möet Hennessy Louis Vuitton Inc., Forbes Magazine, Mr. Rupert Murdoch, and Mr. Conrad Black. We are also grateful to the Minolta Corporation and the Polaroid Corporation for providing technical support to the conference.

I want to mention a few individuals who have been staunch advocates from the first: Charles Powell, my former colleague at Downing Street; Louise Oliver from the Donner Foundation; Adrian Karatnycky of Freedom House, who did much to make this a genuinely bipartisan enterprise; and Peter Rodman of the Nixon Center and *National Review*. I am grateful to our research director, Gerald Frost, who drafted the document that produced the debate, and to Géza Jezsenszky, who helped start the program in Eastern Europe over a splendid dinner we shared in Budapest. I want to thank my friends Georges Liébert in France and Antxón Sarasqueta in Spain as well.

I want to thank in particular my colleague at *National Review*, Dorothy McCartney, who did all the real work and made sure that all the ideas that I was trying to get off the ground actually lifted off.

To all our patrons, whose eminence added a luster to our efforts and ensured that we were taken seriously, I am indeed grateful: Václav Havel, Margaret Thatcher, Helmut Schmidt, Leszek Balcerowicz, Henry Kissinger, and George Shultz. I single out for special thanks my former boss, Lady Thatcher, who has been helpful from the very first to the very last.

And, finally, my thanks to Edward Streator, that model of effortless superiority: everything he had to do, he did without fuss or apparent effort, and often the day before he was asked.

JOHN O'SULLIVAN
Founder and Cochairman
The New Atlantic Initiative

Name Index

A Note on the Book

This book was edited by
Dana Lane and the publications staff
of the American Enterprise Institute.
The text was set in Palatino, a typeface
designed by the twentieth-century Swiss designer
Hermann Zapf. Jennifer Lesiak set the type,
and Edwards Brothers, Incorporated,
of Lillington, North Carolina,
printed and bound the book,
using permanent acid-free paper.

The AEI Press is the publisher for the American Enterprise Institute for Public Policy Research, 1150 Seventeenth Street, N.W., Washington, D.C. 20036; *Christopher DeMuth,* publisher; *Dana Lane,* director; *Ann Petty,* editor, *Leigh Tripoli,* editor; *Cheryl Weissman,* editor; *Jennifer Lesiak,* editorial assistant.